# OPTIMIZING
# GROWTH

# OPTIMIZING
# GROWTH

Predictive and Profitable Strategies
to Understand Demand
and Outsmart Your Competitors

JASON GREEN | MARK HENNEMAN | DIMITAR ANTOV

Published by John Wiley & Sons, Inc., Hoboken, New Jersey.
Published simultaneously in Canada.

For general information on our other products and services or for technical support, please contact our Customer Care Department within the United States at (800) 762-2974, outside the United States at (317) 572-3993 or fax (317) 572-4002.

Wiley publishes in a variety of print and electronic formats and by print-on-demand. Some material included with standard print versions of this book may not be included in e-books or in print-on-demand. If this book refers to media such as a CD or DVD that is not included in the version you purchased, you may download this material at http://booksupport.wiley.com. For more information about Wiley products, visit www.wiley.com.

*Library of Congress Cataloging-in-Publication Data*

Names: Green, Jason, 1963- author. | Henneman, Mark, 1961- author. | Antov,
    Dimitar, 1978- author.
Title: Optimizing growth : predictive and profitable strategies to understand
    demand and outsmart your competitors / Jason Green, Mark Henneman, Dimitar
    Antov.
Description: Hoboken : Wiley, 2018. | Includes index. |
Identifiers: LCCN 2017058594 (print) | LCCN 2018008033 (ebook) | ISBN
    9781119462194 (pdf) | ISBN 9781119462200 (epub) | ISBN 9781119462224
    (hardback)
Subjects: LCSH: Organizational change. | Creative ability in business. |
    Information technology—Economic aspects. | BISAC: BUSINESS & ECONOMICS /
    Finance. | BUSINESS & ECONOMICS / Development / Economic Development. |
    BUSINESS & ECONOMICS / Economics / General.
Classification: LCC HD58.8 (ebook) | LCC HD58.8 .G723 2018 (print) | DDC
    658.4/06—dc23
LC record available at https://lccn.loc.gov/2017058594

Cover Design: Wiley

Printed in the United States of America

10 9 8 7 6 5 4 3 2 1

# CONTENTS

Preface                                                          vii
Acknowledgments                                                  xi
About the Authors                                                xiii

**SECTION I     Why Greater Precision**                          **1**

CHAPTER 1     The Growth Challenge                               3

CHAPTER 2     Building a Demand-Based Business System            29

CHAPTER 3     A New Business Model                               45

**SECTION II    The Precision to Optimize Your Current
              Business**                                         **67**

CHAPTER 4     Building a Demand "Early Warning
              System"                                            69

CHAPTER 5     Enhanced Demand Landscape                          85

CHAPTER 6     Precisely Locating Demand                          111

CHAPTER 7     Brand Economics: Unlock the Power
              of Your Brand                                      131

CHAPTER 8     Pricing with Precision                            149

**SECTION III**   **Moving to a Demand-Driven Business System: The Big Data Advantage**   **165**

**CHAPTER 9**   Innovation That Works   167

**CHAPTER 10**   Demand-Based Cost Reduction   187

**CHAPTER 11**   Winning in a Digital World   201

Index   221

# PREFACE

This is a book about successfully driving profitable growth in a rapidly changing environment. Our goal is to provide principles, approaches, frameworks, and tools that can be applied to virtually any type of business in any industry, whether business to consumer (B2C) or business to business (B2B), large or small, or local or global, to help drive growth. By describing the key steps in an overarching growth process in enough detail, we hope to make each step and its related components actionable for any manager. We have attempted to provide a range of approaches from simple "back of the envelope" exercises and key questions to sophisticated Big Data analytics to help kick-start any growth effort within any organization.

Throughout the book we use case examples to help bring key concepts alive. Our intent is to provide a range of case examples across industries and situations from market-leading companies that wanted to extend their lead to turnaround situations where there was danger of failing. We hope the cases will be both informative and inspiring. When growth has stalled, it is often a symptom of fundamental changes among customers and markets that may make the tried-and-true playbook that drove prior successes less effective. Beyond having a plan for reigniting growth, it takes personal courage and conviction to undertake a process that might challenge the organization's conventional wisdom and then alter or even rewrite the playbook that built the business in the first place.

The book will reinforce four key themes based on our experiences that we believe are critical for successfully achieving growth objectives:

First, we believe that the most certain path for achieving profitable growth begins with insights into demand. We think of demand as the solutions consumers and customers are seeking across the entire range of situations they experience day in and day out. A solution for feeling more energized in the morning, a solution for transforming my business from selling products to providing services, a solution for paying off credit card debt, and so on. Some groups or segments of consumers/customers are highly satisfied with the current solutions available to them. Others are highly dissatisfied with everything they are aware of or have tried. This is why sales figures are not a true indicator of the actual demand in a given market; sales receipts do not measure unfulfilled demand.

Understanding how demand varies by segment of consumer and customer is a critical aspect of identifying the most attractive growth opportunities in the market. Demand is not one homogeneous block. Developing insights into what we call "demand segments," along with insights into what drives demand, what fulfills demand, and the economics of demand, make up the foundation for building a successful growth strategy.

In addition, we believe much greater precision will be needed to drive growth than ever before. More precise insights leading to more precise investments and actions will reduce waste and create a potentially significant edge. Understanding precisely who to win with and how to win with them will require increasing levels of precision as retail channels expand, media options fragment, and the choices available to consumers and customers increase dramatically. For example, if businesses don't have a precise understanding of the new digital path to purchase, the most critical search terms being used by attractive customers, or the role of ratings and rankings on purchase decisions, their offers may never even make the consideration set for key consumers.

We also believe that growth is best achieved through a comprehensive system that continually identifies and tests potential growth hypotheses. The system we propose is focused on continually answering what we call the How, Who, What, Where, Why, and How To of growth opportunities. Starting from demand, we believe managers have to constantly ask and update their learnings about how demand is shifting and what the drivers of those changes are. The next question to address is to determine who the most attractive segments of consumers and customers are based on their demand within a given category. Then the firm can go deep with those attractive consumers and customers to understand precisely what their demand is for and how to fulfill it. Our goal is to describe a step-by-step system to follow that can be regularly updated to enhance the level of insights into demand.

Finally, almost every aspect of the growth process can be improved by leveraging Big Data capabilities, including digital approaches. Whatever your starting point, we believe the ability to leverage Big Data, including digital approaches, in ways that create a more precise understanding of demand, customers, competitors, and opportunities will become an increasingly important driver of competitive advantage. To be clear, Big Data in and of itself is not a strategy or a panacea for curing growth issues. Nor will sustainable growth be achieved by taking a flawed business model, a set of offers that are not aligned to demand, and a weak brand online. The promise of Big Data is to help identify trends and enhance your understanding of opportunities, not to do the critical thinking for you.

Ultimately, it is our hope that this book will inspire you to drive growth within your organization while providing the tools you will need to achieve your growth objectives.

# ACKNOWLEDGMENTS

Writing this book has been a true team effort. There are many people we wish to thank for their contributions to the content of the book and for their support throughout the process of writing this book.

We'd like to start by thanking our families. Many thanks for all of the encouragement and advice from Gwen Farley Green, Alex Green, and Amanda Green. Thank you to Mary Blue Henneman, a former principal at The Cambridge Group, as well as Nicholas Henneman and Ellie Henneman. We are also grateful for the support from Stanimir and Tzvetanka Antovi. A book like this is an undertaking we could never have completed without ongoing support from each of our families.

Our team was very fortunate to have Linda Deeken, chief marketing officer of The Cambridge Group, engaged throughout the process of developing this book. Linda has been a valuable thought partner throughout this effort. She is also a true problem solver who cleared hurdles that seemed insurmountable and kept everything moving forward by providing insights, conducting research, and suggesting edits. On this team, Linda is our MVP.

We are grateful to our colleagues at The Cambridge Group for their contributions to this book and their guidance throughout the process of writing it. Special thanks to our very talented principal team at The Cambridge Group, including Jim Eckels, Chris Fosdick, Don Johnson, Tim Joyce, and Peter Killian. Thank you for the energy and insight you have brought to our client work and to collaborating with us to continually improve the approaches and intellectual capital we leverage in order to help our clients drive growth.

Special thanks to Tim Joyce for contributing to writing the Facebook "Brand Economics" case. The case is based on the work that Tim, Jim Eckels, and others from The Cambridge Group have conducted with the team at Facebook. We also want to thank Zach Phillips, a consultant at The Cambridge Group, who helped edit the initial manuscript of the book. We recognize the contributions of our former colleague at The Cambridge Group and current data science collaborator Alex Moore, who assisted us with editing the content in the book. Zach and Alex added significant value by continually challenging us to clarify the concepts in the book, simplify language whenever possible, and avoid consulting jargon.

It would be impossible for us to thank Rick Kash adequately. It would also be impossible to fully describe the incredible impact Rick has had on each of us and all of us at The Cambridge Group. Rick, who founded our firm and is the former vice chairman of Nielsen, has been a colleague, a mentor, and a friend to each of us over the past two decades. His absolute passion for helping clients, his insights into customer demand and how companies can win, his creative problem solving, and his boundless energy continue to be an inspiration to all of us. Rick's insights, coaching, and example helped shape much of the thinking behind this book.

When he retired a few years ago, our team learned how truly irreplaceable Dr. Kevin Bowen, our former senior principal, actually is. Kevin created, helped create, or influenced many of the approaches described in this book over his thirty-year career with The Cambridge Group. We miss Kevin's insights, guidance, and camaraderie enormously.

We would also like to acknowledge our many Nielsen colleagues, including Mitch Barns, Steve Hasker, John Lewis, Chris Morley, Karen Fichuk, Susan Dunn, Pat Dodd, and the many others across Nielsen who have collaborated with us to help our many mutual clients succeed. Thank you for your partnership over the past eight years. Having the tremendous advantage of working with the global Nielsen team has enriched every aspect of our work with clients.

We would be remiss if we did not thank our former colleagues, Gloria Cox, Eddie Yoon, Louise Keeley, and Taddy Hall. For many years we had the benefit of their outstanding contributions, partnership, and friendship. Each of them made our firm stronger and better able to help clients achieve their profitable growth goals.

None of this would have been possible without the clients across industries, who have partnered with us to drive profitable growth. Thank you for trusting us to help solve your most difficult growth issues. It has been a privilege to work with these amazing client teams across industries and around the world.

# ABOUT THE AUTHORS

**Jason Green** is a managing director with Alvarez & Marsal and has almost 30 years of consulting experience. He is the former CEO of The Cambridge Group and was a principal with the firm for over 20 years. Jason has worked with senior management teams at companies across industries and global markets to create and sustain profitable growth in their businesses. Prior to joining The Cambridge Group, Jason was with McKinsey & Company. He holds an undergraduate degree from Yale University and an MBA from the Kellogg School at Northwestern University.

**Mark Henneman** has delivered profitable growth for more than two decades as a senior partner with The Cambridge Group, a principal with Booz Allen Hamilton (now Strategy &), and an executive with Motorola, Inc. Mark is the architect of the Demand Business System and collaborates with executive teams to unlock new sources of growth by aligning business activities with the most profitable demand in the marketplace. Mark holds a BA & MA in economics from Northwestern University and an MBA from Dartmouth College.

**Dimitar Antov** (Chicago, IL; www.thecambridgegroup.com) is a current Director and former Principal at The Cambridge Group and previously led IP development at their Economic Center of Excellence. He is also the Managing Director at Straight Forward Concepts, a consultancy specializing in sales and marketing strategy activation. In this role, he leads teams that heavily utilize quantitative analysis, machine learning, predictive modeling, CRM database scoring, BI reporting, and data visualization; he also speaks at conferences covering state-of-the-art techniques in data mining and consumer research. Dimitar holds a PhD in Economics from Northwestern University.

# Why Greater Precision

# The Growth Challenge

---

### The Big Ideas

- Profitable, organic revenue growth is harder than ever to achieve due to economic conditions, demographic shifts, changing consumer demand, and disruptive technologies among other drivers.
- Despite this dynamic, profitable, organic growth remains critical to the success of every business.
- Many of the traditional approaches for driving growth are not as successful as they once were.
- A new, more precise business model built on actionable insights into consumer demand and powered by emerging "Big Data" capabilities is a proven approach to achieving profitable growth.

---

"Net, Net
*Economic Growth Slowing +*
*Margins for Error Declining =*
*Easy Growth Behind Us"*
—Mary Meeker, Kleiner, Perkens, Caufield, Byer[1]

Few quotes sum up the current challenges facing businesses around the world better than this insight from Mary Meeker's annual "Internet Trends Report" from 2016: Perhaps growth was never easy to achieve, but clearly it will only get harder going forward. All of which makes the ability to successfully achieve profitable, organic revenue growth an even greater competitive advantage going forward. But how do managers get from the realities Mary Meeker points out to the systematic growth they need? Answering that question in detail is the purpose of this book: To share the approaches, frameworks, and analyses needed to identify and realize growth opportunities with greater precision, regardless of function or industry and to do so with solutions that range from simple "back of the envelope" exercises to those that use sophisticated Big Data analytics.

## Precision That Pays

Ultimately, achieving profitable growth in a rapidly changing environment requires a more precise business system, complete with actionable insights into customer demand that leverage Big Data capabilities as much as possible. Building a more precise, demand-based business system has helped our clients, across industries and around the world, to attain new levels of growth after years of flat or declining sales, despite challenging market conditions, a changing competitive set, and disruptive new technologies.

In our experience, "precision that pays" starts with new insights into a firm's most valuable customers. Not just who they are and what they buy, but how they think about a category, a firm's offers, the brand, and the competition. Those insights are translated into more precise ways of reaching high-value customers and consumers in their preferred purchase locations and in the forms of media with which they are most engaged through a more compelling message and ultimately with offers that are more closely tailored to their demands. In short, the model we are describing starts by anticipating the demands of your most attractive customers, aligning offers and all business functions to serve those demands, and continually improving every aspect of the business by using a "test and learn" approach to monitor results and adapt as needed. This structure depends upon Big Data, or the growing sets of data that are now available, and analytics, by which we mean the tools for analyzing and making sense of those data. The dynamic growth in available information about consumers, in addition to increased sophistication in the tools and techniques used in synthesizing those data, are essential components in this framework. An overview of the approach and the questions addressed at each step could appear as shown in Figures 1.1 and 1.2.

Precision, in the context of this discussion, has two distinct meanings. One important aspect of precision is assessing how accurately you understand customer demand for your products. A good gauge for determining if you have the insights you need to build from is to ask yourself and your team a question that the founder of our firm, Rick Kash, often asks our clients: "What do you know about the demand of your most profitable customers that your competitors don't know?" Many business leaders take pause at this deceptively simple question in part because they are not exactly certain who their most profitable customers are or how best to describe them. Beyond that, they may have only a rudimentary knowledge of their customers' most important needs and the rational, emotional, and social reasons that really drive their purchase decisions.

The ultimate litmus test is to identify those insights that are truly proprietary to your business. These are the insights that create potentially significant advantages because they are not known to your competitors,

| How | Who | What | Where | Why | How To |
|---|---|---|---|---|---|
| • How will demand shift going forward, what "forces and factors" will drive changes in demand, and what are the implications? | • Who are the most important consumers in the category… sales, growth, and profit? | • What is their current, latent, and emerging demand?<br><br>• What do they consume and buy today?<br><br>• What would they prefer to consume and buy? | • Where do they live?<br><br>• Where do they shop?<br><br>• Where can we reach them through media? | • Why do they consume what they do?<br><br>• Why do they shop where they do?<br><br>• Why do they buy what they do? | • How should we win with them?<br><br>• How should we position brands?<br><br>• How should we innovate?<br><br>• How should we activate demand in the store?<br><br>• How should we allocate resources across the company? |

**Figure 1.1  Optimized business system insights and aligned activation.**

| | How | Who | What | Where | Why | How To |
|---|---|---|---|---|---|---|
| Key Questions | • How will demand shift, what will drive changes, and what are the implications? | • Who are the most attractive customers/consumers to focus on and why? | • What are the most attractive customers' needs/demands? | • Where do they go to learn about, shop for, and fulfill their needs/demands? | • Why do they make the purchase decisions they make? | • How can we win with them? To win, how much should we invest and in which efforts? |
| Traditional Approach | • Traditional forecasting models to develop estimates of market demand | • Market segmentation is often based on demographics and/or behaviors, which is largely backward looking and static | • Often behaviorally based...assumes the product purchased yesterday will be purchased again tomorrow | • Using a broad brush to cover all relevant channels of distribution and media regardless of the actual opportunity **within** each channel | • Insights into the rational, emotional, and social drivers of purchase decisions | • Resources are spread "horizontally" like peanut butter with each BU/brand getting its fair share of increases |
| Optimized Approach | • An ongoing "Early Warning System" with demand signposts and "forces and factors" to track in real time | • Enhanced Demand Landscape segments on demand and adds demographics and behaviors for forward looking, dynamic view | • Insights into the specific problems customers are trying to solve ("Jobs to Be Done") identifies offer improvement and innovation options | • Focusing on specific stores, not just channels or retailers and specific "programs," not just traditional or social media types | • Developing insights into the rational, emotional, and social drivers of purchasing within the context of the purchase decision journey | • Specific "vertical" allocations are made based on roles BUs/brands play in the portfolio; fund the most attractive opportunities on a forward going basis |
| Big Data Options | • Leveraged to track signposts and sense market changes on an ongoing basis | • Ability to append additional data sets to the Enhanced Demand Landscape to enrich profiles and insights in real time | • Conduct ongoing A/B testing to continually improve and optimize offers by customer segment over time based on responses | • Predictive models to assign customers and their households to segments, map home locations, and store trading areas and assess media consumption data | • Build propensity models to determine the likelihood of purchase/response for an offer by customer and/or likelihood of retaining customer | • Real time results of resource allocation investments across critical metrics ...not just sales, but sales with target segment A...ability to monitor and take action closer to real time |

Figure 1.2   The optimized approach to growth goes beyond traditional approaches while leveraging Big Data capabilities.

or at the very least, your competitors are not acting on them. It is the type of insight we uncovered in our work with Allstate Insurance that led Allstate to be the first to offer "Accident Forgiveness" and "Deductible Rewards®" for good drivers.[2]

Prior to introducing the Accident Forgiveness and the Deductible Rewards® features in a new offer Allstate called "Your Choice Auto Insurance," Allstate and other insurance companies that sold through insurance agents were facing significant pressure from insurance companies like GEICO that sold policies directly over the phone or online. The "direct model" had much lower costs than the agent model, which allowed the direct players to charge less for "no-frills" insurance packages. GEICO, the leader among direct players, embodied this approach through its well-known ad slogan, "15 minutes could save you 15% or more on car insurance."[3] As the no-frills, direct insurance players continued to grow, the management team at Allstate was concerned that car insurance was quickly becoming a commodity market in which the lowest-cost provider would always win. Increasingly, the benefits of having a personal insurance agent located close by did not seem to justify the costs of the agent-based model. The team at Allstate wondered how it could break out of the commodity trap by successfully differentiating its offers while also making its agent network an advantage again.

The answer would come from two important, proprietary customer insights. First, Allstate discovered through quantitative research that lowest price was not the only consideration among all car insurance customers. In fact, about 40% of consumers were looking for high-quality coverage and the ability to protect their net worth in the event of a car accident.[4] Second, Allstate came to realize how unfair these highly attractive, quality-focused insurance customers thought car insurance was. These customers did not understand why even the most responsible driver could be penalized for things that they could not possibly control, such as having his or her car damaged by another driver while parked in a parking lot. It also seemed incredibly unfair that consumers paid insurance premiums for coverage year after year, but if the consumer ever actually needed to use his or her insurance policy by filing a claim for an at-fault accident, those premiums would suddenly spike upward. What these valuable consumers really wanted was to make the current relationship with their insurer less one-sided and much more reciprocal. With these insights, Allstate created "Your Choice Auto Insurance" to satisfy those complaints of inequity that the company was hearing from its most valuable consumers.

Allstate's Accident Forgiveness feature was perfectly designed to appeal to the most responsible drivers in the market. This feature allowed an Allstate customer a limited number of at-fault accidents over time that could be "forgiven," meaning the accident would not raise the driver's insurance premiums the way most other auto insurance policies would. The Accident Forgiveness offer was incredibly appealing to good drivers, for they were willing to pay a slight premium for protection against the risk of unexpected rate increases. Moreover, drivers who had frequent accidents over a relatively short period would quickly see their monthly premiums rise and would never realize the type of benefit their low-risk counterparts gained from Accident Forgiveness. Additionally, low-risk drivers were less likely to leave Allstate because they were earning Deductible Rewards® – or period-over-period rate decreases as a reward for a clean driving record – each year they went without an accident.

Allstate's "Your Choice Auto Insurance" became the most successful new auto insurance offer the company had ever introduced at that point.[5] Soon after the new offers were introduced, *The Wall Street Journal* reported that Your Choice was having a significant impact on sales: "Anita Sally, an Allstate agent in Bartlett, Tenn., says her sales of Your Choice products are up 20% to 30% over sales of Allstate's standard product."[6] Ultimately, "Your Choice" was so successful in the car insurance market that the concept was also extended to home insurance.[7]

Beyond the precision behind proprietary insights like those that Allstate leveraged, we also use precision in the context of making the best resource allocation decisions in order to win in the market. Actionable demand insights have helped our clients optimize decisions about where to invest to generate attractive returns and where to avoid spending. Allstate saw this firsthand with the decision to target customers who were seeking higher quality rather than the lowest price, which facilitated the decision to design and launch successful "Your Choice Auto Insurance" offers to win with those customers rather than wasting resources chasing cost-conscious customers.

In many cases, these precise new insights are either identified through, or enabled by, the use of Big Data. This data-driven precision has generated actionable insights that have spurred countless clients to invest in exactly those products or services that are most valued by their key customers while avoiding the wasted spend from adding costly features that those same customers do not value. In addition, for products sold through retail stores, more precise insights into demand allow businesses to determine which stores have the highest potential for selling their products and which stores should be avoided. One approach for identifying the highest potential retail stores for a given product is to map all 117 million U.S. households[8] to the stores where they shop using Nielsen data or other proprietary data sets. The level of precision possible can even determine exactly where within a specific store a given product should be sold and how it should be merchandised. A more refined understanding of demand can also be the catalyst for the development of an entirely new business model instead of simply adapting old models to fit new targets.

The guiding principle is to focus on what we call "precision that pays," or proprietary customer insights that explain the drivers of customer preference and why they *really* choose the products and services they buy. The right level of precision helps guide the best possible resource allocation decisions while avoiding unnecessary waste. Ultimately, "precision that pays" can increase sales while lowering costs, as the case studies in this book will demonstrate.

## A Challenging Growth Environment

We believe greater precision will be needed as the rapid, often dramatic changes taking place in today's business environment make the challenge of achieving profitable growth going forward more difficult than ever. Among the major drivers of these significant shifts are a slowing economy; globalization; demographic changes; digital disruption to traditional business models; other new technologies, such as 3D printing, nanotechnology, and robotics; evolving consumer trends; and changing competitive dynamics. Any one of these factors alone might pose challenges to an individual firm's growth prospects, but taken together, they create major barriers. As Mary Meeker points out, in a business environment with "margins for error declining,"[9] success will require greater precision than ever before.

One of the most significant impediments to corporate growth is the stagnant economic environment that the United States and many other countries are experiencing. Unfortunately, the U.S. economic forecast continues to have bleak short-term prospects, with low growth coupled with increasing uncertainty. The Conference Board projected U.S. GDP growth of 2.2% in 2018,[10] which is far below the historical average from 1948 to 2010 of 3.31%.[11] Long-term projections forecast lower levels of GDP growth as a "new normal" for the U.S. According to the PricewaterhouseCoopers (PwC) report "The World in 2050," published in 2015, average real GDP growth for the U.S. from 2014–2050 is projected to be only 2.4% annually.[12]

In many parts of the developed world, prospects for economic growth are even lower than the U.S. forecast. The same PwC report projects average real GDP growth per year for the European Union at 2.0% for the period from 2014–2050. Notably, key developed markets, including Germany and Japan, are expected to experience GDP growth rates of only 1.5% and 1.4%, respectively. GDP growth rates for both Germany and Japan will be pulled down, in part, by negative population growth rates of −0.4% and −0.5%, respectively, according to the PwC report.[13]

Meanwhile, the rapid growth experienced by many developing markets, especially China, has cooled over the past decade. Over the past 20 years (1996–2015), real global GDP growth averaged 3.8% per year according to the International Monetary Fund's "World Economic Report" from April 2016.[14] During that same period, China experienced average GDP growth of over 9.4%, based on data from The World Bank.[15] As recently as 2007, China had achieved annual real GDP growth of over 14%.[16] However, even China is forecast to regress closer to the global mean with projected annual GDP growth of only 3.4% for 2014–2050, according to PwC.[17] Meanwhile, global GDP growth for 2014–2050 is forecast to decline by almost 25% to about 3.0% annual growth .[18]

## Generational Shifts in the U.S.

One of the drivers of the low growth forecast for the U.S. is a major demographic shift.[19] Consumer spending currently accounts for over two-thirds of the U.S. economy,[20] which is an outcome of the economic growth seen in the U.S. post–World War II, along with the rapid population growth during that period that became commonly known as the "Baby Boom."[21] Throughout the Baby Boom, generally considered the period from 1946 to 1964, the U.S. population increased by an average of about 1.8 percent per year.[22] In contrast, the U.S. population grew by only 0.7 percent from

July 2015 to July of 2016, according to the U.S. Census.[23] The last time that U.S. population growth rates this low were recorded was in 1937 as the U.S. suffered through the Great Depression.[24]

Starting in 2015, Baby Boomers were no longer the largest living age group in the U.S. Instead, the Millennial generation, which is considered by the U.S. Census to have been born between 1982 and 2000,[25] surpassed the Boomers in terms of number of people.[26] Looking forward to 2020, the U.S. Census Bureau predicts that there will be 81 million Millennials and about 71 million Boomers.[27] As Millennials grow as a percentage of the total U.S. population, they will also grow in terms of purchasing power. Household spending attributed to Millennials is projected to eclipse the spending represented by Boomer households starting in 2018 or 2019.[28] By 2020, Millennial households in the U.S. will spend over $1.8 trillion annually while Boomer households are expected to spend under $1.6 trillion per year.[29] All of this evidence shows that, after this inflection point, the U.S. will transition from a Boomer-driven economy to one driven by Millennial spending.

Several interrelated economic and demographic factors will weigh on the U.S. economy during this transition. First, the U.S. middle class continues to shrink. From 1971 to 2015, adults in the U.S. middle class, defined as households with an annual income between $41,000 and $125,000, has dropped from 61% of adults to 50% of adults.[30] At the same time, the two lowest U.S. income brackets have increased by 4 percentage points, from 25% to 29%, and the two highest U.S. income tiers have grown by 7 percentage points, from 14% to 21%. Given these trends, along with the fact that consumer spending represents about two-thirds of U.S. GDP, a vibrant, growing middle class and the millions of purchases that these consumers make every day are absolutely critical to driving GDP growth.[31]

Millennials are just entering what should be their peak earning and spending years. In the U.S., income and spending both tend to increase until age 34 before peaking from ages 35 to 54. Starting at age 55, income and spending begin to decline.[32] The oldest Millennials are just turning 35, but the spending and economic growth this generation should be driving may be delayed as Millennials delay the many major life milestones, including marriage, starting a family, or buying a home, that often trigger significant spending.

One of the reasons Millennials may be delaying key life stages and the spending they typically trigger is the crushing amount of student debt they have accrued. In the span of just a few years, from 2005 to 2012, the average amount of student debt among Americans under 30 almost doubled from $13,340 to $24,897.[33] By 2016, the average graduate had over $37,000 in student loans, and as a generation, Millennials are carrying the majority of the staggering $1.4 trillion in U.S. student loan debt.[34] No wonder the wedding has to wait.

Marriage among Millennials does provide a case in point for how dramatic these generational changes have been. In the 1970s, 80 percent of Americans aged 30 or younger were married.[35] Today, 80 percent of Americans aged 45 or younger are married because most Millennials have significantly delayed marriage versus prior generations. In fact, it is more common for Millennials aged 18 to 34 to live with their parents than to live with a spouse. Compare this to 1975, when the majority of 18- to 34-year-olds, fully 57% of them, lived with their spouse.[36]

The fact that Millennials have delayed leaving home and starting households of their own has slowed housing starts and dampened the housing sector, which is a major part of the U.S. economy as a whole. As officials from the Federal Reserve Bank of San Francisco reported, "The recovery in the housing sector has been even slower than for the overall economy. In particular, the pace of housing starts remains subdued by historical standards. This muted recovery can be traced in part to the slow pace of household formation, especially among young adults. In turn, the share of young adults living with parents has grown in recent years."[37]

Whether or not Millennials will spend at the level of prior generations, as they hit the traditional peak earning and spending years, is an open question. What is not being questioned is the fact that Boomers, who are retiring in record numbers, will begin spending less.[38] By 2060, the number of Americans aged 65 and older is expected to more than double, from about 46 million people today to over 98 million in 2060.[39] According to Derek Thompson of *The Atlantic*, "Of the many significant forces shaping the U.S. economy – including globalization, automation, and housing supply – none is so inevitable and invisible as the sheer march of time for today's adults. In the 1950s, at the height of the U.S. manufacturing supremacy, less than 10 percent of the country was older than 65. That share will double to 20 percent by 2050."[40]

# The Age of Disruption

In addition to an increasingly difficult growth environment, many established companies and industries are facing new types of competitors, often from nontraditional players, as industry disruption becomes the norm. Online models and technology have been broadly leveraged to disrupt major industries, including retailing, media, financial services, and automotive, among others.

In the retail industry, Amazon and other online retailers are changing the face of the nearly $5 trillion U.S. retail industry.[41] Long gone are the days of the general store and its motto, "If we don't have it, you don't need it." The virtually unlimited selection, incredible convenience, and increasingly rapid product delivery of online shopping has put pressure on traditional "brick and mortar" stores of all types, including department stores, specialty retailers, and increasingly, grocery stores. Amazon's acquisition of Whole Foods in June of 2017 certainly seems to underscore how serious online retailers are about growing in grocery.[42]

Online retail sales have more than doubled from 2010 to 2016, going from $153 billion to $387 billion or from about 4% of total sales to 8% of total retail sales.[43, 44] More importantly, the percent of consumers who researched their purchase online but then bought it in a physical store has jumped from 24% in 2010 to 58% in 2016.[45] While retail sales as a whole increased at a rate of about 3.4% per year from 2010 to 2016, the portion of sales that was either digitally influenced or completed online grew by 17% per year. At the same time, traditional store-based retail sales with no online research or any type of online involvement declined by over $1 trillion from 2010 to 2016.[46]

Meanwhile, looking beyond retail, Facebook, Google, and Netflix, along with other social media sites, search engines, and streaming media services, are changing the ways people consume media, find information, and spend their free time, all of which has had an enormous impact on traditional media including television, radio, and newspapers. As audiences have increasingly moved online, the advertisers have followed by using their ad budgets to target digital consumers with greater frequency. In 2016, advertising spend in the U.S. topped $200 billion, making the U.S. by far the largest advertising market in the world in terms of dollars.[47]

2016 represented an inflection point in the advertising world, as for the first time digital ad spending eclipsed TV ad spend.[48] This shift marked a dramatic change for an industry that was dominated by the "Big Three" TV networks – ABC, CBS, and NBC – from the late 1940s to the early 1990s. During that period, almost any advertiser could reach the audience it wanted to influence on one of the three major TV networks. Now, TV audiences are much more fragmented across hundreds of channels while the two biggest digital players, Google and Facebook, provide access to huge audiences and offer the ability to target customers more precisely than ever before. The shift from TV to digital will continue to swing, as digital ad spend is projected to grow to over $105 billion by 2020 while TV ad spend will increase more modestly to about $77 billion.[49] Clearly, in this new Age of Disruption, the real question is not who or when your business will be disrupted, but how can you best disrupt your own industry.

Technology is not the only driver of disruption, however: Changes in consumer preferences are bringing significant disruption to many industries, including the U.S. food and beverage industry. Industry veteran Steve Hughes, who had leadership roles at ConAgra, Tropicana, Celestial Seasonings, and White Wave before founding Boulder Brands, told *Fortune* magazine, "I've been doing this for 37 years, and this is the most dynamic, disruptive, and transformational time that I've seen in my career."[50] A similarly stark picture for the packaged food industry is painted by Bob Wheatley, who is the CEO of Emergent. Wheatley, whose firm helps companies understand the potential business opportunities as consumers pursue healthier living, noted in a blog post, "The single most important and disruptive change in food culture, now winding its way through virtually every part of the industry, is the overwhelming desire for fresh foods . . .[.] The packaged food world finds itself facing a state of transition as fresh versions overtake and replace their processed cousins . . .[.] We are moving from a production-fueled system to a demand-driven system, founded on the consumer's interest in real foods."[51]

In an interesting reversal taking place across industries, the traditional "barriers to entry" that have long protected established industries and businesses have increasingly become impediments to their success. Economies of scale and vertical integration across the supply chain once allowed large firms with familiar, mass-marketed brands to consolidate industries by buying up smaller rivals or making it nearly impossible for them to compete successfully. Now many fast-growing businesses across industries, including food, beverage, clothing, and fashion accessories, are the small, "authentic" brands that charge a premium price for products that are hand-crafted, artisanal, small-batch, or bespoke. These brands do not have huge economies of scale, massive advertising and promotion budgets, or dominant distribution networks. As Denise Morrison, CEO of the Campbell Soup Company, noted, "We understand that increasing numbers of consumers are seeking authentic, genuine food experiences, and we know that they are very skeptical of the ability of large, long-established food companies to deliver them."[52]

Meanwhile the "sharing economy" has created platforms for ride sharing (Uber and Lyft), peer-to-peer lending (Go Fund Me), home rental (Airbnb), and even sharing power tools and other equipment with neighbors (Peerby). In many respects, the sharing economy really demonstrates a fundamental shift from the traditional definition of businesses as one of two types: Businesses that sell to other businesses (B2B), or businesses that sell to consumers (B2C). The sharing economy is typically made up of platforms that allow consumer-to-consumer (C2C) transactions to provide goods and services. These C2C transactions generally focus on "monetizing" the many underutilized items consumers own, from renting out infrequently used items, such as power saws, prom dresses, or weekend homes, to using extra cash to provide loans to others. These sharing economy platforms allow people to use sporadic periods of free time to engage in a "side hustle" to earn extra money. One of the major reasons that the sharing economy is a relatively recent phenomenon is that virtually all sharing economy businesses rely on Big Data, complex analytics, and emerging technologies and platforms to make them possible.

## The Profitable Growth Imperative

Despite the potential headwinds, profitable growth is still the key to a successful business. As a *McKinsey Quarterly* article from 2015 noted, "There's no escaping the fact that growth is a critical driver of performance as measured by total returns to shareholders (TRS). And TRS underperformers are far more likely to be acquired."[53] The most successful businesses reliably generate meaningful levels of growth for shareholders and remain independent, while those publicly traded firms that fail to drive consistent growth are more likely to be taken over by new owners. Simply put, growth separates the winners from the also-rans.

When evaluating firms to invest in or acquire, Warren Buffett, arguably the world's most successful investor, uses consistent, profitable growth as his preliminary search criterion.[54] One measure of profitable growth is return on shareholders' equity (ROE), which is a robust metric for assessing the underlying health of a business while also providing a benchmark versus other companies. In addition, ROE, which is calculated as a firm's net income divided by its shareholders' equity, can be a useful indicator of a firm's future potential. As noted by the aforementioned equation, ROE will grow as net income increases, assuming constant shareholders' equity. However, simply having a brief spike in ROE, driven by cost cutting or a "one-off" new product, is not enough to demonstrate the strong trend for which Buffett is searching. Instead, he and his team at Berkshire Hathaway focus on acquiring publicly traded companies with long histories of independently audited results that can be analyzed to determine the drivers of net income growth, along with the sustainability of those drivers.[55]

Warren Buffett looks for other key metrics in addition to ROE, such as the uniqueness of the company's product offerings, the firm's profit margins, the firm's debt levels, and the strength of the management team, among others.[56] As a value investor, Buffett also looks to purchase businesses with attractive growth prospects at a discount to what he believes to be the intrinsic value of the company;[57] however, the business's potential to drive profitable growth going forward is the real key. In an interview with the Financial Crisis Inquiry Commission in 2010, Buffett summed this up as "pricing power," noting, "The single most important decision in evaluating a business is pricing power. If you've got the power to raise prices without losing business to a competitor, you've got a very good business. And if you have to have a prayer session before raising prices by ten percent, then you've got a terrible business."[58] Raising prices without losing share to a competitor is one driver of profitable growth and is a reflection of a highly differentiated set of products or services without meaningful substitutes.

# The Innovation Edge

Some businesses, like Apple, drive organic growth and pricing power through successful innovation. As Walter Isaacson noted in his best-selling biography, *Steve Jobs*, "At a time when the United States is seeking ways to sustain its innovative edge, and when societies around the world are trying to build creative digital-age economies, Jobs stands as the ultimate icon of inventiveness, imagination, and sustained innovation . . .[.] He and his colleagues at Apple were able to think differently: They developed not merely modest product advances based on focus groups, but whole new devices and services that consumers did not yet know they needed."[59] So why not use innovation as a means of driving growth by introducing exciting new "must have" products to customers as Steve Jobs did?

The problem, of course, is that Steve Jobs was the exception rather than the rule, for achieving successful innovation is incredibly difficult to execute and sustain. In fact, a recent study published in the *Harvard Business Review* reported that "84% of corporate leaders say innovation is a high priority" and that "94% are dissatisfied with their firms' innovation performance."[60] Without Steve Jobs, even Apple appears to have lost some of its innovation edge. Adam Lashinsky, author of *Inside Apple*, had this to say one year after Steve Jobs' death: "Apple just had one of the most extraordinary 15-year runs [in business history]. It is unreasonable to duplicate that, even if Jobs were still alive."[61] And, a *National Public Radio* report from 2017 argues, "Both Apple fans and analysts who follow the company are beginning to wonder whether Apple has lost its mojo."[62] Even Apple co-founder Steve Wozniak told *Bloomberg Canada* in a 2017 interview that his bet is that the next great innovation, or "moonshot," as he called it, "will not come from Apple but from Tesla."[63]

None of this is to say that innovation is impossible or that innovation should not be explored as a means of driving growth. It simply points out the reality that meaningful innovation, like profitable growth overall, has become more difficult for most businesses to achieve. The good news, as we will discuss later, is that a more precise understanding of demand, customers, competitors, and market opportunities has helped our clients across industries to identify and introduce many of the most successful new offers they have ever launched.

## Big Data's Role

Could Big Data be the answer for finding profitable growth? Big Data has become a common buzzword that many business managers use today without a very deep understanding of what it means or how it could be used to support their growth initiatives. As Floyd Yager, SVP at Allstate, put it,

"Everyone is saying Big Data is going to change the world. But companies have to figure out what's important to them and get out of the hyped world."[64] In other words, most businesses need to stop talking about Big Data and must go beyond merely collecting massive amounts of information. They need to start leveraging those data in ways that tangibly impact business performance.

We define Big Data as a vast ecosystem of diverse pieces of information sourced from different domains that are supported by computer science, machine learning, and data visualization technologies. The power and the promise of Big Data can be harnessed across all aspects of the business, especially in support of identifying and executing profitable growth. Specifically, Big Data can be used to help form new hypotheses, generate insights, conduct statistical testing, create simulations, and build predictive models to answer the whys, the hows, the wheres, and the whens of consumer needs and behavior, competitive dynamics, and market evolution. These approaches could yield unprecedented levels of proprietary, actionable knowledge of your customers along with precise strategic and tactical plans to satisfy their demand.

Despite its promise, Big Data alone is not the answer to profitable growth. In many cases, business practitioners make the mistake of attributing causal effects to spurious correlations found in the data. One example of this issue that many consumers experience is the seemingly endless stream of ads that pop up on every website you visit. These ads will invite customers to purchase the exact same chinos, Mother's Day gift, or coffeemaker that they recently purchased online. This example is a mistaken use of what is called "behavioral data." The underlying logic is that the behavior observed is strongly correlated to something this individual will do again or is highly interested in purchasing again. In this case, the behavior of buying some chinos leads to the mistaken assumption that the person who recently bought chinos will buy more chinos today. So, as the person who bought chinos explores his or her favorite websites, social media outlets, and search engines, the algorithms keep serving up offers for chinos even though that person may not be interested in buying chinos again in the short or long run.

When used effectively, past historical information that is backward-looking in nature actually can be very predictive of future outcomes. Winston Churchill highlighted this point when he said, "The farther back you can look, the farther forward you are likely to see."[65] The meaningful correlation for the person buying chinos might be that he or she purchases chinos every other year, or that the chinos are purchased each spring, or even whenever the weather in his or her town gets back above 60 degrees each year. Big Data, if used correctly, can help firms pinpoint which of these cases is true, and enable decision-making regarding how and when to promote appropriate products.

Several years ago, we identified an actionable correlation for a client who makes an antacid relief product: The people who used the product most often experienced more stress than most other people do, and that stress often translated into an upset stomach. Like many people, money and personal finances were among the greatest sources of stress for those who frequently experienced an upset stomach. One behavior these people commonly exhibited was to check their investments and their retirement funds whenever the stock market went down. So, rather than be one of dozens of remedies for an upset stomach on the health websites where all of their competitors advertised, our client broke through the clutter by being the only antacid on financial sites whenever the roller coaster ride of Wall Street created the greatest stress among the heaviest users of antacids.

We believe Big Data should be part of the answer now and that it will become an increasingly important part of the answer going forward. But, we also believe that a clear-eyed understanding of the limitations of Big Data is necessary. Big Data is really a vast amount of information that can be mined and analyzed, not a solution for driving profitable growth in and of itself. One of the best ways to leverage Big Data is to make the insights derived from it part of a continuous "learning lab" for driving growth. What this means is to constantly test new hypotheses and insights gleaned from Big Data and then learn how to improve approaches based on the results of each test. Did consumers respond more often to e-mail message A or message B? What drove the biggest increase in sales, a 5% discount or free shipping? The key to building this structure is to cultivate an environment for rapid testing and evaluation of outcomes so that any strategies evolve in a continuous iterative fashion. The result is greater precision in planning your actions along with better results from your actions.

## Cost Cutting and Its Limitations

Given how much more difficult profitable growth is to achieve, it is no wonder that many companies are on a cost-cutting binge. Cost reduction programs such as Zero-Based Budgeting (ZBB) seem to be *the* strategy for many companies that can't find organic, top line growth. According to *Seeking Alpha*, a U.S. stock market analysis website, the number of companies mentioning their ZBB programs during their earnings calls increased more than sixfold in the span of just two years, from only 14 in 2013 to 90 companies in 2015.[66] Cutting costs can certainly improve the bottom line for companies, but these programs have obvious limitations. As a result, Wall Street has historically rewarded predictable growth much more than it has rewarded cost takeouts.

Clearly, costs always need to be managed: Unnecessary waste should be eliminated whenever possible, and, at times, costs need to be reevaluated and reined in. While cost-cutting programs are sometimes required, they have several potentially significant downsides of which business leaders must be mindful. First, there is a limit to the amount of cost that can be taken out over a given period. A cost reduction program may have meaningful success in year one, but could then run out of costs that can be squeezed in year two. As Nestle's CEO, Ulf Mark Schneider, said at a 2017 shareholder's meeting, "Many companies are focusing on radical cost-cutting to deliver higher profits in the short term. This approach is not sustainable."[67]

Beyond the potential lack of sustainability, there is no doubt that cost cutting can go only so far before it potentially damages the business. Identifying the cost boundaries that should not be crossed during a "radical" cost-cutting exercise can be difficult, especially when the organization has created strong incentives to achieve significant savings. The potential damage done if the line is crossed could include reducing quality so much that it causes customers to leave, deferring investments that might eventually hobble the business, or drain employee morale. Any one of these unintended consequences of a cost-cutting program could take years to repair.

In addition, cost reduction programs may not create competitive advantages as competitors often follow suit and streamline their cost structures. The jump from 14 to 90 companies announcing ZBB programs seems to suggest that many companies could find themselves right back to the status quo as their own cost reduction efforts are matched by their key competitors. In other words, conducting a program like ZBB may become table stakes for competing rather than something that creates any type of sustainable competitive advantage.

However, ZBB and other cost-cutting programs have their proponents and have successfully delivered results in terms of profit gains. Perhaps the most famous proponent of the approach is the Private Equity firm 3G Capital, which owns Anheuser-Busch InBev, Kraft Heinz, and Burger King, among other companies. While controversial, the 3G approach has had success, as noted by the *Financial Times*: "The founders of 3G have transformed the beer, fast food and food manufacturing industries with bold acquisitions, which are quickly followed by a brutal but disciplined attack on costs, a surge in profitability and high returns to shareholders."[68] It should also be noted that Warren Buffett worked with 3G to create Kraft Heinz and to acquire Canadian fast food and coffee chain Tim Horton's.

Other industry observers believe that 3G's unrelenting focus on costs results in a poor track record of organic growth, brand building, and innovation. According to *Fortune* magazine, "Kraft Heinz today illustrates the essential 3G: quite possibly the world's best at creating value by eliminating costs and focusing on the most promising opportunities, but not adept at growing the top line organically."[69] In addition, *Fortune* notes that growth is driven by acquisitions rather than through organic growth, and that finding attractive acquisitions can't go on forever: "The 3G managers developed extraordinary skill and greatly increased the value of every company they bought, but they were not great innovators . . .[.] And there's the rub: a central feature of this model is it can't work forever."[70]

The 3G team and its proponents argue that they have invested in and achieved organic growth. According to Alex Behring, chairman of Kraft Heinz and a founding partner of 3G, "We build brands. We aggressively reinvest in our product innovation, expansion into global white spaces and brand health."[71] Mr. Behring says that by freeing up funds through cost cutting, 3G has been able to invest in strategies that have resulted in successful organic growth.

While a traditional cost-cutting program like ZBB is unlikely to drive organic growth in and of itself, it certainly can free up the dollars to invest in growth. As a *McKinsey Quarterly* article aimed at dispelling common "myths" about ZBB programs stated, "ZBB frees up unproductive costs and allows those savings to be taken to the bottom line or redirected to more productive areas that will drive future growth."[72] Savings generated from ZBB can be used to invest in brand building and innovation to enhance the long-term health of the business, but those savings often drop to the bottom line to immediately improve margins and shareholder returns instead.

In our experience, companies across industries can capture cost savings that go beyond what cost-cutting programs like ZBB can identify *in addition to* creating the insights required to drive profitable, organic growth. The key to optimizing costs and maximizing growth opportunities simultaneously is developing more precise, proprietary insights into customer demand and how to win with the most attractive customers in the market using the latest Big Data advances as much as possible.

## Getting to Growth

Achieving profitable growth is still critical to every business's success. However, successfully driving profitable growth has become harder than ever. It seems clear that in this new environment, many of the traditional approaches to driving growth and profitability, including innovation efforts, a reliance on historical "barriers to entry," and cost-cutting programs, are not working as well as they once did. We believe there is a better way – a more precise, more predictable way – of achieving growth, which we will discuss throughout this book through a series of framework overviews and discussions of client success stories. First, however, we will introduce a critical framework, called the "Demand-Based Business System," that we have deployed in many organizations to drive growth and, in turn, help them rise to the top in the incredibly competitive industries in which they operate.

## Questions for Monday Morning

1. Who are your most profitable customers?
2. What do you know about the demand of your most profitable customers that your competitors don't know?
3. How would you describe your most profitable customers, in terms of demographics, behaviors, category engagement, or other key descriptors?

4. Where do you see opportunities to be more precise with your target consumer?

5. How can your firm leverage Big Data to gain a better understanding of what your customers are demanding?

6. How can you ensure that your firm is using Big Data and analytics effectively, while also avoiding "analysis paralysis"?

7. What new competitors are you seeing in your industry? From where might additional disruption to your business come?

# Endnotes

1. Meeker, Mary. "Internet Trends Report." 2016 Internet Trends Report. 1 June 2016. https://www.youtube.com/watch?v=334Gfug 5OL0. Accessed July 2017.

2. "The Allstate Corporation. 2005 Summary Annual Report." The Allstate Corporation. 2005. https://www.allstate.com/resources/allstate/attachments/about/allstate-sar-2005.pdf.

3. "Geico Advertising Campaigns." Wikipedia. https://en.wikipedia.org/wiki/GEICO_advertising_campaigns.com. Accessed July 2017.

4. Kash, Rick and Dave Calhoun. *How Companies Win*. New York: HarperCollins. 2010. 133.

5. Ibid.

6. Saranow, Jennifer. "A Rewards Plan for Auto Insurance." *The Wall Street Journal*. 3 May 2005. https://www.wsj.com/articles/SB111508167634322842. Accessed July 2017.

7. Ibid.

8. Lofquist, Daphne, Terry Logaila, Martin O'Connell, and Sarah Feliz. "Households and Families. 2010 Census Briefs." United States Census Bureau. April 2012. https://www.census.gov/prod/cen2010/briefs/c2010br-14.pdf. Accessed July 2017.

9. Meeker, Mary. "Internet Trends Report." 2016 Internet Trends Report. 1 June 2016. https://www.youtube.com/watch?v=334Gfug 5OL0. Accessed July 2017.

10. "Global Economic Outlook 2018." The Conference Board. https://www.conference-board.org/economic-outlook-2018/, https://www.conference-board.org/data/usforecast.cfm. Accessed July 2017.

11. "US Real GDP Growth Rate by Year." http://www.multpl.com/us-real-gdp-growth-rate/table/by-year. Accessed July 2017.

12. "The World in 2050." PwC. February 2017. https://www.pwc.com/gx/en/issues/economy/the-world-in-2050.html. Accessed July 2017.

13. Ibid.

14. "World Economic Report." International Monetary Fund. April 2016. http://www.imf.org/external/pubs/ft/weo/2016/01/. Accessed July 2017.

15. "China." The World Bank. http://data.worldbank.org/country/china. Accessed July 2017.

16. Ibid.

17. "The World in 2016." PwC. https://www.pwc.com/gx/en/issues/economy/the-world-in-2050.html. Accessed July 2017.

18. Ibid.

19. Smialek, Jeanna. "Here's a Reason Baby Boomers Will Curb U.S. Growth This Decade." *Bloomberg*. July 29, 2016. https://www.bloomberg.com/news/articles/2016-07-29/here-s-a-reason-baby-boomers-will-curb-u-s-growth-this-decade. Accessed July 2017.

20. Mutikani, Lucia. "U.S. Economic Growth Revised Higher, Boosted by Consumer Spending." *Reuters*. March 31, 2017. http://www.reuters.com/article/us-usa-economy-gdp-idUSKBN1711MX. Accessed July 2017.

21. Colby, Sandra L. and Jennifer M. Ortman. "The Baby Boom Cohort in the United States: 2012 to 2060." United States Census Bureau. May 2014. https://www.census.gov/prod/2014pubs/p25-1141.pdf. Accessed July 2017.

22. Chokshi, Niraj. "Growth of U.S. Population Is at Slowest Pace Since 1937." *The New York Times*. 22 December 2016. https://www.nytimes.com/2016/12/22/us/usa-population-growth.html. Accessed July 2017.

23. Ibid.

24. Ibid.

25. "Millennials Outnumber Baby Boomers and Are Far More Diverse, Census Bureau Reports." United States Census Bureau. 25 July 2015. https://www.census.gov/newsroom/press-releases/2015/cb15-113.html. Accessed July 2017.

26. Fry, Richard. "Millennials Overtake Baby Boomers as America's Largest Generation." Pew Research Center. April 25, 2016. http://www.pewresearch.org/fact-tank/2016/04/25/millennials-overtake-baby-boomers/. Accessed July 2017.

27. Colby, Sandra L. and Jennifer M. Ortman. "The Baby Boom Cohort in the United States. 2012 to 2060." United States Census Bureau. May 2014. https://www.census.gov/prod/2014pubs/p25-1141.pdf. Accessed July 2017.

28. Toossi, Mitra. "Labor Force Projections to 2018. Older Workers Staying More Active." Bureau of Labor Statistics. 24 November 2009. https://www.bls.gov/opub/mlr/2009/11/art3full.pdf. Accessed July 2017.

29. Shin, Laura. "How the Millennial Generation Could Affect the Economy Over the Next Five Years." *Forbes*. 30 April 2015. https://www.forbes.com/sites/laurashin/2015/04/30/how-the-millennial-generation-could-affect-the-economy-over-the-next-five-years/#4758d90832e1. Accessed July 2017.

30. "The American Middle Class Is Losing Ground." Pew Research Center. 9 December 2015. http://www.pewsocialtrends.org/2015/12/09/the-american-middle-class-is-losing-ground/. Accessed July 2017.

31. Ibid.

32. "Generations Change How Spending Is Trending." Morgan Stanley. 26 August 2016. https://www.morganstanley.com/ideas/millennial-boomer-spending. Accessed July 2017.

33. Ibid.

34. "A Look at the Shocking Student Loan Debt Statistics for 2017." Student Loan Hero. 13 September 2017. https://studentloanhero.com/student-loan-debt-statistics/. Accessed September 2017.

35. Vespa, Jonathan. "The Changing Economics and Demographics of Young Adulthood. 1975–2016." United States Census Bureau. April 2017. https://www.census.gov/content/dam/Census/library/publications/2017/demo/p20-579.pdf. Accessed July 2017.

36. Ibid.

37. Furlong, Fred. "Household Formation among Young Adults." Federal Reserve Bank of San Francisco. 19 May 2016. http://www.frbsf.org/economic-research/publications/economic-letter/2016/may/household-formation-among-young-adults/. Accessed July 2017.

38. "Baby Boomers Retire." Pew Research Center. 29 December 2010. http://www.pewresearch.org/fact-tank/2010/12/29/baby-boomers-retire/. Accessed July 2017.

39. Mather, Mark. "Fact Sheet. Aging in the United States." Population Reference Bureau. January 2016. http://www.prb.org/Publications/Media-Guides/2016/aging-unitedstates-fact-sheet.aspx. Accessed July 2017.

40. Thompson, Derek. "The Invisible Revolution. How Aging Is Quietly Changing America." *The Atlantic*. 6 October 2016. https://www.theatlantic.com/business/archive/2016/10/aging-america/503177/. Accessed July 2017.

41. "US Retail Sales to Near $5 Trillion in 2016." *eMarketer*. 21 December 2015. https://www.emarketer.com/Article/US-Retail-Sales-Near-5-Trillion-2016/1013368. Accessed July 2017.

42. Turner, Nick, Selina Wang, and Spencer Soper. "Amazon to Acquire Whole Foods for $13.7 Billion." *Bloomberg*. 16 June 2017. https://www.bloomberg.com/news/articles/2017-06-16/amazon-to-acquire-whole-foods-in-13-7-billion-bet-on-groceries. Accessed July 2017.

43. The Cambridge Group analysis, leveraging Nielsen data.

44. Zaroban, Stefany. "U.S. e-Commerce Grows 14.6% in 2015." *Digital Commerce 360*. 17 February 2016. https://www.digitalcommerce360.com/2016/02/17/us-e-commerce-grows-146-2015/. Accessed July 2017.

45. Zaroban, Stefany. "U.S. e-Commerce Sales Grow 15.6% in 2016." *Digital Commerce 360*. 17 February 2017. https://www.digitalcommerce360.com/2017/02/17/us-e-commerce-sales-grow-156-2016/. Accessed July 2017.

46. Ibid.

47. "Statistics & Facts on the U.S. Advertising Industry." *Statista*. August 2017. https://www.statista.com/topics/979/advertising-in-the-us/. Accessed September 2017.

48. "US Digital Ad Spending to Surpass TV This Year," *eMarketer*. 13 September 2016. https://www.emarketer.com/Article/US-Digital-Ad-Spending-Surpass-TV-this-Year/1014469. Accessed July 2017.

49. "Digital Ad Spending to Surpass TV Next Year." *eMarketer*. 8 March 2016. https://www.emarketer.com/Article/Digital-Ad-Spending-Surpass-TV-Next-Year/1013671. Accessed July 2017.

50. Kowitt, Beth. "The War on Big Food." *Fortune.* 21 May 2015. http://fortune.com/2015/05/21/the-war-on-big-food/. Accessed July 2017.
51. "The Real-Food Uprising." *Emergent: The Healthy Food Agency.* 6 June 2017. http://www.emergenthealthyliving.com/2017/06/06/the-real-food-uprising/. Accessed July 2017.
52. Render, Jessica. "Why Consumers Trust Each Other More Than Brands." *Consumer Affairs for Brands.* 27 April 2016. http://blog.consumeraffairs.com/why-consumers-trust-each-other-more-than-brands-908a440ed8d7. Accessed July 2017.
53. Atsmon, Yuval and Sven Smit. "Why It's Still a World of 'Grow or Go.'" *McKinsey Quarterly.* October 2015. http://www.mckinsey.com/global-themes/employment-and-growth/why-its-still-a-world-of-grow-or-go. Accessed July 2017.
54. Reese, John P. "Warren Buffett's Investing Formula Revealed." *Forbes.* 11 October 2011. https://www.forbes.com/sites/investor/2011/10/11/warren-buffetts-investing-formula-revealed/#669ad7852fcd. Accessed July 2017.
55. Ibid.
56. Ro, Sam. "Warren Buffett Might Consider Buying Your Company If It Meets These 6 Criteria." *Business Insider.* 28 February 2015. http://www.businessinsider.com/berkshire-hathaway-acquisition-criteria-2015-2. Accessed July 2017.
57. Szramiak, John. "Warren Buffett's 4 Stock Investing Principles." *Business Insider.* 30 January 2016. http://www.businessinsider.com/warren-buffetts-4-investing-principles-2016-1. Accessed July 2017.
58. Ritholtz, Barry. "TRANSCRIPT: FCIC Interview of Warren Buffett, May 26, 2010." *The Big Picture.* 28 March 2016. http://ritholtz.com/2016/03/fcic-buffett/. Original audio file is stored on the Federal Crisis Inquiry Commission Database (https://fcic.law.stanford.edu/resource/interviews). Accessed July 2017.
59. Issacson, Walter. *Steve Jobs.* New York: Simon & Schuster. 2011.
60. Gerdemen, Dina. "Clayton Christensen: Customers Don't Simply Buy Products—They Hire Them." *Forbes.* 4 October 2016. https://www.forbes.com/sites/hbsworkingknowledge/2016/10/04/clayton-christensen-customers-dont-simply-buy-products-they-hire-them/#62d8e49bb5cf. Accessed July 2017.

61. Swartz, Jon. "Year After Jobs' Death, How High Can Apple Fly?" *USA Today.* 2 October 2012. https://www.usatoday.com/story/tech/2012/10/04/steve-jobs-apple-year-later/1577271/. Accessed July 2017.

62. Sydell, Laura. "Has Apple Lost Its Innovation Mojo?" *National Public Radio: Morning Edition.* 10 April 2017. http://www.npr.org/sections/alltechconsidered/2017/04/10/523035456/has-apple-lost-its-innovation-mojo. Accessed July 2017.

63. "Apple's Other Steve Says Apple Lost Its Mojo, Tesla Is Taking Over." *Wall Street Pit.* 4 June 2017. http://wallstreetpit.com/113555-apple-lost-its-mojo-tesla-taking-over-tsla/. Accessed July 2017.

64. Alseyer, Jennifer. "How Allstate Overhauled Its Business with Data." *Fortune.* 30 October 2014. http://fortune.com/2014/10/30/allstate-insurance-big-data/. Accessed July 2017.

65. "Winston Churchill: Quotable Quotes." *Goodreads.* https://www.goodreads.com/quotes/535242-the-farther-back-you-can-look-the-farther-forward-you. Accessed July 2017.

66. Daneshkhu, Scheherazade, Lindsay Whipp, and James Fontanella-Khan. "The Lean and Mean Approach of 3G Capital." *Financial Times.* 7 May 2017. https://www.ft.com/content/268f73e6-31a3-11e7-9555-23ef563ecf9a. Accessed July 2017.

67. Ibid.

68. Ibid.

69. Colvin, Geoff. "Buy. Squeeze. Repeat." *Fortune.* 1 February 2017. https://backissues.fortune.com/storefront/2017/kraft-s-heinz-recipe-buy-squeeze-repeat-/prodFO20170201.html. Accessed July 2017.

70. Ibid.

71. Ibid.

72. Callaghan, Shaun, Kyle Hawke, and Carey Mignerey. "Five Myths (and Realities) about Zero-Based Budgeting." *McKinsey & Company.* October 2014. http://www.mckinsey.com/business-functions/strategy-and-corporate-finance/our-insights/five-myths-and-realities-about-zero-based-budgeting. Accessed July 2017.

CHAPTER

2

# Building a Demand-Based Business System

---

### The Big Ideas

- Winning in the "new normal" of fragmented demand and slow growth requires a new management model that aligns your entire business to attract, motivate, and retain your most profitable customers.

- This demand-based business system uses a common framework for understanding and activating demand to more precisely link strategy to execution and align activities across functions.

- Building a demand-based business system requires a change in how leaders across the company see opportunities for profitable growth and jointly act to capture them.

---

As demonstrated with the Allstate example in the preceding chapter, the demand-based business system provides a compelling solution for how companies can profitably grow in an increasingly fragmented and slow-growth marketplace by bringing the precision and alignment associated with supply chain management to demand-oriented functions. The Hershey Company achieved similar successes from the demand-based business system we developed with them. As J.P. Bilbrey, then CEO of the Hershey Company, commented in an interview at the time with *Ivey Business Journal*: "After years of growth and success, we had hit a difficult period. Senior management was not aligned on how we were going to compete.... We needed to go from a supply-driven approach to a demand-driven, consumer-focused one.... Our new approach strengthened our brands, lowered inventories, reduced SKUs, created tremendous efficiencies, and generated greater cash flow.... I've never seen a jump in performance like this before."[1]

Companies that are able to sense and activate demand further down the supply chain – particularly the demand of their most profitable customers – can transform their business performance. By better synchronizing their demand and supply plans, both internally across functions and externally with distribution partners, companies are able to unlock new levels of efficiency. Our clients that have fully embedded a demand-based system across their businesses have grown 2.2 times faster than their competitors and increased their operating margins by nearly 4 points. They have optimized product portfolios, innovation pipelines, trade spend, and marketing activities to capture more of the demand of their most important customers. They have realized the old mantra of "the right product, in the right place, at the right time." In short, they have optimized growth.

At this point, you might be thinking: "What's new?" Cross-functional alignment has long been known to drive superior business results, yet, despite countless initiatives and much good faith effort, many organizations have failed at effectively managing across boundaries. In our experience, the underlying reason is that each function has a slightly different view of market opportunities that they use to establish growth strategies and operating plans. For example, the marketing organization may use a psychographic view of consumers to inform brand positioning, while the sales organization may prioritize investments based on heavy-buyer insights, and the innovation organization may fill its pipeline based on analyses of the most common attributes of the fastest growing products in the market. These conflicting views of demand actually existed at one of our clients before they started building a demand-based business model throughout their entire organization, as shown in Figure 2.1.

Given the vastly different frameworks used to create these plans, companies are forced into adopting complex and time-consuming processes

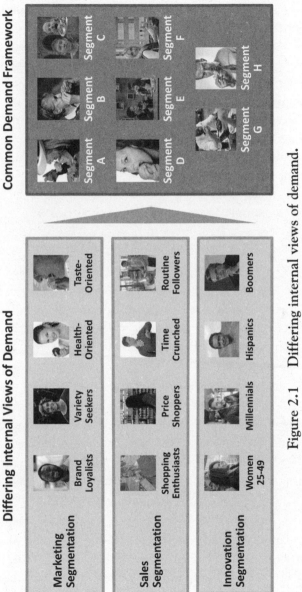

Figure 2.1    Differing internal views of demand.

to align them – and then launching equally time-consuming efforts to diagnose results when actual performance falls short of plan. The vast resources that many companies devote to their annual planning processes are the strongest testament to the challenges that still remain in achieving true cross-functional alignment.

The demand-based business system attacks the challenge at its core by creating a single, common view of demand that can be used across all parts of the company. This demand framework – the "Demand Landscape," or the "Enhanced Demand Landscape," which leverages advanced analytics and Big Data capabilities, as described in Chapter 5 – provides a fully integrated view of current, latent, and emerging customer demand. It answers the essential questions for aligning strategies and plans across organizational boundaries:

**Who are the most important customers in the market?**
To answer this question, it is important to analyze the demographic and attitudinal composition of each group, along with relative segment growth and an understanding of which new segments are emerging.

**How do they act, and what brands and products do they use?**
To address these questions, it is also important to know where they purchase, for what purpose – or job, as we will describe in Chapter 9 – are they seeking to accomplish, and why a certain brand or product "wins" on each occasion.

**What drives customers' actions?**
To answer this question, it is important to know what functional and emotional benefits drive usage and consumption, and what drives where consumers shop and purchase. Additionally, how customers characterize their "ideal" products is key, as well as how well do brands, products, services, distribution channels, and retailers deliver the benefits sought.

**What value do these customers provide to the firm?**
To answer this question, it is critical to understand the revenue and profit drivers associated with each customer segment, and how we expect revenue and profit to change in the future. Additionally, how each segment's demand is being served, how profitably that demand could be served, and under what conditions it would take to win with each segment are all critical factors to analyze.

By describing and, more importantly, quantifying the "who, what, where, when, why, and how" of marketplace demand, the Demand Landscape becomes the shared mental model for managing the business.

How does the model work in practice? Let's continue with the supply chain analogy. Supply chain management achieves alignment by building all plans and tracking results using the common element of the stock keeping unit (SKU). Sourcing, manufacturing, and logistics all develop plans and track performance through that common lens. Because each function defines terms the same way, relies on shared data to make decisions, and measures performance using aligned metrics, there is inherently tight alignment – particularly when compared to functions on the revenue-generating side of the business.

The demand business system achieves the same degree of alignment – but rather than using the SKU to coordinate activities, it uses the customer segmentation, which anchors the Demand Landscape. Marketing uses the customer segments to position brands and buy media. Innovation uses the customer segments to understand emerging need states and identify ideal product characteristics. Sales uses the customer segments to understand the demand profile of each retailer and distribution outlet to develop the right in-store assortment and programs. And supply chain aligns its activities with these demand functions by forecasting national, regional, and local demand through the lens of the customer segments. While the demand system does not eliminate the need for formal coordinating processes, it greatly simplifies the effort. But more importantly, it delivers higher return on investment (ROI) and reduces costs by ensuring that each brand, customer, and functional plan is based on the same assumptions and targeted at the same consumer or end-customer.

Figure 2.2 illustrates the central, coordinating role that a robust demand framework plays in aligning priorities, activities, and investments across a company's business system:

Creating a common demand framework is a significant achievement for any organization. As noted in the previous chapter, many of our clients capture immediate benefit from these core insights. However, to ensure sustained improvement, companies must embed the new mental model in all aspects of their day-to-day operations.

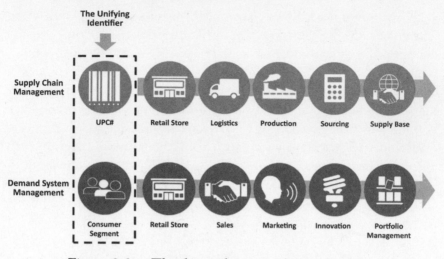

Figure 2.2    The demand system aligns activities.

Historically, accomplishing this alignment has been a challenge. Using the supply chain analogy again, it was relatively easy to coordinate activities across sourcing, manufacturing, and logistics once point-of-sale or shipment data became readily available. And these data became available because bar codes were universally adopted. There has been no similar universal data element adopted for demand-side functions, and there should not be. A company's strategy is strongly defined by the way it views market opportunities, so it would be competitive suicide for all but the largest, most financially secure companies to adopt a universal point-of-view on market demand. This inability to link robust data back to proprietary demand frameworks has been one of the primary reasons why inefficiencies have persisted across most revenue-generating functions.

But now, Big Data and advanced analytics have broken down this historical barrier. Using the extensive data routinely captured at the household or individual level, any demand framework can be linked to core operating data. This breakthrough is the foundation for the demand business system. And the wide availability of disaggregated data means that companies of all scales can build their own system. Figure 2.3 illustrates the data linkages typical of a company activating its demand framework.

Building a demand-based business system typically follows four major phases: Creating a common, integrated view of demand; grounding all

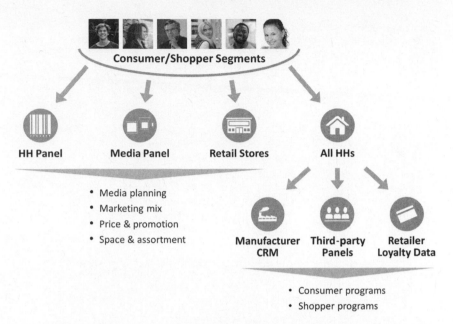

**Figure 2.3    The demand system aligns data.**

strategies and plans in the new demand framework; deploying the new demand framework through the core databases and decision tools used to manage the business; and activating the new demand framework across the company's business system – both internally across functions and externally with customers, partners, and investors (see Figure 2.4).

When sharing this roadmap, many clients' initial reaction is that "this is too much for us to take on." Visions of prior implementation horrors like the first ERP installation or the last company-wide re-engineering effort quickly spring to mind. And those fears are completely reasonable. The word "system" implies a complex undertaking with many moving parts. But the demand business system is different. Although it is anchored in Big Data and employs rigorous analytics, the demand system is primarily based on a new model for decision-making. Unlike IT or re-engineering initiatives, a demand-based transformation does not upend existing processes. As our clients have discovered, existing demand frameworks often can be enriched with new research and analytics, so they are applicable to multiple functions. Current planning processes can be augmented with new demand-based decision rules, and core data sets can be linked with new predictive analytics or other typing tools. While all of these activities

| 1 | 2 | 3 | 4 |
|---|---|---|---|
| **Create an Integrated View of Demand** | **Ground All Strategies & Plans in It** | **Deploy It through Core Data & Tools** | **Activate It across the Business System** |
| • Attitudes & motivations<br>• Purchases & usage<br>• Shopping behaviors<br>• Decision factors<br>• Perceptions | • Portfolio<br>• Brand<br>• Media<br>• Innovation<br>• Channel<br>• Customer<br>• Shopper | **Data**<br>• Public data<br>• Company data<br>• Partner data<br>• Customer data<br>**Tools**<br>• Product testing<br>• Marketing mix<br>• Pricing<br>• Retail activation | • Agencies<br>• Distribution partners<br>• Retailers<br>• Investors |

**Figure 2.4    Building the demand business system.**

require an experienced and expert hand to guide them, they do not rise to the level of infrastructure transformations.

So if a demand-based transformation is not daunting from a technical perspective, what is the holdup? If companies that embed a demand-based system outperform their peers, why is every business struggling to gain share not embracing the opportunity? Clients ask us these questions all the time. Our response is that it requires determined executive leadership. Unlike process re-engineering, demand-based change cannot be delegated to mid-level managers. Executives must set the example by changing the information they use to make decisions, the lens they use for assessing performance, and the criteria they use for the allocation of resources.

Unfortunately, many leadership teams feel so pressured to improve near-term performance that they believe they cannot lead another initiative. But ask the leadership team at Allstate, who will tell you that leading a demand-based transformation is no different from running the day-to-day business. As leaders who have managed this process can attest, often it's no more difficult than changing the way monthly leadership meetings are managed. Rather than have each functional leader report on overall performance, ask them to describe the specific activities underway in their areas of responsibility to win with each priority customer segment. In this way, an organization's shifting mental model can be effectively used to manage day-to-day operations.

By embedding new demand frameworks into existing business reviews, management can design a new model and activate it across the company simultaneously. Invariably this translates into visibility of the key drivers of category growth across employees, external business partners, and investors alike. Here is a good roadmap to follow:

1. Build internal business reviews around the common demand framework:
   - How are we performing with our most profitable and important consumers?
   - What are our marketing and sales plans to improve performance?
   - What new initiatives should we consider?
   - How should resources be (re)deployed?

2. Incorporate the new demand framework into customer business reviews:
   - Is the retailer gaining share with the targeted consumers?
   - Which shopper segments are causing category leakage to competitors?
   - What in-store initiatives will increase conversion and improve trends?

3. Require agency partners to use the common demand framework:
   - Does creative align with consumer segment motivations?
   - Does media buy align with consumer segment behaviors?
   - Does investment/spend have the highest ROI with target consumers?

4. Make the demand framework a core part of investor communications:
   - Communicate business plans through new frameworks.
   - Attribute success to new insights.
   - Link new investments to a new demand model.

At this point, you might be thinking, "Okay, embedding a demand-based approach in my organization may not be as complicated or risky as installing an ERP system, but it can't be as simple as changing a few meeting agendas." And you would be absolutely correct. After creating the common demand framework and adopting it as the mental model for decision-making at senior levels, much work remains to embed the new model throughout the company.

So where should you start? We typically take our clients through a brief but rigorous diagnostic to identify their greatest capability gaps when compared to a prototypical demand business system. The diagnostic starts with a baseline assessment of how precisely the leadership team understands demand for its company's products. In many cases, this assessment is sufficient to define an action plan to guide organizational initiatives. Figure 2.5 is an example assessment of demand understandings that we conducted for a consumer products client.

In this case, the diagnostic surfaced disagreements over portfolio priorities. With that discovery, we dove deeper to identify whether the lack of agreement was due to different insights or management processes (see Figure 2.6). (All diagnostic templates are at the end of this chapter.)

At the end of the diagnostic, the client had a clear action plan (see Figure 2.7).

We are entering the age of precision. The mass market and steady growth are dead. Winning in the "new normal" of fragmented demand and slow growth requires new levels of precision. The demand business system aligns your entire business to attract, motivate, and retain your most profitable customers. It brings the precision and alignment associated with supply chain management to demand-oriented functions. The starting point is a common view of demand used across the company for managing the business. This Demand Landscape fully explains the

| Identify | Prioritize | Locate | Collaborate | Activate |
|---|---|---|---|---|
| • Who are the most profitable consumers/ end-customers?<br><br>• What do they demand?<br><br>• How do they decide what to buy and where to shop?<br><br>• What is our share and performance with them? | • What is our offer to these consumers?<br><br>• Where and how should we enhance our offerings?<br><br>• Are we aligned on these priorities?<br><br>• How should we allocate resources? | • Where do the most profitable consumers shop?<br><br>• How can we best reach and serve them?<br><br>• What is the consumer demand profile of our distribution & retail partners? | • How can we work with retailers to capture more demand?<br><br>• What is our joint business plan for profit and growth?<br><br>• How can we integrate our insights with distribution partners/ retailers? | • How should in-store activation vary by channel and retailer?<br><br>• How can loyalty programs be more precisely targeted at the most profitable consumers? |

Figure 2.5    A demand-based business system.

| Identify | Prioritize | Locate | Collaborate | Activate |
|---|---|---|---|---|
| • Identify the most profitable consumers and shoppers<br>• Profile in detail what they demand<br>• Understand how they decide what to buy and where to shop<br>• Measure how you are performing with them<br>• Determine who you are competing against for their demand | • Decide what consumers you should target<br>• Determine how you will win ... what benefits must we own<br>• Assign the role each function will play in delivering these benefits<br>• Determine where and how you should enhance your offerings<br>• Ensure that everyone is aligned on these priorities<br>• Allocate resources across sales, marketing, and innovation based on strategy | • Identify where the most profitable consumers shop<br>• Identify what the most profitable consumers watch<br>• Assess how you can best reach and serve them<br>• Profile the consumer demand profile of each retail partner | • Determine how you should work with retailers to capture more demand<br>• Create a shared understanding of category demand & shopping missions<br>• Determine the right category growth strategy for each retailer<br>• Develop a joint business plan for profit and growth<br>• Develop a joint learning plan | • Develop a total program to capture more of the most profitable demand<br>• Optimize in-store assortment, promo, merchandising based on demand<br>• Optimize media ... TV, circular, DTC based on demand<br>• Create loyalty program offers precisely targeted at demand<br>• Measure & track business performance with the most profitable demand |

**Figure 2.6    Action plan to build a demand business system.**

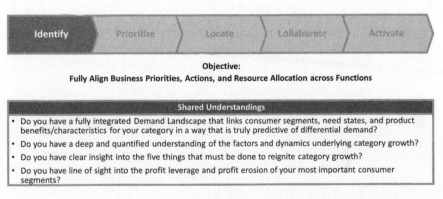

**Objective:**
**Fully Align Business Priorities, Actions, and Resource Allocation across Functions**

| Shared Understandings |
|---|
| • Do you have a fully integrated Demand Landscape that links consumer segments, need states, and product benefits/characteristics for your category in a way that is truly predictive of differential demand? |
| • Do you have a deep and quantified understanding of the factors and dynamics underlying category growth? |
| • Do you have clear insight into the five things that must be done to reignite category growth? |
| • Do you have line of sight into the profit leverage and profit erosion of your most important consumer segments? |

**Figure 2.7    Demand chain business system: diagnostic questions.**

"whats" and "whys" driving a purchase. As a result, the demand business system creates strategic and operational roadmaps that capture a greater share of market growth and profit. To build a demand-based business system, you as a leader must change the way you see opportunities for profitable growth and jointly act to capture them (Figures 2.8–2.13).

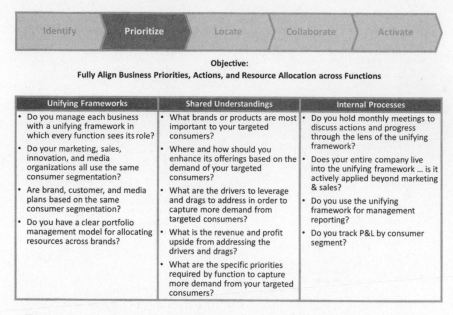

**Figure 2.8    Demand chain business system: diagnostic questions.**

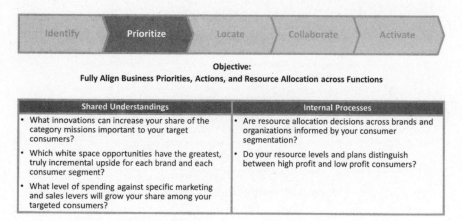

**Figure 2.9    Demand chain business system: diagnostic questions.**

| Identify | Prioritize | **Locate** | Collaborate | Activate |

**Objective:**
Identify the Demand Profile of Every Retailer, Store and Household to Enable Precise Activation of Your Demand Framework

| Analytic Techniques | Activation Databases | Activation Insights |
| --- | --- | --- |
| • Do you build proprietary econometric models to type 400k retail stores and 120mm households by your consumer segments?<br><br>• Do the econometric models include multiple demand indices beyond basket purchase profile and demographics?<br><br>• Do you link typed households to typed stores using channel-specific trading areas? | • Do you create a matrix of consumer segments and missions to provide unique IC for each retailer?<br><br>• Do you measure and track retailer performance across the segment-mission matrix?<br><br>• Do you profile all 400k stores by your consumer segments?<br><br>• Do you profile all 120mm households by your consumer segments?<br><br>• Do you cluster stores by your consumer segmentation for retail activation? | • Where and how can you best participate with the fastest growing channels and retailers?<br><br>• Where do your targeted consumers live? Where do they shop?<br><br>• Where across the segment-mission matrix does each retailer have the greatest growth opportunity?<br><br>• Which retailers have the greatest potential to grow your brands based on their alignment with your target consumer demand? |

**Figure 2.10   Demand chain business system: diagnostic questions.**

| Identify | Prioritize | Locate | **Collaborate** | Activate |

**Objective:**
Create a Shared Understanding of Category Demand and Opportunities with Each Retailer to Grow the Category and Your Share

| Collaborative Databases | Activation Insights | Recommended Strategies |
| --- | --- | --- |
| • Do you provide retailers with banner, local market, and store cluster-level insights into category demand based on your consumer segmentation?<br><br>• Do you align your consumer segmentation with retailers' own shopper segmentations?<br><br>• Have you typed your consumer segmentation into retailers' own loyalty program databases?<br><br>• Do you have a proprietary category performance measurement system, delivered to retailers, that builds the category? | • What is the greatest source of category leakage by consumer segment for each retailer?<br><br>• What are the individual actions and activities that determine success with each segment?<br><br>• What are the common success factors among each retailer's priority shoppers and your targeted consumers?<br><br>• What are the highest potential sources of growth (segment or mission) for you and each retailer?<br><br>• What are the opportunities to increase pricing power for both you and retailers? | • Do you create multi-year JBPs with customers that grow both the category and your share?<br><br>• Are the multi-year joint business plans aligned with the prioritized sources of growth and purchase drivers?<br><br>• Do you and retailers jointly allocate resources consistent with each retailer's prioritized sources of growth?<br><br>• What actions, other than trade spend, can result in your capturing a greater share of customer resources (e.g., ads, displays, space)?<br><br>• Do you recommend to retailers how to differentially price by store cluster based on price elasticity and profit opportunity? |

**Figure 2.11   Demand chain business system: diagnostic questions.**

| Identify | Prioritize | Locate | Collaborate | Activate |

**Objective:**
**Precisely Activate Demand Based on the Consumer Segment Profile of Each Store Cluster and Shopper Household**

| Assortment | Merchandising | Pricing/Promotion |
|---|---|---|
| • Are your add/delete recommendations based on consumer demand at the store cluster level? | • Does aisle layout reflect the demand preferences of each store cluster's consumer segment profile? | • Do promotion plans incorporate consumer segment/shopper insights at the local market or store cluster level? |
| • Are assortment guidelines based on the consumer segment profile and retailer performance of each store cluster? | • Do displays and aisle communications reflect opportunities to capture more latent demand? | • Are promotion plans based on the alignment of brands or products with the consumer segment profile of each store cluster? |
| • Are planograms customized based on the consumer segment profile of each store cluster? | • Do cross-merchandising programs align with consumer demand within each store cluster? | • Do pricing strategies incorporate perceived category and item value based on the consumer segment profile of each store cluster? |
| | | • Are price elasticities and feature/display lifts calculated at the store level based on the consumer segment profile? |

Figure 2.12    Demand chain business system: diagnostic questions.

| Identify | Prioritize | Locate | Collaborate | Activate |

**Objective:**
**Precisely Activate Demand Based on the Consumer Segment Profile of Each Store Cluster and Shopper Household**

| Loyalty/Shopper Marketing | Performance Tracking |
|---|---|
| • Are loyalty/shopper marketing tailored by card member based on her consumer segment profile? | • Do customer business reviews track performance among the most important consumers and shoppers? |
| • Are loyalty/shopper marketing programs tied to the success factors specific to each consumer segment? | • Do customer business reviews track how each retailer is performing against the success factors for each mission? |
| • Are loyalty/shopper marketing investments targeted at the most profitable consumers/shoppers to drive ROI? | |
| • Beyond price discount, what shopper marketing programs have the greatest potential to grow the category and your brands among target consumers? | |

Figure 2.13    Demand chain business system: diagnostic questions.

## Questions for Monday Morning

1. Do marketing, sales, and innovation share a common view of demand?

2. Are all brand and product line plans grounded in this common framework?

3. Are all customer plans grounded in this common framework?

4. Do you use this common framework to manage channel and retail execution?

5. Are your core data and analytics grounded in the common framework?

6. Have you aligned performance tracking with the shared view of demand?

## Endnote

1. Kash, Rick. "The Hershey Company: Aligning Inside to Win on the Outside." *Ivey Business Journal.* March/April 2012. https://iveybusinessjournal.com/publication/the-hershey-company-aligning-inside-to-win-on-the-outside-2/. Accessed July 2017.

CHAPTER

3

# A New Business Model

---

### The Big Ideas

- A more precise system for driving growth that is built on insights into customer demand and leverages the power of Big Data is a proven approach for success.
- This approach drives growth while optimizing costs at the same time, so managers do not have to choose to focus on either growth or cost cutting.
- This approach and its major elements can be applied to any type of business.

---

Given all we've discussed so far, how can businesses consistently deliver meaningful levels of profitable, organic revenue growth despite economic headwinds, shifting consumer trends, and ongoing industry disruption? In our experience the solution is to develop a much more precise business system that starts with actionable insights into demand and is powered, as much as possible, by the emerging tools and capabilities of Big Data, including digital approaches. Done correctly, this new business system not only drives profitable growth but also optimizes costs. While driving profitable growth and bringing costs down to their optimal level are often seen as opposing objectives, they are actually highly compatible once demand is understood more thoroughly.

This more precise, demand-based business system has the following eight major characteristics:

1. Anticipates and takes advantage of shifts in demand.

2. Develops more precise, more actionable insights into target consumers/customers than competitors.

3. Optimizes go-to-market approaches including selling, distribution channels, messaging, and media based on precise demand insights.

4. Achieves much higher rates of innovation success.

5. Optimizes costs across the business based on its more precise understanding of demand.

6. Aligns the entire organization around the strategy for winning and clarifies each function's role in driving success.

7. Leverages Big Data, including digital capabilities, as much as possible.

8. Continuously improves all aspects of the business system by precisely monitoring results.

A more precise business model that brings these eight characteristics together maximizes the potential to be had from current offers, eliminates wasted spending, and builds the foundation for successful innovation. Efforts to develop this business model can be sequenced in order to quickly generate wins in terms of both higher growth and lower costs. These "early wins" serve two important purposes.

First, the early wins quickly demonstrate to a potentially skeptical or demoralized organization that there is a path forward, a way to win. After years of being undercut by their lower-cost, direct to consumer competitors, Allstate's insurance agents felt the positive momentum of the company's new Your Choice offers almost immediately. Recall that, at the time, Allstate insurance agent Anita Sally told the *Wall Street Journal*, "... sales of the Your Choice products are up 20% to 30% over sales of Allstate's standard product."[1] That jump in sales was energizing and was particularly important to an organization that really began to wonder how it could compete more successfully against the lower-cost direct model.

Second, the early wins help create internal demand to move forward with the transition to a more precise business model. Change is often threatening to organizations and is frequently met with resistance as a result. Changing existing processes, challenging conventional wisdom, and altering familiar routines is uncomfortable and can become overwhelming for some people in an organization. It's simply human nature. One of the best ways to alleviate these concerns is to demonstrate early wins. Putting some points on the board early is one of the best ways to build momentum and show the team that the changes required are well worth the effort.

Another common issue we run into with this work is based on the belief that achieving growth and optimizing costs are opposing objectives and that one has to be chosen over the other. The fact is that developing a more precise, demand-based view of growth opportunities also identifies significant amounts of waste from spending that is misaligned with profitable demand. In aggregate, this wasted spending can be 20% or more of total cost, which can represent billions of dollars of waste that can be eliminated while simultaneously growing the top line.

We typically find demand-based cost opportunities in four broad areas: Supply chain costs, distribution/retail investment, media spend, and innovation efforts. By developing a more precise, demand-based approach, we've identified billions in savings from these areas across global markets and across industries ranging from consumer packaged goods and retail to financial services and commercial printing. In our experience, the growth opportunities identified from a demand-based growth assessment can be funded through the cost savings identified from the same assessment. In fact, the typical savings realized are so significant they often fund the new growth initiatives identified and much more. Our work with brewing giant Anheuser-Busch is a good example of the impact a more precise, demand-based model can have.

## Expanding the Kingdom of the King of Beers

The growth of Anheuser-Busch (AB) is a classic American success story. AB went from being one of thousands of local brewers established by German immigrants in the nineteenth century to the largest, most profitable brewer in the world by the late twentieth century. Budweiser, with its distinctive beachwood aging, became the best-selling regular (or full-calorie) beer brand in the U.S., and Bud Light became the best-selling beer of any style in the world. For decades, Anheuser-Busch was synonymous with beer.

However, as the third millennium started, AB began to lose steam as consumer preferences shifted. For nearly 20 years, per capita beer consumption had been declining – and the trend finally caught up to AB as sales had been flat from 2001–2005. The company found itself fighting a two-front war: First, the beer category overall was losing volume to spirits and wine; and second, within the beer category, mainstream U.S. brands were losing ground to imports and craft beers. Following a ruinous price war in 2005, the leadership of Anheuser-Busch decided that it needed to adopt a new model for its business.

Several major issues weighed on AB's leadership team. First, they needed to grow. Beyond their desire to increase profitable sales, AB's senior team was concerned that their portfolio – which included nearly 90 brands in addition to Budweiser and Bud Light – all seemed to be fighting with each other to win with the same set of consumers. One reason was that the company had not had a really significant new product hit in many years. Stagnant category growth and low innovation success led some to question whether there was any growth left in the beer market. Given this situation, some senior leaders at AB felt that the best opportunities going forward might be captured by entering the spirits or the wine market instead of focusing on the beer market. With all of this uncertainty, AB engaged us to help them build a demand business model in late 2006.

## Changing the Existing "Mental Model"

The team, which included our client partners from AB as well as members of our firm, felt the most critical initial action was to understand how demand, adoption, and consumption of alcoholic beverages in the U.S. had changed over time. The purpose of building this historical review was to anticipate how demand for Anheuser-Busch's beers might evolve going forward. Historically, AB had believed that 21- to 29-year-old males drove the beer category – and that they wanted easy-to-drink, refreshing beers. But this "mental model" could not be squared with category trends. If the most important consumers wanted light beer, why were full calorie imported beers growing? And why were spirits and wine stealing volume?

As we assessed alcoholic beverages in greater depth, we discovered that a substantial amount of the market's growth had been driven by the introduction of sweeter beverages – flavored vodkas in particular. These new vodkas appealed to a new generation of young adults by providing an almost endless variety of flavors including lemon, vanilla, raspberry, and black cherry, among others. Whether flavored or unflavored, these new vodkas also mixed well with other beverages, such as Red Bull energy drinks, which were popular among 21- to 34-year-old consumers.

The popularity of these sweeter vodkas pointed to a major generational shift in consumer demand. Baby Boomers had accepted the fact that beer was an acquired taste with a pleasant bitterness to it. When Boomers first reached the legal drinking age, they adopted beer as the beverage of choice for socializing among young adults like themselves. Wine and spirits, on the other hand, were considered the domain of more mature consumers and much more appropriate to their social set. But unlike previous generations, the young adults from post–Baby Boomer generations did not adopt beer as their alcoholic beverage of choice.

This new generation of young adults appeared to have much sweeter taste preferences. In part, this stemmed from the fact that many had grown up eating and drinking sweeter foods and beverages like carbonated soft drinks, breakfast cereals, and many types of snacks. Their preference for sweeter taste also affected the ways they had adopted coffee, which, like beer, is a pleasantly bitter beverage with an acquired taste. When it came to coffee, these young adults chose coffees with foamed milk and added flavors like chocolate and caramel. Given this context, it is not too surprising that as they turned 21, they saw no reason to acquire a taste for bitter tasting beer, so they gravitated to the hip, new, flavored vodkas instead.

Using the success of flavored vodkas as an analogous example, the team wondered if a new, slightly sweeter beer could break through to the current generation of 21- to 34-year-olds. This led the team to another analogous example within the beer category itself: The popular Mexican "beach beer," Corona. While Corona is not an inherently sweet beer, the nearly universal habit of adding a slice of lime to Corona does create a sweeter taste experience. Taken together, sweeter beverages – whether flavored vodkas or sweetened beer – were driving most of the growth across the macro beverage alcohol category. AB's mental model needed an update.

## Building the Quantitative "Demand Landscape"

Our next step was to test the initial growth hypotheses we'd developed and create a quantitative view of demand for alcoholic beverages and AB's offers by building what we call the "Demand Landscape." The Demand Landscape is an advanced means of segmenting a market in order to develop new consumer insights while also quantifying and sizing potential opportunities within the market. We'll go into details about how to build a quantitative Demand Landscape later in Chapter 5. For now, we'll focus on how Anheuser-Busch was able to use the Demand Landscape to understand WHO the most important consumers in the market were and WHY they bought alcoholic beverages. These foundational insights were critical to turning AB's performance around.

At the outset of building the Demand Landscape, we had to define the market we wanted to assess. Our combined team decided that the relevant market to examine was the "alcoholic beverage market," which included beer, wine, and spirits. A lot of healthy debate went into the market definition because it is such an important consideration. A definition that is too broad becomes unwieldy and very difficult to take action on. For example, AB's beers technically compete with all other beverages for "share of stomach," but in practice it would have been impossible to understand AB's opportunities in the context of all beverages. Even narrowing the definition to include only carbonated soft drinks in addition to all alcoholic beverages would have been too broad because of the many sub-categories such as cola, root beer, lemon-lime, orange, and so on, that have little or no overlap with alcohol. A market definition that is too broad simply won't generate the deep, proprietary insights needed to drive growth and optimize costs.

At the same time, a definition that is too narrow runs the risk of missing important insights and potential new opportunities. At a minimum, it makes sense to understand your major competitors and how your offers perform with the different segments of consumers in the Demand Landscape versus your competitive set. Most categories also have some close substitutes for your own product that are important to understand as well. This is why the team settled on understanding the total alcoholic beverage market for Anheuser-Busch. This definition was broad enough to encompass major opportunities within AB's core business but was also specific enough to result in actionable outcomes. Weighing the pros and cons of the potential market definition is an important step in getting to the level of precision that will help drive growth.

The Demand Landscape provides a view of the distinctly different groups of consumers in the market, which we call "Demand Segments" or "Demand Profit Pools." For AB, we found that there are five distinctly different groups of consumers in the U.S. that are defined primarily by their demand for alcoholic beverages. In other words, conducting statistical analyses of consumers from across the U.S. identifies five distinctly different groups of people who buy beer, wine, and spirits based on their interest in, attitudes toward, and behaviors regarding alcoholic beverages. Demand Segments identify who is in the market and who is most and least attractive in terms of amount of spend, types of products purchased, and level of engagement or interest in the category. Figure 3.1 provides an overview of the five Demand Segments as shared by AB InBev at its St. Louis Investor Conference on June 2–3 in 2010.

Note the names of the five different segments at the top of the chart from the "Experimenters" at far left to the "Sippers" on the far right. Each segment is named to reflect that group's core essence. As you might guess from the description of the "Loyalists" segment, including their interest in sports and their preference for mainstream beers, they are extremely important to the beer category overall and to AB specifically. In many respects, AB had become the "King of Brewers" by winning with Loyalists.

With the quantitative Demand Landscape view of the market completed, one of AB's major growth opportunities became clear. While AB was winning significant share among the Loyalists who buy about 40% of

**Figure 3.1     Dimension 1 – distinct consumer segments.**

*Source:* ABI Investor Relations

the beer sold in the U.S., they had little to offer other attractive segments of consumers. Of particular interest were the Experimenters, Trendsetters, and Aspirers who in aggregate represent about half of the beer consumed in the U.S. market. How could AB maintain its base with Loyalists while gaining more market share among these other attractive segments?

To answer this question we had to understand WHY people in each Demand Segment purchase the beverages they buy. This dimension is explained within the Demand Landscape through the lens of "Need States." Need States are the circumstances or the occasions people experience that cause them to want something. While most people generally experience similar Need States when it comes to any given category, they will solve for those Need States in very different ways based on the Demand Segment they represent. Bringing the Demand Segments and the Need States they experience together completes the Demand Landscape and assigns spending levels and brands purchased to the intersections of segments and Need States. These intersections highlight areas where spending is high or low while also identifying "white spaces" where there is demand that is unfulfilled by either AB specifically or the beer industry as a whole.

Figure 3.2 shows the illustrative Demand Landscape for alcoholic beverages, which includes beer. You'll notice that in this view the Demand Segments are still at the top of the page. Now, another dimension has been added down the left side of the framework. This new dimension describes the six distinctly different Need States that consumers experience related to alcoholic beverages.

The Need State at the top of the chart, "Party Time," is all about socializing with others at large events, smaller gatherings, or out at a bar or restaurant. In this Need State, beer adds to the fun whether it is celebrating a major milestone, enjoying a holiday, or simply being with friends and family. In contrast, the "Sports Companion" Need State is built around watching sports live or on TV. Alcoholic beverages, especially beer, might be served at the tailgate before the big game, at the sports bar where fans have come together to watch, or at home with a few friends who have come over to catch the game on TV.

One critically important point to make about Need States is that the people in different Demand Segments tend to solve for Need States in different ways while people in the same Demand Segment tend to solve for the same Need State in similar ways. While this sounds like the setup

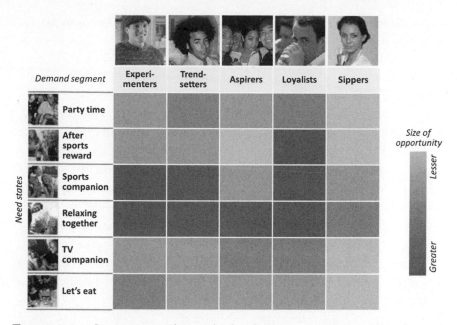

**Figure 3.2** Consumer demand landscape – U.S. hypothetical example.

*Source:* ABI Investor Relations

to a bad joke, imagine that a Loyalist, an Experimenter, and a Sipper all meet at a sports bar to watch their favorite team play. Although they are all in the same "Sports Companion" Need State, the Loyalist is most likely to have a mainstream light beer, such as Bud Light, while the Experimenter might order a darker beer like an India Pale Ale (IPA) from a local craft brewer; and the Sipper might have a glass of white wine. If all three of these people were in the Loyalist Demand Segment, they would probably have the same type of beer (mainstream light beer), but each of them might choose a different brand of light beer (Bud Light, Coors Light, Miller Lite). These fundamental differences are critical to understand thoroughly and to value in terms of economic opportunity.

Anyone who is a consumer of a given category tends to experience the same Need States over time. The major difference to keep in mind is the frequency of experiencing each Need State and the spending per Need State. Clearly, some people will watch or attend many more sporting events than others while some people host or go to parties much more often than others. This is why quantifying the number of Need

States experienced, the amount of alcoholic beverages purchased for each, and the spending on alcoholic beverages for each Need State is so important.

Understanding and valuing the specific Demand Segments, the Need States they experience, and the economics of each intersection of the two are among the insights that made the Demand Landscape so powerful for Anheuser-Busch. The detailed information included the volume or the amount of alcoholic beverages purchased, the specific brands purchased, AB's share of market for each intersection, the dollars spent as well as media consumed by each Demand Segment, and where they shop, among other insights. These aspects of the Demand Landscape are incredibly valuable, but they generally describe what happened in the past.

More forward-looking insights about the underlying demand for each intersection of Demand Segments and Need States, how well that demand is or is not fulfilled currently, and where there are potential white spaces for innovation are also included in the Demand Landscape. The details behind each of these intersections showed that AB could capture some of the potential growth opportunities in the short term with its existing portfolio of products while other growth options would take longer to access because they required developing innovative new products. Note that AB did not share all of the details about spending and volumes purchased that make up this proprietary fact base in public forums such as its Investor Day.

## From Insights to More Precise Actions

With the foundational Demand Landscape established, AB began to build out other parts of the demand business system. In particular, the demand system gave AB opportunities to optimize media spend and improve retail activation. Given the social nature of beer consumption, brand imagery plays an important role in consumers' purchase decisions. Recognizing this, AB makes significant investments in media each year. With its sizable investment (often in the hundreds of millions of dollars), AB had developed industry-leading competencies in media purchasing and management. But AB's leadership team quickly realized that the precise insights into each demand segment's media consumption that are embedded in the demand system gave them a new capability to capture even more value from their media spend.

AB's executives also saw opportunities for the demand system to substantially enhance retail execution. As noted earlier, beer drinkers consume different brands or types of beer in different Need State occasions. To satisfy Need State–specific demand, brewers had greatly expanded their offerings. The result was a large assortment that exceeded the available shelf space in any single store. To decide what to stock, retailers had used historical sales data and judgment. In categories with limited innovation or very strong brand loyalty, relying on historical sales data is a reasonable approach for decision-making. But in the incredibly innovative beer category, this approach resulted in many retail shelving decisions being made on judgment. The demand system could replace judgment with precise, quantified recommendations.

Given its significant spend and ability to quickly take action, AB started activating the demand system with its media spend. The opportunities were significant. The Demand Landscape quantified the types of media that each Demand Segment consumed across TV, radio, print, and online, including social media. The Demand Landscape also provided insights into the specific types of content, from sports to news to situation comedies to cooking blogs, each of the different Demand Segments was most interested in and engaged with. By aligning each segment's media preferences with their category motivations, AB was able to increase both the efficiency and effectiveness of its spend – as well as options to enhance the messaging itself.

Most media plans are built on demographics. Marketers start by creating demographic profiles of their target consumers. These profiles primarily consist of age, gender, ethnicity, and a few other demographic markers. Then media buying companies determine what specific TV programs, radio stations, social media, online sites, magazines, and so on are consumed most by these demographic groups. Frequent demographic targets are men between 21 and 34 years old or female head of household aged 35 to 54 years old. While it is relatively easy to find these demographic groups and identify the media they consume, demographic targeting can create significant waste. The fact is, not all men who happen to be age 21 to 34 have the same interest in beer or electronics or cars. Marketers would prefer to be more precise and buy the exact media that aligns with each consumer segment's behaviors and motivations, but traditional approaches gave them no other choice. The demand system breaks that compromise.

To increase the efficiency of AB's media spend, we applied sophisticated statistical models to profile Nielsen and other media data sets according to AB's Demand Segments. By mapping AB's Demand Segments to the media they consume most, we were able to identify media spend efficiencies of 12% to 18% depending on the specific Demand Segment and the specific media plan. AB spends hundreds of millions of dollars on media each year. (In 2016, AB InBev's U.S. advertising budget was estimated at $716 million.)[2] By generating media spend efficiencies of about 15%, the demand system enabled AB to grow their bottom line while also making investments to further accelerate growth.

Now that media dollars were being spent more efficiently, the team wanted every dollar spent to be as effective as possible. Driving effectiveness had two aspects. To start, the message being communicated had to be as compelling to target Demand Segments as possible. In addition, that message had to break through the advertising clutter and get noticed on programs or in content AB's key Demand Segments were highly engaged with.

With the initial insights from the Demand Landscape, the team was able to conduct further work to develop messaging elements that were more compelling to Loyalists, Experimenters, and other key Demand Segments. Now that we knew how to identify these important groups of consumers, we were able to talk to them in greater detail in qualitative research discussions. One topic these consumers helped us understand in more depth was the type of messages and the critical elements of messages they found most compelling for their favorite AB brands.

To further enhance effectiveness, we had to develop measures for audience engagement by specific program or content. Not all of the content or programs our most attractive Demand Segments consumed were equally valuable. What we really needed to identify were those programs or content our key Demand Segments paid the most attention to. For example, a program they consume regularly, say the evening news, might just serve as background noise while they make dinner each night. It's true that they have the program on frequently, which makes it a potential opportunity to reach those target Demand Segments. But it was also true that these consumers did not pay much attention to that program. Once again, we were able to leverage Nielsen and other data sets to zero in on the most effective content, the content target Demand Segments really leaned into, in order to make AB's advertising and media spend more effective.

# Getting It Right at Retail

As the team developed more insights into the beer category demand, we learned that not all retail channels and not all stores were equally attractive. To understand shopping behaviors in greater detail, we conducted additional quantitative research with consumers to map the proprietary Demand Segments to the beer-related "Shopping Missions" they experienced most. This new analysis is what we call a "Shopper Landscape." It starts from the same WHO – the Demand Segments – but rather than answer WHY they choose the type of beer they drink, it now answers WHERE they make most of their purchases and WHAT beer category–specific shopping benefits they seek that cause them to purchase beer from a retailer. For example, a Loyalist who is on a "Stock Up" mission might decide to make his purchases at a mass merchant that has a wide selection of pack sizes of mainstream beer brands, while an Experimenter might choose a liquor store that has a wide assortment of craft beers.

The Shopping Landscape was a powerful new tool that allowed AB to create more effective joint business plans with retailers. It provided precise insights that were specific to the beer category – and more importantly, specific to each retailer. AB was able to tell each retailer what assortment, merchandising, pricing, and promotion factors caused shoppers to select their store rather than a competitor's. It also quantified how well shoppers perceived the retailer is delivering on these purchase decision factors compared to its competitors. As a result, AB and each retailer could jointly prioritize action plans that would grow the category. And, crucially, grow the category in a way that is distinctive for each retailer. The uniqueness of each plan ensured that AB would not cannibalize its own business across retailers and that each retailer would not be offering the same programs and promotions as its competitor.

These new demand-based plans, by themselves, gave AB a clear advantage. But the demand system provided even greater activation insight. As was the case with media activation, the demand system applied sophisticated statistical models to profile core data sets according to AB's Demand Segments – in this case all 400,000 retail outlets that sold beer in the U.S. Thus AB knew which stores had the most Loyalists as shoppers and which stores had the most Experimenters. This provided unmatched guidance for product distribution. AB – or more specifically,

AB's 600+ independent distributors – could tell each retailer and store manager what specific assortment of beers would result in the most category sales. Rather than using national or local market averages to determine what beers to stock, AB made recommendations based on each store's specific demand profile.

Armed with these new data, the team developed comprehensive programs for AB's distributors and major retail partners. Now instead of spreading resources to all stores equally, AB worked with each retailer to target which of their own individual stores had the most significant upside – and how in-store signage, product assortments, and merchandising should vary across stores. Investing in the right product assortments at the right stores increased sales for the retailer and for AB, all while reducing the costs associated with distribution, inventory, and lost sales/out-of-stocks.

The combination of more insightful joint business plans and more precise in-store activation plans further cemented AB's category leadership with retailers. As AB rolled out the demand system across its distributors and retailers, store tests proved the new, more precise approach successful over and over again. As AB noted to *Beer Business Daily*, a leading industry newsletter, "What we've seen is that 100% – it used to be 85% but now 100% – of those retailers that are using the balanced approach are actually outperforming the market" (*Beer Business Daily*, June 22, 2012). Now the AB team had a unique approach for helping retailers maximize their sales opportunities for the beer category while saving money. This valuable capability made AB an increasingly important and trusted partner for retailers by creating an attractive win-win-win for consumers, retailers, and AB.

## Hitting the Sweet Spot

Having successfully captured most of its near-term and mid-term growth opportunities by making smarter investments in media, improving collaboration with retail partners, and enhancing the in-store experience for beer category shoppers, the Anheuser-Busch team now turned its attention to addressing the longer-term innovation opportunities that had been identified. While there were several successful innovation efforts that came out of the work, the most important of these addressed the largest white space identified in the Demand Landscape: The opportunity for a slightly sweeter light beer.

As the team began investigating the potential of introducing a slightly sweeter new beer from AB in greater detail, the opportunity became increasingly attractive. We conducted statistical discrete choice testing to understand exactly what features and benefits of a potential new offer appealed to the most consumers and to determine which Demand Segments those consumers represented. This quantitative assessment indicated that the demand for the new offer could be quite significant and that it would primarily attract consumers who did not already drink AB products. In other words, there were a lot of consumers who did not love the current choices available in the beer market, including AB's offers, who were very interested in a slightly sweeter beer. The testing also revealed that very few of the consumers in AB's critical Loyalist segment were interested in the slightly sweeter new beer, so there would be very little cannibalization of existing AB sales.

The discrete choice testing allowed us to architect the specific benefits and features that would optimize the new offer. Importantly, the testing showed us that the best option for making a slightly sweeter beer was to add natural lime juice. Another very clear finding was that the new beer had to be a light beer rather than a regular, full-calorie beer. The testing also showed us how to optimize the new offer in terms of its overall taste, appearance, amount of carbonation, level of alcohol, pricing, packaging, and branding. While most of these recommendations were readily adopted, a few were debated among the team and would require further testing to get to a decision.

Getting to the right brand name for the new beer was a particularly difficult decision. Our testing showed that sales of the new offer would benefit significantly if it were branded as "Bud Light Lime." Recall that at the time Bud Light generated billions of dollars in sales per year and was not only the best-selling beer in the U.S., it was also the best-selling beer brand in the world. In addition, Bud Light was primarily consumed by men, was strongly associated with sports, and was often consumed while watching sports on TV or at the game. As a result, the internal team at AB was concerned, and very rightly so, about the potential impact that introducing a new, slightly sweeter Bud Light Lime offer might have on the Bud Light brand. Would the new, sweeter beer alienate Bud Light's core consumers? Could the Bud Light brand be stretched to include a sub-brand called Bud Light Lime? Would AB be better off launching an entirely new brand for their new lime-infused light beer?

The team put all of these questions and more to the test. Additional testing showed us that the Bud Light brand was much more elastic, meaning it could be stretched across new offers and did not have to stand for only one product, than anyone had initially believed. This is frequently the case. Fans of a given brand often want to follow that brand to other offers as long as the new offers really fit with the essence of that original brand. This was certainly true of Bud Light, which has always been seen as a very social, outgoing brand. It turned out that Bud Light's core consumers wanted everyone to love Bud Light as much as they do. Even though Bud Light Lime was not something loyal Bud Light drinkers would switch to, they wanted Bud Light Lime and its fans to literally join the fun.

Further qualitative and quantitative analysis with consumers answered several critical questions. First, no other brand name had as much positive impact on projected sales as the Bud Light Lime name. Multiple existing brands from AB's portfolio were tested as were many potential new brand names. None were as powerful as Bud Light.

Second, Bud Light Lime appealed to a different consumer than Bud Light. Most of Bud Light Lime's consumers were 21- to 34-year-olds who had never really found a beer that appealed to them. By and large, they were consumers who had never acquired the taste for traditional beers. And, unlike the young men who were Bud Light's core consumers, many of Bud Light Lime's new consumers were women who switched from sweeter white wines and mixed drinks to Bud Light Lime.

Far from hurting the Bud Light brand, we found that introducing Bud Light Lime would actually enhance perceptions of Bud Light. Recall that while Bud Light was still a multi-billion dollar brand and a powerhouse in the beer category, its sales were slowing down. AB's marketing team worried that the brand was getting tired and was increasingly associated with consumers who were over 35 years old. They worried that Bud Light might be less relevant to 21- to 25-year-olds who might choose other beers or other beverages instead. In reality, Bud Light Lime's slightly sweeter taste and fun, Mexican beach beer vibe helped energize and contemporize the Bud Light franchise. Bud Light Lime also reflected a more active, outdoor lifestyle that helped make the more traditional Bud Light brand hipper and helped connect it to a younger, more diverse set of consumers.

After further study of demand and after extensive product testing, AB introduced Bud Light Lime on Cinco de Mayo (May 5) in 2008. As is often the case when tapping into a previously neglected source of demand, Bud Light Lime was an instant success. Unlike the typical adoption curve for new product introductions, which builds slowly, Bud Light Lime jumped off the shelf, even at a price premium. In fact, Bud Light Lime grew so surprisingly fast that AB initially had trouble keeping up with demand for their blockbuster new beer.

Ultimately, Bud Light Lime became the most successful new consumer packaged goods product to be introduced in 2008. By 2011, Bud Light Lime had already added $250 million in profits to AB's bottom line and had restored the profitable growth the brewer had been seeking. In addition, the Demand Landscape had shown us that the Bud Light brand could be extended further. The team began to see Bud Light not as one brand of beer, but as a platform for innovative new products including beers and new malt beverages.

After the successful introduction of Bud Light Lime, the team began work on other successful new offers from the growing Bud Light family including Bud Light Platinum, Bud Light Lime-a-Rita, and a series of other new "Rita" malt beverages. At the outset of our work together, the AB team was concerned that there was no growth left in the beer market, that there were no big innovation ideas left, that their portfolio of brands was fighting among itself for the same consumers, and that their biggest brand, Bud Light, was losing steam. Now Bud Light was a platform for exciting new innovations and a growth engine within AB.

## AB and the Eight Demand-Based Business System Characteristics

The AB case illustrates the eight characteristics of the more precise, demand-driven business system we believe will be critical to driving successful growth going forward:

1. Anticipates and takes advantage of shifts in demand: Anheuser-Busch took advantage of the significant shift toward sweeter taste preferences across many food and beverage categories in the U.S. – including alcoholic beverages.

2. Develops more precise, more actionable insights into target consumers/customers than competitors: Anheuser-Busch identified the most attractive segments of consumers in the "Demand Landscape," especially the "Loyalists," the "Trendsetters," and the "Aspirers." Developing deeper insights into Trendsetters and Aspirers than any other competitor allowed Anheuser-Busch to have more success with this group and launch more new offers for this group than any other competitor.

3. Optimizes go-to-market approaches including selling, distribution channels, and media based on precise demand insights: Anheuser-Busch used its fact base about demand to optimize media spend, re-energize the key Bud Light brand, and focus on the right stores in the Shopper Landscape where the most attractive beer Demand Segments shopped.

4. Achieves much higher rates of innovation success: The Demand Landscape helped identify several highly successful areas for new innovation, including the demand for slightly sweeter beer and malt beverage offers such as Bud Light Lime and the family of "Rita" offers as well as Bud Light Platinum.

5. Optimizes costs across the business based on its more precise understanding of demand: More precise insights into demand allowed Anheuser-Busch to drive much greater cost efficiencies across media spend, retail distribution costs, and investments in innovation.

6. Aligns the entire organization around the strategy for winning and clarifies each function's role in driving success: The new demand insights were reinforced with investors and across the organization with every function from procurement and production to sales and marketing working together to make it a success.

7. Leverages Big Data as much as possible: At the time, the Anheuser-Busch team was able to assign all 117 million U.S. households to a Demand Segment and then mapped those households to the stores where they shop most often. Big Data was also used to refine media buying to get the right advertising to the right consumers as much as possible. New advances in Big Data continue to make these approaches more robust over time.

8. Continuously improves all aspects of the business system by precisely monitoring results: AB can now track their results with key Demand Segments, and this precise knowledge about AB's most valuable customers serves as an important ongoing barometer for the overall health of the business.

## Banking on a New Model

Our work for a major retail banking, investment, and wealth management firm further illustrates the benefits of increased precision. Our analysis revealed the fact that the firm was missing out on some of the most attractive investors in the market. Their traditional approach to the market lacked precision and essentially treated all customers as the same, despite investors' very different demands. This lack of precision was one of the major reasons growth had slowed down to the point that more cost cutting was being contemplated. But, cutting costs alone would not have solved the real issue: Their business model was ineffective because it was fundamentally mismatched with market demand. Instead, we piloted a new approach to the market.

The insights we developed with our client into new groups of investors extended to their media habits. Understanding precisely what TV shows, online sites, and other media the three most attractive segments of investors consumed most helped our client's agency zero in on the right media in ways that demographics alone could not. Importantly, the new media plan also identified the media our key investors were most engaged in and were paying the most attention to, not just what happened to be on. The resulting media plan generated the same reach as the prior plan but was reaching new audiences that were much more engaged and was using 20% fewer dollars to do so.

Next, the agency mined the insights we developed to create messaging that resonated with each of our three key investor groups. It was now clear not only what messages appealed to each group, but exactly how to reach each of them across media types. The new approach was piloted through online advertising, which allowed for tailored messaging to each investor group.

Response rates for the new tailored approach were high and were driving significant traffic and inquiries to our client's call centers.

The call center reps had been trained in advance to ask a few simple questions to help determine which type of investor was on the line. If they were among the three most attractive groups, they were transferred to a financial advisor who was trained to understand the unique needs and concerns of each of the three groups of investors.

Overall, this client's investment in precision paid off in increased inquiries among potential customers, a call center experience that went from being rated one of the industry's worst to one of the best, higher win rates among prospective customers, and higher satisfaction and retention among existing customers. As our client noted, "Investing in greater precision paid off in ways that cost cutting alone never could have. As a result of this work we have an approach that is more efficient and effective. We've built skill sets that help us win with clients much more often ... and winning with clients has dramatically improved morale."

These client experiences were not "one-off" occurrences or the exceptions to the rule. What we've found across industries and global markets is that really understanding consumer demand and then aligning all activities, including the supply chain, to more precise demand insights drives growth while optimizing costs. Many businesses build in unnecessary costs and inefficiencies over time by chasing the wrong demand opportunities. Once the business system is aligned to focus on profitable demand, it becomes much more efficient and optimizes supply chain, media, distribution, and innovation costs all while growing the top line.

## Questions for Monday Morning

1. How do you define your market today?
   a. What substitutes for your products/services are "closest in"?
   b. Are there other substitutes that are further out that should be considered?
   c. Are there other meaningful alternatives to your products/services ... including doing nothing?
2. How far could you stretch your current view of your market? When does it become too broad?
3. What is the narrowest definition of your market? Does that narrow view make sense or is it too restrictive?

4. As you explore different definitions of your market, what do those broader and narrower definitions imply about your competitive set?

5. Who are your most valuable consumer segments and how would you describe them?

6. Will your most valuable consumers continue to be highly valuable over the next five to ten years or will you need to win with other consumers as well?

7. How well are your current offers meeting the most critical demands of attractive Demand Segments in the market?

8. What are the key Need States experienced by attractive segments of consumers/customers that motivate them to make a purchase?

9. Do gaps in the delivery of current product benefits or gaps meeting needs for specific Need States point to potential innovation opportunities?

10. How might insights into the Demand Landscape and the Shopper Landscape inform opportunities to optimize costs across your business model?

# Endnotes

1. Saranow, Jennifer. "A Rewards Plan for Auto Insurance." The *Wall Street Journal*. 3 May 2005. https://www.wsj.com/articles/SB111508167634322842. Accessed July 2017.

2. "Advertising spending of Selected Beer Manufacturers in the United States in 2016." Statista, 2017; "Alcohol Companies Are Placing a Huge Bet That Cable TV Isn't Dead" by Seth Archer, *Business Insider*. 22 July 2016.

# The Precision to Optimize Your Current Business

# CHAPTER 4

# Building a Demand "Early Warning System"

---

## The Big Ideas

- Anticipating how demand for your business will evolve creates an important "Early Warning System" with potentially significant benefits.
- Understanding Demand Trends and the "forces and factors" that drive them helps create context and a long-term roadmap of demand for your business.
- One way to develop insights into Demand Trends is to assess the current, emerging, and latent forms of demand in your market.
- Demand Triggers are the close-in drivers that influence consumers to make a purchase, and these are equally important to assess in order to have more precise insights into opportunities to win the most profitable market demand for your business/offers.

---

How well can you predict the future of demand for your industry? Will demand grow steadily over the next three to five years? Is there reason to believe demand for your offers will grow rapidly, or perhaps drop suddenly?

What will have the greatest impact on demand for your business going forward? Are there signposts that can be observed or indicators that can be tracked? Can you influence the way demand will unfold or its impact on your business?

These may seem like theoretical questions but they can be answered, or at least assessed, in ways that can provide meaningful competitive advantages. Understanding and anticipating shifts in demand and what drives them can give your business an important "Early Warning System" for taking advantage of positive changes before competitors can do so or for getting ahead of potentially negative threats. The more precisely your business can identify the drivers and signposts related to demand, the better prepared you will be as demand shifts going forward.

What we find most helpful in these assessments is to have an ongoing dialogue among your cross-functional team about what has shaped demand in the past and what is most likely to drive demand going forward. This approach is different from most traditional forecasting exercises where numbers are calculated and updated over time. Our approach does involve background research, but it also involves discussion about potential hypotheses and scenarios that can be tested over time and shared during regularly scheduled updates. By revisiting this topic at regular intervals, scenarios can be updated, and key assumptions can be validated, rejected, or refined. The process of stepping back from the day-to-day in order to identify the most critical drivers of demand for your business and to develop "what if" scenarios with your team becomes more valuable as the team learns from the various hypotheses that are tested over time.

By knowing what to look for, managers can begin to identify and read the signposts of shifting demand ahead of major changes in their industry. One helpful example of how demand evolves over time is the emergence of what *BusinessWeek* dubbed the "pet economy" in 2007.[1] Examining the transition to the pet economy helps to illustrate principles that can be used to develop a more precise understanding of demand in any category.

## Pet Industry Trends: From the Dog House to the Penthouse

How did we become "pet parents"? The term not only reflects a fundamental shift in our relationships with our beloved pets, but also represents an enormous shift in consumer demand and spending. In 2016, American pet parents spent a staggering $66.8 billion on their four-legged children, a figure that includes spending on food, vets, toys, gifts, grooming services, and boarding services. For context, pet spending has grown by about 5.4% annually since 2002, which is much stronger than U.S. GDP growth over the same period.[2] In fact, the $66 billion spent on pets is substantially higher than the estimated $50 billion Americans spend annually on alcoholic beverages.[3]

One of the major forces driving the pet economy is demographics. Millions of Boomers have become empty nesters as their children have left home, despite many Millennials "boomeranging" back home as adults. Pets have become the surrogate children, filling the void many of these empty nesters feel. According to the U.S. Bureau of Labor Statistics, Americans aged 55 to 64 spend more on pets than any other group.[4] Interestingly, pet spending is one of the major exceptions to the general rule that aging Boomers spend less on almost everything, especially once they retire. The net result is that today's Boomers now spend lavishly on their pets, at levels never seen by prior generations. Perhaps this trend is highly predictable, given that Boomers have redefined every life stage transition they have experienced. Why would becoming empty nesters be any different?

In just a few generations, dogs have gone from farm implements to family pets to surrogate children (Figure 4.1). Hollywood and popular culture may have helped prime this pump. As the Boomers were growing up, both Lassie and Rin Tin Tin were box office and television stars that helped change the image of dogs while also elevating their roles in the family.

| Year | 1900 | 1954 | 2007 |
|---|---|---|---|
| Role | Farm Hand | Part of Family | Favorite Child |
| Relationship | Master | Owner | Loving Parent |

**Figure 4.1** **The evolving role and relationship of dogs in the U.S., 1900–2007.**

One other observable change is the disappearance of doghouses. It seems downright cruel today to send the dog outside to a tiny shed with no heat or air conditioning. In fact, a recent survey found that almost half of American dog owners now allow their dogs to sleep in bed with them.[5] This would have been absolutely unthinkable a century ago. In 1900, most dogs in the U.S. were likely to be found outside of the house and most had a job herding livestock, tracking or retrieving game, or guarding hearth and home.

There were also category-specific developments at play as the pet economy emerged. One signpost on the way to the pet economy focused on services. In 1960, a man on the Upper East Side of New York City named Jim Buck launched his long career as a professional dog walker. Buck is credited with becoming the first of thousands of professional dog walkers who participate in a U.S. pet services industry that has estimated revenues of over $5 billion per year today for services including grooming, walking, and boarding.[6] In 1965, a few years after Buck got started, Petco launched the first major pet specialty superstore to serve the growing demand for pet products.

Pet food has also followed trends in human food, which is not surprising given the fact that pets often command "favorite child" status in many homes. Take dog food for example: Dog parents can choose from all natural, organic, and even gluten-free dog foods in flavors that range from chicken to buffalo to salmon. Additionally, as with many of the organic and gluten-free foods intended for humans, the price premium for these dog foods can be eye-popping.

Now imagine that in the late 1990s, as all of these changes are taking place, you are a senior manager at a large pet food manufacturer. How might you take advantage of the trends reshaping the pet food market if you had observed them? If you were our client, you would have seen the opportunity to launch the most successful new dog food your company had ever introduced: A brand that not only fulfilled the demand pet parents had for pampering their beloved pets but also for maintaining their health.

Prior to the launch of this new brand, pet parents often had to fight with their pets to coax them into eating the healthy foods they needed. Alternatively, they could simply throw in the towel and feed their pets the indulgent foods that their pets loved most. This compromise was a no-win for loving pet parents: They wanted their pets to love them and did not want to turn every meal into a battle, but they also did not want to kill their pets with kindness by feeding them rich, indulgent foods that were not good for them. By breaking this compromise with a healthy offer that pets loved eating, we helped our client create a new brand that still generates over $1 billion in sales each year about 20 years after first being introduced.[7]

## Demand Trends

To structure these discussions about demand, we first think about the broad context of demand in which the business operates, including what is shaping demand and what the implications are for the business. We call this level of analysis "Demand Trends." Demand Trends are typically driven by changes in broad macro forces along with micro-level factors closer to the specific industry or the categories in which the business competes. The macro forces shaping demand often include drivers such as demographics, economic conditions, and technological advances. Shifts in category-specific factors might be driven by changing consumer tastes, growth in niche competitor offerings, or the emergence of channels designed to fulfill this new demand. Emerging digital capabilities can help a promising new idea scale quickly while leaping over the many traditional barriers to entry that helped protect established businesses. Uber, Blue Apron, Diapers.com, and many other examples come to mind.

In many cases, shifts in demand also include an element of borrowing from an entirely unrelated industry or a different global market, which means that a broad lens should be used whenever possible in examining potential Demand Trends. One well-established trend of borrowing from one category to another is the trickle down of commercial grade equipment to the consumer market. Companies have had success tapping into consumer demand for "professional" offers in categories as diverse as ovens, hand tools, electronics, and cars. If this trend has not already impacted your industry, does it represent an opportunity to fulfill a new segment of demand? If it has impacted your industry, are there signs indicating that the trend will expand or that it has plateaued? Assessing an analogous industry or another region to see how demand unfolded in that situation can often provide a template for your own industry. We often find that the pattern of how demand was generated and evolved in another industry or region can be observed in your own industry.

One of the most critical questions to ask is, "How could our business/industry be disrupted?" The next logical question to ask is, "How could we disrupt our business/industry ourselves?" Based on the disruption taking place across industries, there are several common patterns that reflect initial areas to examine. A few of the most prevalent include:

## Direct/online models

Could your business go direct to your consumer or customer without intermediaries (such as retail stores) in the same way that Dollar Shave Club and Blue Apron have?

## Small batch/premium

Established companies across many industries are being disrupted by smaller, "authentic" players that offer premium offers crafted using superior ingredients. Examples include everything from Shinola watches to the explosion of microbreweries in the United States.

## Leverage a C2C platform

Is there an opportunity to leverage an existing Consumer to Consumer (C2C) platform or to create one in order to help consumers monetize underused items or engage in a "side hustle" of some sort, in the mold of Airbnb or Uber?

## Unbundle/restructure pricing

Can you change the pricing model, usually to lower costs and prices, through unbundling or some other model? Car insurance premiums can now be calculated by the mile due to advances in telematics, while cable packages that once had to be purchased as "blocks" of programming are going a la carte. Both of these approaches lower prices, but prices can also move in the other direction. Most movie theaters charged the exact same price for the best seat in the house and for the worst seat. Now, for a premium, some movie theaters allow patrons to reserve seats in advance and show seat maps almost like the airlines. Are there ways to open new markets for your offers by unbundling or otherwise restructuring pricing?

## Leverage emerging technologies

Could new technologies such as the internet of things, artificial intelligence, location based technologies, payment devices, or self-driving vehicles be leveraged to disrupt your industry or a segment of it?

## Current, Emerging, and Latent Demand

One of the best ways to understand how demand will evolve going forward is to break demand down into what we call "current, emerging, and latent demand," which can be identified through a thorough assessment of the "forces and factors" that shape industry demand. One industry that provides many familiar examples of forces and factors at work is the beverage industry. In addition, beverages illustrate how some businesses have taken advantage of insights into demand to drive significant profitable growth by tapping into current, emerging, and latent demand opportunities. From the explosion of bottled waters to the nearly endless array of flavored vodkas to the phenomenon of energy drinks started by Red Bull to the entirely new experience and language of Starbucks, the beverage market holds lessons in understanding and tapping into current, emerging, and latent demand from which every business can learn.

## Current Demand: Growth Opportunities Hidden in Plain View

Current demand is readily observable in the market and should be relatively easy to identify. The signposts pointing to new ways to serve current demand often exist in some other category or some other part of the world that can serve as an analogous example. In many cases, important new opportunities stem from successfully importing a benefit available in another product or category but not available in your category. Recall that one aspect of Allstate's successful Your Choice offer, Deductible Rewards®, was essentially a loyalty benefit borrowed from the points programs used by hotels and airlines to recognize and reward frequent customers.

Although shifts in current demand are typically close at hand, businesses frequently fail to miss these changes for two major reasons. The first is related to the fact that demand is dynamic. It would certainly be easier and completely predictable to serve market demand if it never changed, and, unfortunately, too many managers operate as if this were the case. In reality, demand is shifting at an increasing pace today due, in part, to both globalization and the impact of the World Wide Web.

Today, a great new idea can get its start anywhere – from Bangalore to Beijing to Baltimore – and quickly find global demand to fulfill.

Second, many organizations focus so completely on their existing products and markets that they simply don't see the demand shifts happening before their eyes. In some cases, they only recognize significant shifts in current demand after it is too late and the market has passed them by. Harvard Business School marketing professor Theodore Levitt coined the term "marketing myopia" to describe this almost willful blindness, and it is as true today as when he first identified it over fifty years ago.[8]

One instructive example of recognizing and successfully tapping into current demand opportunities comes from the work we described earlier with Anheuser-Busch (AB, which is now AB InBev). As you'll recall, AB was struggling to drive profitable growth in the first half of the 2000s. By examining the forces and factors shaping the alcoholic beverage market, which includes beer, wine, and spirits, in depth, our team, along with our AB client partners, discovered that the majority of market growth had been driven by sweeter, flavored vodkas. These new flavored vodkas appealed to a new generation of young adults who had never really acquired the taste for beer. Unlike Baby Boomers, whose first alcoholic beverage was beer, this new generation of young adults skipped over beer altogether and gravitated to the new vodkas and some sweeter wines instead.

To capture this demand, AB introduced a slightly sweeter, lime-infused version of Bud Light called Bud Light Lime in 2008. Bud Light Lime brilliantly addressed an unfulfilled current demand among significant numbers of consumers and grew rapidly as a result. Just three years after it was introduced, Bud Light Lime had already added $250 million in profits to AB's bottom line and had restored the profitable growth the brewer had been seeking.[9]

Importantly, the Bud Light Lime case highlights the fact that current demand opportunities can often be uncovered in your existing category or industry. Although it is often tempting to pursue growth outside of your core category, doing so is also a much riskier approach than finding new opportunities for growth within your existing category or industry. While studying flavored vodkas, for example, AB might have been tempted to enter the spirits industry rather than taking the analogous learnings from flavored vodkas and launching a blockbuster new beer.

# Emerging Demand: Getting Beyond the Tip of the Iceberg

Unlike current demand that can be readily observed and readily accessed, emerging demand is typically a small but growing demand for new and different products that can be sighted from multiple vantage points. In some cases, several trends can be connected and interpreted to correctly determine that demand that represents only a small niche market today will grow significantly going forward. Emerging demand is critical to monitor because it has the power to radically transform an existing industry or create an entirely new industry that renders existing offers obsolete. For an example of emerging demand, consider the phenomenal growth of Red Bull and the forces and factors that helped give it wings.

Starting in the 1980s, our increasingly frenetic, 24/7 lifestyles led, not too surprisingly, to growing complaints of a lack of both physical and mental energy. Existing solutions that consumers turned to for an energy boost included coffee, colas, and candy bars, among others. However, none of these brought together the instant energy boost, convenience, and cool cachet that consumers, especially younger consumers, were seeking.

Famously, a former Austrian salesman named Dietrich Mateschitz came across a potential solution in the form of a relatively obscure beverage from Thailand called Krating Daeng.[10] What Mateschitz recognized was that this unique beverage could tap into an emerging demand opportunity among a new generation of European and U.S. consumers who had not been targeted to date. Unlike the current demand for a slightly sweeter beer that AB had observed in the U.S. that was being addressed by Corona with a lime and Miller Chill, there was no established, current market in Europe or the U.S. for what became Red Bull.

In launching Red Bull, Mateschitz was really creating an entirely new category of "energy drinks" and needed to both introduce consumers to the category and educate them about it. In doing so, he made several brilliant choices. First, while still retaining the unique flavor and ingredients that denote and deliver Red Bull's signature energy boost, he altered the taste of the original Krating Daeng to appeal more readily to Western tastes. Second, he introduced Red Bull's distinctive cylindrical package: A tall, slim 250-milliliter can unlike that of any other beverage. In addition, he priced the product significantly above carbonated soft drinks and most other nonalcoholic beverages, which reinforced the drink's premium image. Finally, the brand name, Red Bull, was unusual, intriguing especially to younger consumers, and symbolized the energy boost that was packed in each can.[11]

The potentially vast market Mateschitz imagined for Red Bull in 1987 has since become the global energy drink category with dozens of competitors generating estimated 2014 sales of over $50 billion.[12] The market is forecast to enjoy continued growth and ring up sales of as much as $62 billion by 2021.[13] Red Bull, the original category creator, still leads the pack with an estimated 40% share of the global market.[14]

## Latent Demand: Tapping into Unarticulated Opportunities

Latent demand is the most difficult to identify and anticipate but can also lead to the greatest rewards. In essence, latent demand represents the unarticulated demand consumers have for solutions they did not even realize they were seeking. In general, consumers will not know they ever wanted or would benefit from the new product or solution until they have actually experienced it. Once consumers experience a successful solution, it unlocks this previously dormant type of demand.

One of the most familiar examples of successfully tapping into latent demand is the rise of the now ubiquitous coffee chain, Starbucks. Unlike Red Bull, where consumers complained about fatigue and low energy, there were no consumers telling Starbucks founder and CEO, Howard Schultz, that they wanted a better way to enjoy coffee. In fact, per capita coffee consumption in the U.S. had been declining every year since 1963. If anything, all of the discernable signposts pointed to coffee as a dying market with rapidly declining demand.[15]

Although the demand was not articulated, Schultz was convinced that if he reinvented the coffee experience along the lines of the neighborhood coffeehouses he had visited in Italy, consumers would quickly realize what they had been missing. Schultz envisioned a "third place" between home and work where consumers could enjoy an "everyday indulgence" in the form of any one of hundreds of high-quality, carefully crafted coffee drinks. Given that consumers were not aware of or asking for a solution like Starbucks, Schultz's vision for the coffeehouse ultimately had to be experienced to be understood.[16]

The fact that Schultz was aiming for latent demand posed a significant issue as he attempted to gain support from potential investors. He was turned down by over 200 potential investors who reviewed his plans for Starbucks. Some scoffed that no one in their right mind would ever pay $3 for a cup of coffee. Others pointed out that coffee was a declining market that was already dominated by consumer packaged goods giants Procter & Gamble (Folger's coffee, since sold to J. M. Smucker's) and General Foods (Maxwell House), among others. The small handful of investors who believed in Schultz and his vision reaped outsized rewards for their investment in the nascent chain of coffeehouses.[17]

Although we've drawn on examples from the beverage industry, the same dynamics can be seen at work in any industry. Step back and think about the forces and factors shaping demand in your business and the potential signposts to watch over time. As usual, demographics and economics will probably play big roles in the future of your industry. Important demographic changes shaping demand in the U.S. might include the aging of Boomers, the emergence of Hispanics, and the coming of age of Millennials. To date, Millennials have altered the way banking relationships are formed, how alcoholic beverages are adopted, and when cars are purchased. At the same time, these demographic groups face new economic challenges such as living on retirement income, paying off college loan debt, and navigating the new normal of our post-recession economy. All of these forces and factors and more could have important implications for your business and your industry.

## Demand Triggers

An equally important exercise is to assess what we call "Demand Triggers." If Demand Trends analyze the context of demand and look several years ahead to anticipate shifts, Demand Triggers are the close-in drivers that might trigger a purchase among potential customers. There are several common categories of Demand Triggers that often apply across categories, including seasons/weather, holidays, life events, and life stages.

Consider, for example, getting married. Getting married is a major life event that triggers so much spending that weddings have become a more than $50 billion industry in the U.S.[18] Each year, over two million Americans get married[19] and the average cost of a U.S. wedding has more than doubled from $15,208 in 1990 to a record high of $35,329 in 2016.[20]

Ever more elaborate and expensive weddings are part of a broader trend toward amplifying all types of celebrations. Every year, birthdays, graduations, Halloween, and, of course, Christmas trigger ever-greater spending on gifts, themed decorations, parties, and more. For Halloween alone, recent statistics show that spending jumped an astounding $1.5 billion in just a few years,[21] going from $6.9 billion in 2013 to $8.4 billion in 2016 as a record 171 million Americans celebrated the spooky holiday.[22] Not to be left out, these numbers include an estimated $350 million spent on Halloween costumes for cats and dogs.[23]

Beyond broad life event or life stage triggers, there are also the triggers that are specific to each industry. Several years ago we worked with a hardware/home improvement retailer and determined that the age of housing stock in each neighborhood in which their stores operated was a significant trigger for both home repairs and remodeling. Not surprisingly, the owners of the oldest housing stock tended to spend the most not only on repairs but on much bigger ticket home remodeling projects. Fortunately, for this effort we were able to leverage detailed data on the age of U.S. housing stock by city that is available from the U.S. Census Bureau's American Community Survey. These data allowed us to help identify neighborhoods to focus on promoting the store while also tailoring the message to highlight our client's expertise in working on and providing hardware appropriate for all home styles, ranging from Victorian-era homes to Craftsman-style bungalows.

One familiar use of triggers online is the recommendation engine in the form of the "customers who bought that often buy this" section that was popularized by Amazon. The fact that someone bought a specific shirt triggers the potential for selling pants, a sweater, or shoes that match the shirt. These applications across the consumer "purchase funnel" are getting more sophisticated with advances in analytics and more access to a variety of Big Data resources. The purchase funnel is the decision-making process we all go through that narrows our choices down to the product or service that is eventually purchased.

Typically, the purchase funnel starts with a demand trigger: Something happens, such as a life stage, a life event, or a holiday, that causes the consumer to want something. Now that person searches for information regarding potential choices and purchase locations. From an initial "consideration set," the consumer keeps evaluating options on the decision criteria that matter most to him or her: Price, quality, convenience, and so on. Those decision criteria often vary by the need state or occasion that the consumer is experiencing: For example, a beverage choice to provide a boost in the morning (coffee, orange juice, energy drink) is usually quite different from a beverage for winding down at the end of the day (wine, herbal tea, beer). Ultimately, this decision-making process funnels choices down to the product or service that is purchased.

This is why understanding Demand Triggers, and, if possible, the key steps along the purchase funnel are both so important. Anticipating critical Demand Triggers is one of the best ways to get your offer into your customer's initial consideration set of products/services. In some industries, if your offer doesn't make the top three brands/offers in the consumer's consideration set, the chances of winning with that consumer are virtually zero. While intercepting consumers at or as close to the Demand Trigger is critical, it also helps to understand the entire purchase funnel and how your brand/offer can remain top of mind throughout the process in order to drive a successful outcome.

## Final Thoughts

Attempting to anticipate demand shifts is unlikely to result in a perfect forecast for your business. But done correctly, the exercise should yield valuable insights into how demand might evolve and what potential opportunities may exist as a result. Who will be the equivalent of pet parents for your industry? What will drive demand? Building scenarios for how demand might evolve, understanding the macro forces and industry factors that could drive shifts, and identifying the signposts to gauge progress can help prepare any business for what's ahead and how to win.

While understanding demand can help identify new growth opportunities, it also helps create greater certainty for your business. Having a more precise view of how demand will evolve, while still not perfect, does mean you are less likely to be caught by dramatic shifts in demand or to be caught napping while competitors tap into new opportunities that you missed. The Demand Trends at current, emerging, and latent levels, along with their underlying signposts, macro forces, and category-specific factors, in addition to the Demand Triggers that will give you insights into the buying process and how to win are generally available to anyone willing to look.

# Questions for Monday Morning

1. What are the major Demand Trends that could impact your industry and your business over the next three to five years?

2. Which "forces and factors" can you track as they shape Demand Trends?

   a. How will demographic changes impact your business?

   b. How will economic shifts impact your business?

   c. What consumer trends will create changes?

3. How well does your industry, including your offers, serve current demand?

   a. Do you have a "Bud Light Lime" opportunity to better serve shifting demand?

4. Are there important emerging and latent demand opportunities on the horizon?

5. How might your business be disrupted by a company outside of your industry or by a competitor within your industry?

6. How could you disrupt your industry in ways that create competitive advantages for you?

7. What are the most important Demand Triggers that cause consumers to buy your offers or your competitors' offers?

   a. How might you anticipate or intercept these Demand Triggers to be top of mind as customers begin the purchase process or purchase funnel?

8. How well do you understand the discrete steps and the criteria used by your most important consumers at each point in the purchase funnel?

   a. What could be done at each point in the purchase funnel to provide competitive advantages for your business?

# Endnotes

1. Brady, Diane and Christopher Palmer. "The Pet Economy." *Bloomberg Businessweek.* 5 August 2007. https://www.bloomberg .com/news/articles/2007-08-05/the-pet-economy. Accessed July 2017.
2. "Pet Industry Spending Topped US$66 Billion in 2016." Petfood Industry.com. 3 April 2017. http://www.petfoodindustry.com/ articles/6370-pet-industry-spending-topped-us66-billion-in-2016. Accessed July 2017.
3. Nielsen Sales Tracker Estimate, 2016.
4. Henderson, Steve. "Spending on Pets: 'Tails' from the Consumer Expenditure Survey." *Bureau of Labor Statistics: Beyond the Numbers.* Volume 2, Number 16 (May 2013). https://www.bls.gov/opub/btn/ volume-2/spending-on-pets.htm. Accessed July 2017.
5. "Pets in Your Bed." *WebMD.* http://pets.webmd.com/features/pets-in-your-bed#1. Accessed July 2017.
6. "Pet Care Industry Analysis 2017 – Cost & Trends." *Franchise Help.* https://www.franchisehelp.com/industry-reports/pet-care-industry-report/. Accessed July 2017.
7. Interview with client.
8. Levitt, Theodore. "Marketing Myopia." *Harvard Business Review.* August 2004. https://hbr.org/2004/07/marketing-myopia. Accessed July 2017.
9. Interview with client.
10. Nicatpunim, Chiratas and Busrin Treerapongpichit. "Red Bull Still Charging Ahead." *Bangkok Post.* 28 December 2015. https://www .bangkokpost.com/archive/red-bull-still-charging-ahead/808868. Accessed July 2017.
11. Ibid.
12. "The Energy Drinks Industry." *Investopedia.* 23 February 2015. http://www.investopedia.com/articles/investing/022315/energy-drinks-industry.asp?lgl=rira-baseline-vertical. Accessed July 2015.
13. "Global Energy Drinks Market 2015–2021." *Research and Markets.* 3 September 2015. https://www.prnewswire.com/news-releases/ global-energy-drinks-market-2015-2021-insights-market-size-share-growth-trends-analysis-and-forecasts-for-the-61-billion-industry-300137637.html. Accessed July 2017.

14. "Energy Drinks Market." *Mordor Intelligence*. March 2017. https://www.mordorintelligence.com/industry-reports/energy-drinks-market. Accessed July 2017.

15. Loudenback, Tanza. "The Incredible Rags to Riches Story of Starbucks Billionaire Howard Schultz." *Business Insider*. 15 October 2015. http://www.businessinsider.com/howard-schultz-profile-2015-10/#in-1985-schultz-left-starbucks-after-his-ideas-to-cultivate-an-italian-like-experience-for-coffee-lovers-was-rejected-by-the-founders-he-soon-started-his-own-coffee-company-il-giornale-italian-for-the-daily-9. Accessed July 2017.

16. Ibid.

17. Ibid.

18. Chhabra, Esha. "How The $50 Billion Dollar Wedding Industry Could Be A Platform for Philanthropy." *Forbes*. 30 July 2016. https://www.forbes.com/sites/eshachhabra/2016/07/30/how-the-50-billion-dollar-wedding-industry-could-be-a-platform-for-philanthropy/#15464b4e3af0. Accessed July 2017.

19. Bialik, Carl. "Weddings Are Not the Budget Drains Some Surveys Suggest." *Wall Street Journal*. 24 August 2007. https://ctjpmarie.com/average-wedding-cost/; https://www.wsj.com/articles/SB118790518546107112. Accessed July 2017.

20. "The National Average Cost of a Wedding Hits $35,329." *The Knot*. 2 February 2017. https://www.theknot.com/content/average-wedding-cost-2016. Accessed July 2017.

21. Smith, Ana Serafin. "Halloween Spending to Reach $8.4 Billion, Highest in Survey History." *National Retail Federation*. 22 September 2016. https://nrf.com/media/press-releases/halloween-spending-reach-84-billion-highest-survey-history. Accessed July 2017.

22. Amadeo, Kimberly. "Halloween Spending Statistics, Facts and Trends." *The Balance*. https://www.thebalance.com/halloween-spending-statistics-facts-and-trends-3305716. Accessed July 2017.

23. "20 Million Pet Owners Expected to Spend $350 Million on Their Pets This Halloween." Dogtime.com. September 2016. http://dogtime.com/trending/18630-pet-costumes-a-multi-million-dollar-industry. Accessed July 2017.

CHAPTER

# 5

# Enhanced Demand Landscape

---

### The Big Ideas

- While traditional market segmentation approaches continue to offer valuable insights, the increased availability of data and advances in technology are creating an opportunity to enhance these approaches.

- Enhanced techniques for segmenting consumers are already present and growing in acceptance and effectiveness. A new world of opportunity awaits – a modern approach to customer segmentation incorporates new data to increase actionability and improve customer reach.

- A modern approach to segmentation can be achieved through the following four steps:

  1. Start with the simplest segmentation framework and determine what additional desirable dimensions can be added to it.

  2. Identify all of the information that is captured in your internal data as well as any external sources to fill in gaps on the dimensions of interest.

3. Tie observable metrics to your segmentation in order to monitor segment behaviors over time and evaluate both upstream and downstream activities.

4. Refine the segmentation iteratively over time.

---

*"Worry about being better; bigger will take care of itself. Think one customer at a time and take care of each one the best way you can."*
—Gary Comer[1]

At the height of the Cold War, correctly diagnosing a heart attack for a crewmember on a nuclear submarine was of critical importance. Balancing the risk of remaining undetected by staying submerged and resurfacing to coordinate an airlift for the sufferer was of utmost importance. This decision required a swift determination of whether the crewmember with symptoms was indeed experiencing a heart attack or simply feeling momentary discomfort, possibly caused by variations in pressure or temperature common in a submarine. The stakes were high. Too much care for the mission without proper regard for the crewmember could lead to the death of a crewmember; conversely, the mission could be jeopardized unnecessarily if too much conservatism is displayed for the health of the crewmember. It was of utmost importance to increase the precision of this diagnosis to allow for the best course of action in these situations.

The military devised a set of guidelines to apply in making these decisions. Before the start of the mission, all crewmembers' health had been screened, and both vitals and family history were assessed to categorize crewmembers into risk cohorts. When suspected of experiencing a heart attack, a simple set of questions requiring "yes/no" answers were devised to apply in sequence, eventually leading to a determination of risk. The answer of the first question determined subsequent ones, thus formulating a dynamic decision tool. Do you have chest discomfort? How long have you experienced it? Does it spread to other areas of the upper body? Are you breaking out in a cold sweat? Do you experience nausea?

This sequence of questions resulted in a risk classification of whether a heart attack was taking place or not. The answers to the questions placed the crewmember into one of several risk groups that each had a different likelihood of heart attack ranging from high to low. Those classification outcomes offered clear recommendations on the next course of action. Effectively, this system enabled the military to segment the crew into groups with assigned risks of fatality and a corresponding action plan to counteract the threat.

Imagine how a submarine captain could improve this process with modern technology and all of the additional data available that were not available during the Cold War! Rather than wait until people experience heart attacks, he could constantly monitor risk factors and vitals to continuously predict whether a crewmember is at risk of a heart attack. Wearable technology, wireless transmission of data, real-time analysis, and machine-learning capabilities could all be combined to improve the captain's ability to detect health risks. With these tools, a submarine captain could discover new patterns that reveal risk factors, increasing the accuracy and speed with which he could distinguish between a heart attack and a false alarm. The Cold War submarine example is about the past – but imagine the outcome if we really applied the latest technology to the problem. If one collects data passively and analyzes it proactively, risk could be substantially mitigated and handled more effectively.

The notion of applying segmentation frameworks to consumers is not new. Marketing experts have been partitioning customers into groups of relative levels of attractiveness for years. Unlike the submarine example, in marketing, rather than partitioning crewmembers based on risk of a heart attack, we partition customers based on business criteria. For a brand manager, segmentations are relevant frameworks for prioritizing customer outbound communication or new product introductions. For a retailer, segmentations can inform price, advertising, and promotional activities. For a bank, segments might help prioritize loan amounts and associated interest rates, or even potential locations for new branches. Traditionally, segmentations enabled these types of applications, but the increased availability of data from diverse sources, along with improved technical and analytical capabilities, allow for an enhanced framework that offers new insights and the applications for your existing segmentations!

## The Failures of Traditional Market Segmentations

Traditional market segmentation techniques have remained largely unchanged for decades despite monumental advances in technology, computer science, and the availability of new data. While these techniques have served practitioners well, they can be enhanced with modern technology. Today, in a world where rich, up-to-date data sets on millions of consumers are readily available, practitioners of market segmentation continue to rely exclusively on decades-old statistical techniques and small data sets, often derived through primary research.

While traditional segmentations will remain valuable for getting a general view of the market, they don't adequately capture the rich nuances of the real world due to their reliance on smaller data sources. These segmentations typically use either internal or external data that rarely include more than one data asset. For example, a segmentation may rely solely on the outputs of primary research conducted on a few thousand respondents, which makes them basic and not sufficiently rich to capture the complex realities of consumer behavior. They are also static: In a world where new data are constantly being generated, they represent the marketplace at a given point of time rather than adapting dynamically to market conditions. These shortcomings mean that traditional segmentations are not flexible enough to adapt to constantly evolving consumer tastes and disruptions brought about by competitors.

From a methodological standpoint, there have not been any notable advances in statistical techniques for performing segmentations. Instead, it is the availability of data and the low cost of data storage and processing that have evolved drastically in recent years. Today, there are new types of geographic data, improved coverage of population trends, and higher frequency of data updates. New cloud technologies have vastly improved data storage and processing through fast, inexpensive, and, in some cases, free tools. Take the costs per megabyte in hard drive storage space as an example: In 1981, when Apple went magnetic with its 5MB hard drive at $3,500, the price of 1MB equaled $700. In 1995, Seagate introduced the first 1GB hard drive for $859, bringing the cost of 1MB to under $0.12. In 2007, Hitachi introduced the first terabyte drive at $399, implying $0.0004 per MB. By 2010, the cost per MB had dropped to $0.00002.[2] Today's cloud technologies offer further cost savings, with Amazon Web Services offering 1MB at $0.000004. These trends have converged to create new opportunities to understand the customer and to apply segmentations for real business applications and uses. These advances have revealed an entirely new spectrum of uses for segmentations, which we call "Enhanced Demand Landscapes."

Surprisingly, despite being proven to be effective for decades, many Fortune 500 firms continue to avoid even the traditional market segmentation approach. While corporate executives are familiar with the benefits of adopting the differentiated customer approach, a number of obstacles have prevented them from using segmentations. One major obstacle is their desire to reach the highest percentage of the total market and increase penetration as much as possible with a single product or brand. These executives believe that their brand should target the entire market rather than individual segments in order to reach the highest level of penetration. Thus, we observe some organizations pushing to build larger brands and amass portfolios that deliver on mass appeal and serve everybody in the marketplace. The problem with mass-market strategies is that they are not founded on individual consumer cohorts with distinct tastes and preferences. As markets continue to fragment to serve niches with tailored offerings, the mass-market model will cave under increasing pressure.

We have used the Enhanced Demand Landscape to address many of the issues above for a number of our clients. This robust segmentation framework integrates a variety of large data assets and naturally adapts to changing market conditions. It enables the implementation of a concrete, differentiated approach to managing consumers' complex behaviors and offers major upgrades over traditional segmentations.

The Enhanced Demand Landscape is designed to combat our concern that inertia at perennially profitable companies will prevent them from embracing crucial new technologies. Technological advancements are applying more pressure to innovate in marketing and customer management: As new entrants are upending traditional business models with refined targeting to complement their competitive offerings, the executives of today are recognizing the competitive threat and looking for dynamic ways to remain relevant. I recall the CEO of a major U.S. beer producer acknowledging that "he is flying an airplane without any of the avionics" and that his company has been applying very little strategy in marketing, saying that he feels his firm is "throwing money against the wall and hoping some of it will stick." Are you wondering how to improve precision and deliver higher ROI for your marketing campaigns?[3]

## The Benefits of the Enhanced Demand Landscape

The opportunity is ripe to use Big Data and advanced analytics capabilities to gain a deeper understanding of what consumers want and think, how they behave, and where to locate them. The Enhanced Demand Landscape is a more refined segmentation framework that relies on multiple data sources to precisely identify target consumers, along with their needs, and enables the execution of strategies with tactical and concrete action plans to deliver on those needs.

How does the Enhanced Demand Landscape work? At a high level, it uses these new technologies to supercharge a traditional segmentation and delivers an improved understanding of the consumer. It represents a framework where data flows into clustering algorithms to create the segments in modeling samples and feeds those into modern analytical tools and technologies to recreate these segments onto additional data assets. It then flows through predictive algorithms into downstream applications to tie back to the segments. For example, this framework might allow a company to evaluate changes in the size and composition of their segments and find members of these segments in their CRM database automatically on a monthly basis. The framework evolves continuously, enabling the creation of a holistic view of the consumer through continuous refinement, tracking, and evaluation of outcomes.

Compare this more sophisticated approach to traditional segmentations that typically start with qualitative research investigations to formulate hypotheses and provide a foundation for primary research. This process informs the type of data we need to collect, most often through custom surveys. Once the segmentation is built, we can then move on to creating the tools needed to recreate the segmentation on new data assets. There are two main limitations to the traditional approach of segmentation, the first of which is that the clustering is performed on partial and static data. As a result, the segment groupings are relatively simple and do not capture the rich underlying characteristics of the consumers. The segment groupings also represent a single snapshot of the marketplace and do not account for evolution over time. The second limitation is that the algorithms used to identify the segments in outside databases, as well as the tools to track and monitor segment behavior and profiles, are often outdated. The Enhanced Demand Landscape augments the traditional segmentation approach to overcome these limitations, offering companies exciting new capabilities.

The advances in Big Data have changed the paradigm in data collection and analytic approaches. Today, we have countless new sources of data and improved abilities to clearly analyze that information. Moreover, the availability of data and the sophistication of analytical capabilities enable the deconstruction of traditional segmentation processes. Specifically, instead of starting with qualitative research, you can commence directly with segmentation and then simultaneously build the algorithms to find these segments in other databases. At that point, you can revert to qualitative work to fill in gaps and probe deeper in areas where observable data are not readily available. This process saves significant time and produces segmentation insights much more quickly than traditional approaches. This process improves the efficiency of your marketing efforts, allowing use of the segmentation in targeting applications immediately after the framework is built along with the algorithms to classify customers into the segments onto your CRM domains, for example.

Many of these advances are possible thanks to the staggering amount of data we have available today, ranging from social media to the improved ability to capture purchase data and track the habits of your consumers. Many of these data assets appear segmented at first sight, but innovative data storage and database management systems like Hadoop enable these data to be linked together and used for the development of the segmentation instead of using only primary research. Integrating these dynamic data sources results in a holistic view of the consumer that traditional segmentations have not been able to capture.

In addition to creating a more holistic view of the consumer, the Enhanced Demand Landscape is also dynamic, in that it adapts to changes in underlying market forces and evolving consumer preferences by constantly updating itself to match variations in the observable data. Allowing for the underlying data to get refreshed enables any algorithm to update with the latest indicators and improve on the quality of the learnings it produces. Take, for example, category purchases: Observing that consumption of a given consumer is rotating through different brands over time would indicate that he or she may value variety. Incorporating different measurable and trackable information, including location of retail outlets shopped or total basket size, not only supplements the learnings but also creates links to tie data back to the segments and evaluate how accurate any individual classifications are. This flow of information back to the segments creates a flexible system where the consumer segments are dynamic and evolve over time, which enables time-series or trend analyses of segment sizes, taste preferences, and purchase patterns, among other key characteristics, all of which would have been impossible in traditional segmentations. Knowing such key characteristics positions your firm to adopt new strategies and maintain relevance with its consumers. These insights also feed into your continual analyses of consumer tastes and preferences, which iteratively builds on your knowledge of the consumer and allows incorporating new and additional segmentation dimensions. This dynamic process is incredibly powerful, for it enables us to refine our initial hypothesis on who our target customer is and the messaging for consumers, to create pricing and promotions that will be most appealing to them, and to optimize channel placement, among other key decisions.

Replicating the output in samples outside of the modeled segmentation is of critical importance, and Machine Learning algorithms provide this necessary replicability and automation. The richness of available data and new quantitative technologies can lead to an unprecedented level of accuracy, allowing you to precisely locate your consumers. Machine Learning techniques enable the use of data to build algorithms that project the segmentation extremely accurately. They can also be used to create simulations, which can help business leaders construct tactical action plans related to a segmentation framework prior to the rollout of new strategies. Finally, these processes can also be easily connected to data visualization and dashboarding tools, which can also be tied to existing data sources to create incredibly powerful and dynamic reporting tools that can be widely used across an organization.

Finally, the Enhanced Demand Landscape can also use Machine Learning to tie segments to their predicted and observed outcomes, which enables the translation of insights into concrete action. For example, algorithms can be used to analyze the likelihood of individuals in a given segment to purchase a certain product. Similarly, algorithms can be used to track attrition risk, predicted customer lifetime value, or the impact of promotional activity through the segment lens, among other critical metrics. By tying segments to predictions and outcomes, the Enhanced Demand Landscape offers companies concrete steps for using segmentations to stay several steps ahead of both consumer trends and competition.

By linking the vastness of the capabilities of Big Data and Machine Learning with traditional segmentation approaches, the Enhanced Demand Landscape creates fertile ground for the design of efficient tools that capture the nuances of the marketplace while providing concrete steps to take advantage of new findings. In essence, the Enhanced Demand Landscape provides a segmentation solution that is incredibly quick in generating precise insights, agile enough to adapt to changing consumer preferences, and expansive through the ability to be integrated into existing client frameworks and data streams. All of these aspects combine to improve decision-making capabilities and, ultimately, strong results that will immediately be seen in the firm's bottom line.

## The Benefits of Enhanced Segmentation

Growth in today's world is rarely achieved by expanding scale and attempting to serve all your customers with megabrands. Some products serve a niche before quickly gaining broader market appeal. We have witnessed this phenomenon repeatedly across many industries, ranging from craft beer to instant messaging platforms and applications. One specific case we encountered in the implementation of an Enhanced Demand Landscape was with a major telecom company that focused on smartphone adoption and data usage. Once we built the segments on survey attitudes and motivations, we used the predicted risk of attrition and favorability preferences to create micro-groupings of consumers. In addition, we introduced additional characteristics for further refinement of the groupings based on demographics and geographies, zeroing in on a select and targeted population in the market, which appeared small today but was predicted to grow in size and revenue opportunity very quickly. After having formulated initial insights, we tested and fine-tuned them, before building an Enhanced Demand Landscape that considerably strengthened our clients' competitive position. Our work significantly increased the ROI for retention campaigns and new customer acquisitions by focusing on customers most likely to favorably respond to campaign offers.

The client credits our Enhanced Demand Landscape for helping it in navigating through cutthroat competitive pressures and a disruptive technological environment. Since working with us, our client has expanded its footprint and coverage at a time when many other service providers experienced losses and customer attrition. This firm understood how the preferences of customers to communicate have been evolving: Demand for traditional telephone calls was quickly being overtaken by texting, instant messaging, and other features. As this was happening, we positioned the client right at the forefront of the category, continuously refining their customer groupings through the use of newly available observed data. Thanks to the Enhanced Demand Landscape, our client successfully introduced new services, innovative device plan programs, targeted customer outreach, and customized customer service.

The Enhanced Demand Landscape makes your go-to-market strategies more actionable and effective. In addition, the introduction of the framework into your organization breaks silos and brings transparency across divisions. The Enhanced Demand Landscape also increases reliability of self-reported data while linking external and internal assets to primary research. This use of the data yields a nuanced understanding of the many types of customers and how they interact within a product or category. Linking results directly back to the segmentation and evaluating programs, not by their impact overall but instead against a specific target population, enables keeping the segments current and monitoring how they evolve over time. It also allows for connection to other data streams, including geo-location tools, as well as existing models, to optimize effectiveness and organizational efficiency.

## *Taking Full Advantage of the Data in Your Organization*

Aligning your organization with the Enhanced Demand Landscape is an effort that is well worth the investment. The first thing that the framework accomplishes is to remove barriers between different divisions at a company, which in turn allows for improved use of internal data. We often find that different divisions of a company do not know what data other divisions are collecting or purchasing: This lack of transparency leads many companies to underutilize their internal data assets that could be used successfully in marketing efforts. With the Enhanced Demand Landscape, these assets are immediately put to use to provide a richer understanding of consumers' desires and motivations. This new understanding can then be used to create strategies that more effectively address the needs of customers and get the right message to the right consumer.

By integrating different data sources, we are able to establish linkages between internal customer data, self-reported primary research data, and other external third-party data, each of which complement each other in unique ways. Primary research complements behaviors and demographics with attitudes and motivations that are not directly observable. Conversely, the inherent errors or biases that stem from self-reporting, like quantities purchased, can be validated against and corrected using CRM and other internal databases. Linking data in this way allows a company to connect what customers say to what they actually do, increasing the reliability of data and creating new insights on the connections between attitudes and behaviors. In addition, linking internal data with external retail, macroeconomic, or industry data can further augment a company's understanding of customers. By combining all of these disparate data assets together, a company can create a nuanced understanding of its customers, which in turn will help with tactical choices on various resource allocations.

## Getting a More Nuanced View of the Market

Another key benefit of the Enhanced Demand Landscape is the creation of a nuanced understanding of the different types of customers and how they interact with different offerings, which is achieved through the granularity we gain by increasing the number of segments. The traditional mass-market approach to market segmentations uses a one-size-fits-all approach, which divides the entire population into five to eight distinct groups, though the exact number of segments may vary by analysis. The result of this type of segmentation is a high-level view of the market, which does not fully capture the nuances in shopping and purchase patterns of consumers. While the broad view provided by a traditional segmentation is still valuable, most organizations could also benefit from a more granular view of the market.

With the Enhanced Demand Landscape, we provide this granular view by using all available data to increase the number of segments, which we call micro-segments. There are different ways to incorporate additional segmenting variables to build micro-segments. In some applications it is appropriate to use customer purchase occasions or their observed preferences. In other cases, understanding the products that consumers purchase on a single shopping trip reveals patterns unique to different micro-segments. This type of a nuanced understanding yields improved predictions on what consumers in different micro-segments will purchase in the future, allowing for greater precision and less waste in marketing outreach and promotional activities.

## Taking Full Advantage of Existing Predictive Algorithms

In addition to tying together disparate data sources, the Enhanced Demand Landscape also offers a platform to tie together existing predictive algorithms. Predictions from existing models can be evaluated through the segments, linking modeled predictions to the underlying segment profiles and characteristics. For example, the output from an existing attrition risk model might be combined with micro-segments to determine which customers should be interjected with retention offers that contain monetary rewards and which ones to induce with functional benefits. This process offers additional validation of model performance that extends beyond the standard quantitative evaluation metrics, while also improving those algorithms through testing, comparison, and refinement capabilities.

In addition to evaluating and improving predictive algorithms, by tying predictive algorithms into segmentations, you can improve the effectiveness of your campaigns and consumer outreach. Consider, for example, linking an algorithm that predicts response rates with a customer segmentation tool: This combination would enable an outflow of tailored offers to the micro-segment of customers who are most likely to respond. By prioritizing or ranking certain consumers in a given segment, companies can improve the efficiency of their marketing campaigns. Merging micro-segments with models can further differentiate outbound strategies and make campaigns extremely effective by picking messages that are custom-tailored to the individual. By combining predictive models with segmentations, your firm can increase the likelihood that it is reaching the right customer with the right message.

## Understanding the Location Where the Action Takes Place

Once the Enhanced Demand Landscape has integrated a segmentation framework with the data and models within an organization, it is possible to gain a whole new understanding of the customer. For example, with the right data, your firm can know where customers live, work, and shop. Considering these types of spatial characteristics of customers represents a huge and largely underdeveloped opportunity for corporate executives to think beyond large geographic regions like north and south. The Enhanced Demand Landscape capitalizes on this untapped opportunity by connecting segmentation frameworks to geography. Thinking in terms of geography allows your firm to link a plethora of data to the segmentation and tie that to a physical location.

Once a customer is tied to a location, we gain access to general data characterizing his or her location, which could include broader macroeconomic indicators, weather patterns, real estate trends, health metrics, and labor market activity. Linking this information to your firm's segmentation through the Enhanced Demand Landscape enables a more holistic understanding of consumers, who can then be targeted more dynamically, especially after merging this information with CRM outputs to understand purchase preferences.

## Understanding How the Market Changes over Time

Linking data with the Enhanced Landscape also creates opportunities for your firm to monitor segments over time, which enables businesses to learn more about the constantly fluctuating needs of consumers and how they can be more dynamic in their methods of targeting. This ability is a function of the dynamic updating capabilities of advanced statistical techniques, such as Bayesian methods or Markov chain processes, which enable models to break away from a single static view of the market that grows increasingly inaccurate over time in favor of one that is constantly adapting and improving in terms of precision and accuracy. Specifically, the noise and errors in these segmentations are reduced over time as new and pertinent information is fed into the model. Monitoring consumers in this fashion improves the accuracy of segmentation assignments and thus decreases the likelihood of an errant classification of a consumer into a segment in which he or she does not belong.

The Enhanced Demand Landscape will significantly improve your firm's understanding of consumers so that it can take action to satisfy their needs in more efficient ways. Marrying primary research with internal and external data assets results in a very detailed, rich, and nuanced view of the marketplace. Moreover, adoption of the framework will make your organization more prepared to respond to changing tastes and attitudes among your consumers. The framework will deliver flexibility to course-correct tactical plans as you go and enable experimentation in applying robust and differentiated consumer strategies, all of which will improve the competitiveness of the firm's offerings with its target consumers.

## The Challenge in Implementing a Complex System

While incorporating a segmentation framework into a company's strategy leads to great returns, implementing one in a corporate environment is not necessarily straightforward. Challenges such as achieving organizational alignment, maintaining up-to-date data management, and building robust predictive capabilities often stand in the way of building a segmentation and implementing it in a business setting. For the Enhanced Demand Landscape, these difficulties are further compounded due to the increased demands for data use, analytics, integration with existing processes, and the need for up-to-date systems. Through years of experience on both traditional segmentations and Enhanced Demand Landscapes, we have found that many of these challenges can be overcome by careful design and planning along with disciplined and committed execution.

Part of the challenge of implementing an Enhanced Demand Landscape arises from its complexity and highly customized nature. In order to take full advantage of the available data from multiple sources, the framework cannot be transferred as a template from one company to the next. In other words, it is a highly customized framework that fits into your existing data and analytic ecosystem.

This complexity and highly customized nature of the framework requires broad organizational alignment behind the concept of the Enhanced Demand Landscape itself. Furthermore, it is necessary to get buy-in from managers across the company who will execute the framework. Traditional segmentations usually require coordination between strategy executives, data insights teams, and marketing departments. The Enhanced Demand Landscape, on the other hand, requires additional coordination with predictive analytics departments, third-party data vendors, external data collectors, CRM architects, and other technical experts. This high level of coordination is necessary due to the complexities and vastness of the inputs into the framework and how it all flows into the clustering and predictive algorithms that tie back to the segments, as well as the functioning of analytic processes supporting the framework.

Furthermore, the dynamic nature of the Enhanced Demand Landscape requires continued involvement of different parties both inside and outside your organization. With the Enhanced Demand Landscape, as new data become available, departments responsible for procuring data need to remain engaged in continually updating internal databases. In addition, algorithms need to be updated to match continually changing market conditions.

Implementing a project on the scale of the Enhanced Demand Landscape requires a champion with broad executive powers and support from senior leadership. The design, construction, and implementation of the framework is a lengthy process that requires continued focus, discipline, and persistence from many participants within an organization. Without a committed senior executive at the head of the initiative, the sustained effort needed to implement an Enhanced Demand Landscape is not possible. While implementing the framework will lead to some quick wins, more significant improvements will only come with long-term commitment to the process. While the hurdles to implementing an Enhanced Demand Landscape may seem daunting at first, the results are well worth it. From years of experience, we have seen that organizations committed to overcoming the organizational hurdles of implementing and maintaining this framework reap great benefits over time. In an increasingly crowded and competitive marketplace, the Enhanced Demand Landscape offers a way for a strong, committed leader to unify an organization behind a single vision.

## Constructing an Enhanced Demand Landscape

The Enhanced Demand Landscape needs to be carefully designed for successful implementation in business environments. The high complexity in the system requires detailed planning and a high degree of coordination among different functions and across many stakeholders. Once the segmentation is created in a modeling sample and applied to populations of interest, campaign outcomes will be evaluated against the segments so that they can be refined continuously to keep a differentiated and robust view of your marketplace.

Building the Enhanced Demand Landscape entails a multistep process that starts with identifying the data sets available internally and the ones that can be purchased. Some of the segmentation data will be consumer attitudes and motivations sourced from primary research, while other data will come from internal CRM systems or third-party providers. Fusing data to create a uniform modeling sample should take place before any segmentations can be performed. A subset of these data will be used to construct the segmentation before identifying the data that will be used for developing the predictive capabilities needed for taking concrete actions based on segmentation.

Practical uses of market segmentations, like consumer targeting and profiling, rely on a number of predictive algorithms. Because the modeling sample is small and contains survey data that are not directly observable, finding the segments in a broader population requires building algorithms that use only observable data like that found in a CRM database. While some of these algorithms may already exist in your organization, it's possible that some new algorithms would need to be specifically developed for this project. Once these predictive algorithms are found or developed and then applied onto external data assets, work with a broader population can begin. New uses for segmentation frameworks like linking upstream activities, including product design and offer optimization, with downstream activities, including media optimization and distribution, allows you to improve the effectiveness of your customer outreach and relevance in the marketplace.

To maximize the effectiveness of the new structure, adopting firms must track and report outcomes like sales and customer attrition, and build those inputs back into the model through a feedback loop. Further, they should monitor key performance indicators regularly to allow for the evaluation of resource allocation plans and for the quantification of the efficiencies resulting from your differentiated consumer management approach. All of this work, while arduous, will ensure high precision and relevance of the framework while also maximizing its effectiveness in the short and long term.

The foundation for the Enhanced Demand Landscape is a segmentation framework. This segmentation can be one that your firm already has in place or it can be created specifically for this process. If your firm is creating a new segmentation, you should consider starting with the simplest one possible. Perhaps partitioning the population into lapsed and current customers makes natural sense. Similarly, you could split the market into high-volume and low-volume consumers. Once you have established the basis for this segmentation, find other important

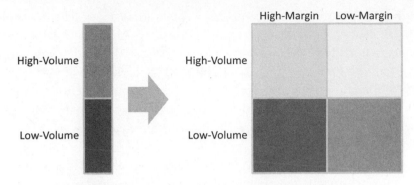

**Figure 5.1    Factors that distinguish consumers.**

factors that distinguish customers and further partition the population. For example, if you start with low-volume and high-volume consumers, further divide those groups into consumers of high-margin and low-margin products (Figure 5.1).

Continue partitioning the market along distinguishing characteristics to create more granular cohorts. There are no strict rules on selecting how many micro-segments exist in the framework. If your capabilities to implement marketing strategies tailored to your segments are limited, consider starting with three to five. If you have experience with a differentiated go-to-market strategy, six to seven segments might be more appropriate. We have worked with up to 12 segments. Depending on the category, larger numbers of micro-segments could work well for you. Selecting the right number of segments requires balancing the specificity of the segments with their practical usability as well as their size. A segment that is too small, for example, would not provide any good, tactical information on what products to offer and what messaging to use. Similarly, a segment that is too large might not possess any meaningful and differentiating profile from the total market.

As you select an existing segmentation or build a new one, it is vital to keep in mind the specific ways it is going to be used. Will your firm's segmentation be used to manage current customers, or to find new ones? Do you want to find the geographic distribution of your segments to align with your retail footprint and physical presence? The answers to these specific questions will inform the type of data you need for segment creation in addition to finding segments in a broader database beyond the modeling sample. To assure stable and predictive models that identify segment composition outside of the segmentation-development sample, it is helpful to build in observable "hooks," which are behavioral and demographic elements that are available for both the initial segmenting data and the broader data that will be used to implement any strategies. These observable data guarantee that you will be able to identify members of segments without additional primary research. Through the use of these hooks, the segmentation, in effect, becomes a bridge from one set of data assets to another one.

In many cases, much of the data needed for developing segmentations and implementing strategies based on them can be found within an organization. In our experience, companies tend to underutilize their internal data assets. When we engaged with a current client of ours in the project management and education space to build an Enhanced Demand Landscape, we discovered that they were capturing rich data on their customers without realizing its potential uses in marketing initiatives. Simply recording information and storing it is not sufficient. You need to take additional steps to determine how the different data elements you capture work together and what new information can be gleaned through some standardization, roll-ups, or aggregations.

For example, sometimes looking at multiple types of data together can reveal more information than looking at each part individually. Our aforementioned education client keeps track of the various course credits customers accrue over time as well as the levels of certification achieved. The total number of credits reveals limited information on its own, but combining those data with other pieces of information can create a nuanced view of the customers. For instance, when does course credit accrual take place? Does accrual happen at the beginning of membership, or is it evenly spread throughout the tenure of membership? We helped our client create this kind of rich view of members by combining several existing pieces of information that they were already collecting. Through this process, we captured how class credits accrue over time, allowing our clients to see their customers with a new level of detail. For example, we constructed flags that inform our client if the member accrues credits because he or she is driven by the desire to learn and enhance his or her education. Instead, if we observed credit accumulation being concentrated right before certification, the flag we create would indicate that the member cares primarily about completing the certification and not so much about continuous learning. Often, combining several pieces of observable information in new ways reveals consumer attitudes and motivations that are not directly observed.

Once the assessment of the internal data is complete, your firm will be able to identify what additional information is needed from external sources to make informed decisions. Third-party aggregators can provide data on areas like lifestyles, financials, demographics, and product ownership, and none of this information is exclusive to a single provider. Today, data powerhouses, ranging from credit bureaus like Experian to consumer data aggregators like Nielsen, make each other's data available, which creates increasingly valuable bundles of data.

The design of the segmentation typically entails the development of algorithms that predict segment assignments in external data assets. The creation of these predictive algorithms relies heavily on Machine Learning techniques, which sift through a large number of models to quickly develop highly accurate algorithms that can predict whether a person belongs to a segment. In the past, only the largest companies could create these kinds of models because of the development costs and the time required to construct them. Today, thanks to the existence of powerful, open-source programming tools such as R, Python, and Spark, this process is within reach for enterprises of all sizes.

The algorithms predicting segment assignments are developed on the same data used to construct the segmentation through statistical clustering that leverages a small number of data elements. These elements would also be available on the entire population that your firm is interested in classifying into segments. They are most commonly applied to internal customer relationship management (CRM) systems, retailer loyalty card databases, or prospect lists available from third-party providers. Once your team has built the algorithms predicting the segment assignments of the members of these databases, they can get assignments for that whole population using those data through a process called "scoring." It is preferable to score your data assets in real time to keep segment assignments current. The frequency of rescoring depends on many factors like rates of new customer acquisitions and data input refreshes. As such, a custom implementation plan needs to be devised to meet the needs of your organization. A roadmap needs to be put in place accounting for how data get refreshed, how models get updated over time, and how often scoring takes place.

Once your team has constructed the segment memberships of the population represented by the outside database, you can use that new information to learn about the market and your customers. Campaign execution and evaluation of outcomes should be tied back to the segmentation framework. More effectively, building a feedback loop from point-of-sale interactions to segments enables your firm to keep sales, promotion, and outreach campaigns current, as well as the relevance of segment assignments. For example, tying segment assignments with outcomes from individual campaigns could be used for market sizing exercises and ROI estimations. Maintaining a pulse on the contribution of your segmentation to the top and bottom line of your business in this way is important to maintain broad organizational support and continue the evolution of the framework. As a living and breathing entity, when appropriately embedded within your organization, the Enhanced Demand Landscape evolves with changing market conditions and steers your firm's go-to-market execution.

Also, when the segments are constructed and projected out to a population of interest, it becomes possible to tie reporting metrics to the segments to continuously profile segment behaviors. The reporting metrics enable the feedback loop from activation initiatives back to the segmentation. This process provides the "avionics," to quote the CEO of the major beer producer we referenced earlier in the chapter.[4] Evaluating downstream activities like outbound marketing communication, through the segment lens, can be used to construct powerful revenue and profitability indicators. Similarly, linking segmentation to upstream activities like new product innovation should also be explored. Optimizing product features and tailoring an offering to the revealed preferences of your target segment groups significantly increases the likelihood that any innovation launched will be successful. Observing the variation in the response rates across different segment groups will allow further optimization of the product in an iterative fashion. This process builds a flow of information originating from the segments, enabling you to evaluate and quantify outcomes that today are mostly decided experientially and subjectively.

Finally, consider fine-tuning and refining the segmentation as you go. The feedback loop connecting outcomes back to the segmentation allows you to gauge whether or not your partitioning of the marketplace needs refinement to improve results. Monitor performance and explore whether segment preferences are becoming more or less homogenous.

Good segments should remain homogenous on any desired underlying characteristics that are useful. At the same time, different segments should demonstrate meaningful differences from each other. If segments become less distinct on observable behavioral and demographic factors, consider combining them. If the variation within the group increases over time, it is time to consider dividing segments and creating new, smaller homogenous groupings.

With time, the internal and external data your firm are capturing about your customers will expand. It is important to incorporate new information into your segmentation to improve upon the distinctiveness of your individual consumer groupings and the precision of the algorithms used to recreate the groupings in outside databases. The framework should continuously evolve to appropriately support the execution of strategies and tactics to improve your standing with consumers, suppliers, and distribution partners.

By adhering to the steps laid out previously, any company with sufficient will can reap the rewards of the Enhanced Demand Landscape. In our experience, implementing these projects has been less a matter of resources and more a matter of unifying management behind a single vision and working toward that vision in a consistent manner. For those companies that can implement a comprehensive system like the Enhanced Demand Landscape, the outcomes will be well worth the effort.

## Case Study in Financial Services

The Financial Crisis of 2007–2009 caused huge tremors across many industries and institutions. The demand for insurance products was also impacted. Not only had consumer spending and saving patterns been altered, almost overnight, but the appetite for risk and the demand for protection also changed dramatically. That was not manifested across the board but with distinct areas of demand demonstrating changes in how consumers were adopting brands and channels in the marketplace. A major provider of property and casualty insurance in the U.S. approached us to stem customer attrition and help them develop a long-term consumer strategy to accelerate their profitable growth.

We developed an Enhanced Demand Landscape for that client with great success. The process started with fielding a custom survey on a representative sample of their internal customer database. We performed clustering and settled on six segments that were strongly differentiated on observable factors like demographics and insurance usage along with self-reported attitudes and motivations from the primary research. The segments were easy to recognize in the general population through the observable differentiation and revealed consumer preferences shaping current and future demand through their strong attitudinal and motivational distinctions.

To increase the richness of our segmentations, we used all available internal data and evaluated third-party data suppliers. After assessing the predictability of incremental data elements from external suppliers, we made recommendations for procuring data to supplement the client's internally available sources. We then moved on to building predictive algorithms to replicate the segmentation in various operational client domains.

The predictive algorithms that reproduced the segments in outside databases we developed had approximately four times the predictive accuracy relative to the random rate. This represented significant gains in predictability and illustrates the power of applying modern Machine Learning methods. After models were scored in the internal CRM databases, all customers were flagged with their corresponding segments.

Statistics from the scored book of business revealed troubling trends. Fifteen percent of customers had not been retained and were likely lost to competitors. Furthermore, the lost customer mix indicated the client was disproportionately losing members of their preferred target customer group. These results underscored the need for targeted retention initiatives rather than broad based ones.

Predictive algorithms that were already in place and used by the client were quickly incorporated into the Enhanced Demand Landscape in order to stem the loss of target customers. Models predicting the likelihood of attrition were immediately tied to the segments. Tying the segments to these models enabled the creation of customer scorecards, which enhanced the individual profiling of our customers. We incorporated customer lifetime value, models predicting renewal of insurance products, and estimated responses to marketing campaigns to further drive agent product and sales focus.

By combining our segmentation with new and existing models, we were able to take immediate steps to improve customer interaction, service, and retention. Training programs for agents to recognize customer segments and tailor experiences to them were designed, local trade areas for each agent were defined, and customers were aggregated according to those areas to produce the segment distribution of consumers for each individual agent's territory. The concentration of specific segments revealed what type of agent characteristics, such as product and service experience, was needed to best serve customer needs and expectations.

Next, over and under performing groups of agents were identified by segmenting them according to a set of standard industry key performance indicators (KPIs). We analyzed groups of agents by market to identify which ones the client should invest in and which should be deprioritized. Also, we analyzed agents by region to assess overall strengths and weaknesses. We found that 16 percent of agents over-performed, and 24 percent were meeting high expectations. Of the remaining 60 percent that under-performed, we found that 24 percent were serving customers with an unfavorable segment composition while 26 percent were associated with an extremely favorable segment mix. The latter group represented a strategic focus for the client to tailor marketing materials and optimize media purchases.

Programs to improve site merchandising were designed for each agent and tailored to the composition of customers she was serving in her trade area. Point of purchase materials and layout of brochure placements were designed and tailored to the local market footprint for each individual agent. The objective was to drive some target households to a local agent and others to a call center depending on which segment they belonged to. The segmentation model sample had already provided deep understanding of what motivates different segments and to which channels of communication they are most likely to respond. Now it was time to activate those action levers.

In order to support local agents and call center representatives, we devised consumer-centric programs with detailed scripts to provide the most relevant offers for coverage and attractive pricing. After addressing customer issues, agents were trained to use a script to identify the most likely needs among customers. Knowing the segment to which a customer belongs enabled the service rep to select the appropriate script and sales method that most resonated with the person sitting on the other end of the line. Then, they would provide targeted options to complete a sale.

Next, we established a system to track the progress and success of various retention initiatives underway. This allowed our client to refine processes and procedures to maximize the future impact of initiatives. The feedback loop between the segments and the initiatives tied to them allowed us to refine the segmentation. Campaign offer responses suggested it might be appropriate to combine two segments, reducing their number from six to five. Monitoring segment assignments over time in the database revealed a significant inflow and outflow between those two segments from one time period to the next. This switching between segments confirmed that it was best to roll these two segments up into a new segment to add stability and increase the effectiveness of outbound marketing initiatives.

The results associated with the introduction of the Enhanced Demand Landscape were most impressive. Over the course of the six months after adoption, customer attrition was reduced by 8 percentage points, representing a 58% improvement in retention. New customer acquisitions represented a disproportionally higher fraction of the desired target segments. Improved conversion of inbound customer calls resulted in increased sales and higher customer satisfaction. Higher loyalty among local agents is also attributed to tailoring the service experience to individual consumer segments. The Enhanced Demand Landscape had broken internal silos and improved customer-centricity widely within the client organization.

## Questions for Monday Morning

1. What type of internal data do we have and what gaps exist that we need to fill in?

2. Do we have a suitable segmentation framework in place we can use or do we need to build a new one?

3. How many distinct consumer groups do we need to gain a nuanced understanding of the marketplace?

4. What observable metrics do we need to tie to the segmentation to link with downstream and upstream activities?

5. How do we construct a process to refine segments iteratively over time?

# Endnotes

1. "Gary Comer Quotes." http://www.quoteland.com/author/Gary-Comer-Quotes/3821/. Accessed July 2017.
2. "Cost of Hard Drive Space." http://ns1758.ca/winch/winchest.html. Accessed July 2017.
3. Client interview.
4. Ibid.

# CHAPTER 6

# Precisely Locating Demand

---

### The Big Ideas

- While companies face many different kinds of demand in the marketplace, they often only satisfy them partially.
- Firms frequently miss opportunities as they focus too much on current categories and obvious markets while ignoring the emerging and unarticulated needs of consumers.
- The traditional mass-marketing approaches for winning consumer demand have become increasingly inadequate as technological change, shifts in media habits, and increased competition have drastically altered the marketplace.
- Innovative data-driven approaches can be used to gain competitive insulation from potential disruptors. This type of system can be implemented by:
  - Segmenting your customers into distinctive groups based on factors like profitability, attitudes, and risk of attrition.
  - Building predictive algorithms to identify these distinct customer segments.
  - Collecting historical or simulated data to validate the predictions of predictive algorithms.

- Applying your framework to external databases using your predictive algorithms.

- Formulating strategy and executing it to capitalize on algorithms' predictions and capture consumer demand.

---

*"I know half the money I spend on advertising is wasted, but I can never find out which half."*

—John Wanamaker[1]

We have all been victims of bad weather reports. The forecast tells you to expect a sunny day, and a few hours later you find yourself stuck outside in the pouring rain without an umbrella. Despite failing to predict the odd surprise downpour, though, our weather predictions have improved dramatically over the years. A century ago, meteorologists would look at past weather events to determine if future weather would be hot or cold, humid or dry. Everything changed in the early 1920s when Lewis Fry Richardson invented mathematical techniques to forecast the weather.[2] Instead of relying solely on past events like previous forecasters, Richardson mathematically modeled environmental conditions like surface temperature using measurements that were gathered from all over Europe and communicated to him via telegraph. While models have improved significantly over the last century, modern weather models still rely on the blueprint created by Richardson.[3]

While the basic principles of weather modeling have not changed since the 1920s, we can now capture reams of data that were not available in Richardson's day. Weather balloons, commercial aircraft, weather stations, and satellites constantly monitor our planet, producing data on everything from wind speeds to cloud patterns to barometric pressure. These data sources provide information for estimating weather patterns and creating more accurate forecasts. In addition, advances in mathematics and the availability of advanced computers with unimaginable storage processing capabilities have allowed for the processing of these data in order to create more accurate and far-reaching forecasts. Thanks to these improvements, today, forecasts for a week in advance are more accurate than three-day forecasts were 15 years ago. Furthermore, meteorologists now have the ability to forecast overarching weather trends several months in advance.

The development of weather forecasting illustrates dynamics we have observed in many business applications, one of which is the desire of manufacturers, service providers, and retailers to increase the precision with which they are targeting consumers. As in the weather example, companies today should not simply observe past sales and transactions. Instead, there is rich information available today that can be incorporated into forecasting algorithms to more accurately pinpoint information about who is consuming, what they are buying, and what messages resonate with their underlying attitudes and motivations. Furthermore, it is now possible to track what channels of delivery consumers prefer, what pricing and promotional materials resonate with them, and what factors are driving sales. Tracking this information often leads to strategies that increase ROI of new product development and marketing campaigns. Just like with weather forecasting, a business stands to benefit tremendously from accurately predicting the demand it will encounter in the marketplace.

## Locating Demand Using Traditional Statistical and Econometric Techniques

In Chapter 4, we discussed in detail the distinction between current, emerging, and latent demand. Finding customers hinges on understanding how each of these types of demand manifests itself in your industry, and requires creating distinctive strategies satisfying each demand type. Failing to address any of the different types of demand can lead to significant misallocation of precious resources, and ultimately a reduction in competitiveness.

Current demand is often located based on experience. While this experience-based approach is easy to implement, data-driven, analytical approaches are far more effective at informing decision-making. Strategies for satisfying current demand are most effective when informed and implemented through the disciplined application of traditional econometric and statistical techniques utilizing historical data. These historical data can be used to develop algorithms that predict relevant market dynamics, including what customers want, the price they are willing to pay, or when they are most likely to purchase a product. A variety of widely accepted statistical techniques enable this kind of learning about consumer behavior. With these techniques, we can understand a population by extrapolating learnings from a smaller, representative sample. These techniques are valuable because they offer quick, in-depth, and inexpensive ways to learn about the demand driving a market.

It is critical to go into quantitative analyses with concrete questions and a clear list of hypotheses. For example, you might want to establish the factors driving customer attrition and find actions you could take to counter it. Maybe you are interested in finding new ways to increase your customer base or increase the frequency of visits to your stores. After you have stated these questions clearly, you can then hypothesize possible answers to them, which will help you identify the data you will need for your analysis. For example, when looking for the cause of reduced traffic at your stores, you might have a hunch that people are not shopping as much due to issues around product assortment and promotional pricing. These hypotheses and their potential answers will help you generate a list of data that you want to analyze as you perform your statistical investigation.

Data used for analyses and the development of predictive algorithms should be tailored to the questions that need to be answered. After all, without the right data, it is impossible to conduct good statistical analysis. Often, the best source of data is an internal CRM database, which, as alluded to in the previous chapter, can be augmented with outside data sets, if necessary. Ultimately, your final data set should combine any CRM data, primary research, and second- and third-party data to help you test your hypotheses. With the right data, new information can be created by combining variables in new ways to get at new phenomena.

Once you have your hypotheses and collected all relevant data into a single data set, it is time to build a model. Generally, there are two types of statistical models: Explanatory models and predictive models. In an explanatory model, the goal is to understand what drives an outcome. For example, if you are modeling store traffic, you might be interested in establishing if price discounts are more effective in expanding your clientele than in-store displays or advertising. In a predictive model, the goal is to obtain estimates on in-store traffic under hypothetical conditions. For example, you might want to predict how many new customers will arrive at the store when prices are discounted by 5%.

To create any model to predict demand, you will need two sets of variables: explanatory variables and response variables. The response variable captures the outcome of the question you are posing. If you are trying to reduce attrition, this variable might be one indicating whether a consumer has left your service for a competitor. Alternatively, if your goal is to increase the frequency of store visits, the response variable would be how often a person shops at your store. Explanatory variables, meanwhile, are the hypothesized factors driving the outcome we are investigating. Those could be hours of operation, cleanliness of the stores, or the breadth of your assortment, for example.

Once a model is created, it will yield a framework that explains the factors that drive demand, which will allow you to test the hypotheses you developed earlier. The model will identify which of the hypothesized drivers are likely to be true in the broader population outside of your modeling sample, as well as establishing the relative importance of various factors. For attrition, for example, a model will differentiate between factors that impact the likelihood a customer will leave for a competitor and those that do not. In addition, for factors that have an effect, the model will indicate those that have higher and lower impact relative to one another.

Once you have developed a good model on your sample, you can apply their findings to the entire population. If you have built an explanatory model, you can use the model results to formulate strategic decisions to manage your business. If you had built a predictive model, the insights it generates can be used for drafting tactical decisions for executing strategy. In either case, models offer statistically valid insights that improve your chances of success and decrease your reliance on intuition and experience.

Companies across many categories are already harnessing these powerful tools to help them with their decision-making. Financial institutions, for example, leverage predictive models to assess risks such as default and attrition. They also use models to improve their chances of deepening client relationships through cross-selling and upselling. Retailers model trade promotion and assortment to guide pricing and merchandising activities. Utility companies leverage models to predict energy demand and plan for production and storage. With the right data and the right models, all companies can develop a rigorous, statistically-based understanding of the factors driving demand in their categories and develop tools to estimate future outcomes.

Still, predictive models have their limitations. Since they are constructed using historical data, they are poor predictors of emerging and latent demand. As such, it is necessary to rely on different qualitative and quantitative methods to understand the emerging, unrealized, and unarticulated needs of consumers. Consumer focus groups and other qualitative concept testing are instrumental for generating insights on breakthrough innovations that can lead to new products or even new categories. When there are no historical data to use for testing, these techniques generate data and enable the formulation and testing of hypotheses for strategy formulation. There are some quantitative methods available for testing as well. Consumer choice models and simulations are also key in identifying and quantifying emerging and latent demand. They allow for the identification and quantification of consumer demand that is not being satisfied in the marketplace. These demands, in turn, can be used to estimate market sizes and shares after the inclusion of new products.

When qualitative insights are generated, it is important to validate them with statistical tests in order to ensure that your findings hold true in the general population. The best way to test these insights is to run a randomized control trial (RCT). This technique, most commonly used in medicine for testing the efficacy of new drugs, seeks to establish whether an intervention causes a measurable change. For example, an RCT might help you establish how well customers will react to a new store layout that reorganizes and repositions products. In this case, the RCT would be implemented by first dividing a group of test subjects into two groups: A treatment group, which would be exposed to the new format, and a control group, which would be left unexposed. We would record sales (or other metrics of interest, such as items in a shopping basket, aisle browsing times, or satisfaction) for each one of the two groups. We would then apply statistical tests to establish if the outcomes in the two populations are statistically different. With this information, we can establish if the new format would yield the necessary increases in sales to justify the expenses that would be incurred in a system-wide rollout of the test plan.

As you can see from the aforementioned examples, traditional statistical and econometric techniques are indispensable in any strategic and tactical planning to satisfy consumer demand. However, analyses on samples of historical data, along with qualitative studies, will never completely eliminate sound business judgment. Instead, they supplement experience and intuition so that you can formulate and execute strategies that lead to present and future growth.

# Disruptions to Traditional Approaches

The emergence of new technology has led to an array of disruptions facing established companies today. Many of these disruptions come from computer science: This field has evolved tremendously in the last two decades, giving rise to Machine Learning techniques that build high-precision predictive algorithms. In addition, Big Data has grown to allow for a whole new set of behaviors to be modeled and predicted. Outside of computer science, increased intensity of competition thanks to globalization, social media, and the diminishing power of mass marketing have all created new vulnerabilities for big and established brands.

In the opening of this chapter, we discussed the ways that technological innovations have changed modern weather forecasting. Over the last century, weather forecasting moved from relying solely from intuition based on past trends to utilizing statistical models requiring vast amounts of computer power and up-to-the minute data. Just as these technologies have impacted weather forecasting, they are now starting to change the way that companies understand their customers and their behaviors. These new insights, in turn, have put pressure on companies to remain competitive by finding new ways to serve the needs of their customers. Gone are the days when brand managers at companies relied solely on their intuition to make strategic decisions. Instead, today's successful managers blend intuition with an abundance of data, as understood through complex statistical models, to accurately predict how and when consumer demand will shift.

Companies armed with these techniques are changing the way that business is done across all sectors of the economy. For example, leading retailers have found new ways of monitoring customers in order to figure out what they want. Instead of simply tracking volumes sold at the registers in their physical stores, as they had done in the past, the emergence of online and mobile sales channels generates vast amounts of transactional data that allow firms to better understand and predict their customers' behaviors and unmet needs. For example, a customer's online "wish list" can be combined with information on past purchases online and a history of product exchanges at physical stores to give retailers information on a customer's interaction with the category. By finding the different ways that customers interact with the category, companies can redesign their sales process to better respond to latent and emerging demand.

For a retailer, changing a sales process can seem risky, but these risks can be minimized by using statistical methods and experimentation to test ideas and concepts at a small scale. It's no longer necessary to undertake expensive redesigns that involve hundreds of locations without an understanding of the different impacts that these changes would have in each place. Today, companies can easily test multiple store layouts and formats, as well as sales techniques, at a small scale by setting up a few test stores that "pilot" these new processes. Metrics from these stores can be collected and statistically analyzed against a group of similar stores that did not change their sales process to determine whether the new process resulted in the desired outcome. If the process is found to offer sufficient benefit, it can be rolled out to a wider set of stores. This process, based on the RCT discussed earlier, is called "A/B testing." It allows companies to quickly roll out a series of new concepts with relatively low risk in ways that were impossible in the past.

In addition to A/B testing, Big Data has introduced new dimensions for tracking consumer behavior. Today, thanks to technological advancements, advanced analytical capabilities, and innovations in database management, data from multiple sources can be combined to create a rich picture of the consumer. In physical outlets customer movements can be tracked through Wi-Fi routers, location counters, and video technologies. "Smart shelves" loaded with sensors can provide valuable information on how people interact with products in stores. This type of information can generate heat maps of traffic patterns within stores, which can help retailers optimize assortment, product placement, and merchandizing. Online storefronts enable further customization and additional experimentation that surpasses what is possible at physical locations. In addition to observing consumers, companies can use third-party consumer panels that help companies understand what consumers are purchasing beyond the reach of their own outlets. Panels like Nielsen's Homescan can provide information on shopping details, including but not limited to basket information and competitor sales, in different channels and geographies. Combining data from these sources can allow companies to gain a deep and complete understanding of the market.

In addition to new technology, new entrants have also increased the intensity of competition. Online retail, in particular, has been effective in harnessing large amounts of data to disrupt established industries. As these companies gain more customers, they collect ever increasing amounts of information that can be used to target customers. Companies like Netflix and Amazon, with millions of customers, analyze customer purchases or preferences to predict future behaviors with technologies called "recommendation engines." These processes allow these companies to draw upon the behavioral patterns of their customers as a whole and compare them with each customer's behavioral history to generate recommendations. These suggestions allow a company to leverage its long tail of products and the diversity of its customer base to offer a potentially superior experience compared with traditional retailers.

Social media has also disrupted traditional marketing functions by offering new forms of interaction between companies and consumers, which can lead to significant opportunities if properly harnessed. Since many customers are passionate about leaving feedback for manufacturers and retailers, social media provides companies with immediate, rich information about customer interactions and pain points. Specifically, mining these user reviews and comments reveals sentiments and preferences that are not expressed or detected in traditional consumer interactions. However, social media requires very detailed management, for these passionate customers do not want their voices to go unheard, and poor management of social media can alienate these customers and damage your brand reputation. Thus, while social media provides a new and innovative way to engage with customers, it must be managed very carefully.

Technology, coupled with consumers' desire for self-expression, has not only led to the rise of social media, but has pushed the boundaries of product customization to new levels. Big brands with mass consumer appeal have been especially vulnerable to this trend. Celebrating one's individuality and uniqueness has given rise to a new desire for customization. Product cycles are shortening across many industries and categories as companies struggle to keep up with rapidly changing consumer preferences. The power of design and customization are shifting to consumers. In the past, the fashion industry, with its seasonal offerings, had the shortest product cycles. Now industries from electronics to beverages need to redesign their products frequently. Today, customers have the ability to not only customize their wedding dress but also their running sneakers and even their fountain drink or morning coffee to match their taste preferences.

All of these factors have combined to make the mass-marketing approach used by many established brands obsolete over the last decade.

Detecting the specific needs consumers have has become easier, and companies are better equipped to design products to deliver on desired benefits. Players who embrace new tools and technologies will reap huge rewards as they increase the precision of their processes and more effectively deliver on consumer demand. They stand to expand their market share, build loyalty, eliminate waste, and remain nimble to adapt to ever-changing market conditions and evolving consumer demand.

## Closing Knowledge Gaps and Vulnerabilities

There was a time when a company could have a single product with a single message and sell it to a whole country. In the early 1900s, for example, Henry Ford famously said that his customers could have the Model T painted in any color they wanted, as long as it was black. At the time, Ford enjoyed tremendous competitive insulation because he was the only one making affordable cars. He did not need to think about specific marketing for different groups of people because he had no competition and did not have the technology available to enable customization. Over a hundred years have passed since Ford first introduced his car, and for much of that time, variants of his one-size-fits-all model remained the dominant way of doing business.

Today, thanks to a convergence of technological, cultural, and economic changes discussed earlier, this approach is quickly losing its effectiveness. Instead, the market is fragmented into countless cohorts of consumers, each seeking different benefits from their purchases. In the supply-driven environment that dominated in the past, consumers were expected to conform to a single product even though they wanted different things. Today, in a demand-driven world, consumers expect that products will conform to their personal tastes, and fierce competition makes this kind of individual targeting necessary to stay relevant. In essence, Henry Ford's attitude would guarantee customer dissatisfaction and disloyalty for any large brand in today's dynamic world.

A consumer segmentation framework like the Enhanced Demand Landscape we reviewed in the previous chapter can help companies design a differentiated strategy built on individual consumer preferences. This kind of framework will not only divide consumers into segments based on their desires and attitudes, but will also help companies better understand the opportunities associated with each group. With this information, it is possible to quantify the level of investment that is justified to deliver the benefits consumers in these different groups are seeking. When the opportunities to win with individual segments are sized, it becomes possible to establish an appropriate level of investment to support strategies targeting them. For example, a cost-benefit analysis can help determine whether a company should pursue incremental product extensions or an entirely new brand to entice members of an attractive segment. This kind of detailed understanding of segments and the opportunities associated with them can help guide innovation geared toward specific consumers.

Our job, though, is not complete after the launch of a new product that is targeted at a "white space" opportunity: As a marketing campaign evolves to attract a specific segment of the population, it is vital to keep learning. Data and statistical analyses can be used to continually test hypotheses to see how a marketing campaign is doing and how the market is changing through analyses of small, representative samples of consumers. In other words, precisely identifying demand is not an exact science. Instead, it is an iterative process that involves continual testing, refinement, and optimization. This notion highlights the need for data-driven approaches to be ingrained in the culture of an organization, for the work does not stop with the rollout. A new product should be monitored constantly, using both quantitative and qualitative analytics, to ensure that it is aligned with the needs of your target and to know when and where it would be appropriate to expand distribution beyond the test areas.

## Major Benefits of the Data-Driven Approach

The data-driven approach to serving consumer demand requires significant effort in planning and execution. For businesses operating with traditional supply-driven mindsets, shifting to this approach may require a substantial organizational transformation. Across the company, many managers will need to learn to collect and analyze vast troves of data in systematic ways and use this information in formulating new strategies. To execute these strategies, others will need to learn to leverage new technologies and adopt consumer-driven frameworks. Despite the effort involved, we have found that businesses that have appropriately implemented data-driven consumer approaches have reaped many benefits.

One key benefit of implementing this approach is the generation of proprietary insights on consumer behavior. In a world where competition is increasingly fierce, this enhanced understanding allows companies to stay ahead of their competitors. As explained earlier in this chapter, many of these insights are generated by applying statistical models on historical or simulated data, which help to explain the factors that influence observed consumer behavior. For example, a property and casualty insurer with which we worked was concerned with customer attrition and interested in establishing the drivers of consumer loyalty. Through statistical analysis of data, we were able to identify and prioritize the factors that led customers to renew policies. These findings enabled the client to prioritize their actions so to focus on interventions that were likely to lead to customers renewing their policies.

Beyond simply explaining consumer behavior, these statistical techniques can also be used for predicting future behavior or even delivering early-warning signs of shifts in consumption. As we discussed in Chapter 4, understanding these signs is critical for capturing "latent and emerging demand." These models can simulate the market under different scenarios, and reveal where demand is headed. Where traditionally companies had to react to market changes after they happened, by predicting demand before it occurs, companies can be proactive in their ability to adapt to future conditions, and, as a result, achieve a significant competitive edge.

Demand systems can also help companies eliminate silos within an organization. When data start flowing between a variety of different departments, the affected departments naturally begin to coordinate with each other. That coordination can serve as a basis for lean and efficient business operations that rapidly adapt to evolving consumer tastes and market conditions. We have seen many examples of a new product rollout that targets a "white space" opportunity breaking down organizational silos in marketing and sales. In one particular case, before our work, sales data were used to measure outcomes at the end of ad campaigns. As the rollout progressed, the sales and marketing departments started sharing data; the departments began working together to determine how many ads to produce and how to target them. This improved communication led to increased efficiency and an increase in innovation within the company. This project also drove shorter cycles of innovation and improved marketing effectiveness.

Data-driven demand systems also eliminate waste from existing processes. Having multiple departments work together often leads to an increase in efficiency as redundant processes are identified and eliminated. Before our project with the property and casualty insurer discussed earlier, its customer retention efforts were divided across four divisions that did not communicate with each other. To help with their retention efforts, we devised customer scorecards that summarized characteristics of individual account holders. One of the metrics reported on the scorecards was the likelihood of a customer renewing a policy derived from predicted risk of attrition that we modeled separately. These scorecards served as a link between the four divisions. They were introduced at call centers and made available to customer service representatives (CSRs). A process for handling inbound calls was put in place where, after a customer called in, he or she would be directed either to the general CSR pool or to CSR groups dedicated to serving members of high-priority segments. Depending on the predicted risk of attrition and the issue reported, an incentive offer was presented. We estimated that retention due to this quantitative risk segmentation–tailored approach improved retention by 80 basis points for the targeted segment groups the insurer was after. In this way, our scorecards linked together customer service with agents, marketing, and risk assessment departments.

In addition to increasing efficiency, consumer-centric transformations based on data have proven effective at increasing customer satisfaction and loyalty. In the preceding insurance example, the Net Promoter Scores for its products improved within nine months of the launch of the Enhanced Demand Landscape. Much of this improvement came as a result of streamlining the inbound customer communication as we pointed out previously. Outbound communication was also improved so that targeted mailings went only to members of specific consumer segments. Predicting the likelihood of the acceptance of new product offers and tying those to customer segments allowed the company to identify to whom it should be mailing offers. This innovation reduced direct marketing expenditures while improving metrics measuring loyalty and customer satisfaction. Furthermore, the reliance on agents handling customer relationships was substantially decreased. Now, agents could focus on new leads, conversion, and on-boarding while online tools and CSRs dealt with claims and customer issues.

Finally, these data-driven approaches deliver higher ROI on new initiatives. For example, we analyzed the drivers of per capita consumption of chocolate across the U.S. for a confectionary manufacturer. Through our research, we found substantial variation in consumption in different parts of the country, and, outside of weather differences, the client did not have hypotheses on what caused this variation. To find the drivers of this pattern, we collected time-series data and combined it with other sources to compile a comprehensive data set. We then analyzed these data by building a statistical model that revealed the source of the pattern. We established that the presence of the sales force in retail channels and states, not weather, was one of the strongest predictors of higher sales. Thanks to this insight, we were able to pinpoint the retailers and states that would benefit the most from increasing its sales force. Since we selectively increased the sales force rather than increasing it for the whole country, the ROI of our approach was extremely high.

By increasing reliance on data and statistical analyses, a consumer-centric framework introduces a rigorous analytic approach to all decision-making done in a company. Aside from the concrete benefits we discussed, there are numerous intangible gains that flow from the approach. For example, increased transparency, higher customer and employee satisfaction, and improved brand equity all result from the approaches recommended here. Applying an empirical mindset and correctly employing predictive analytics results in efficient resource allocations that outperform experience-based approaches and sustain your competitive advantage.

## How to Reap the Benefits of Higher-Precision Systems

How can you introduce a precision-demand system at your company? In this section, we will outline the steps required to build the frameworks, mindsets, and culture necessary to build such a system.

The first key is locating consumer demand, which requires a deep understanding of the entire marketplace. Starting your investigation at a broad, aggregate market level is key to grasping the factors that shape demand in your industry and discovering how consumers interact with your category. The analytical framework of "forces and factors," covered in Chapter 4, is vital for establishing this broad understanding of the market.

Armed with a good grasp of the dynamics affecting your category overall, it is time to use that understanding to investigate at a more granular level. Where previously the market was being viewed at a high level, it is now time to look at distinct segments of customers and even at individuals. The first step toward this detailed understanding of your category is to partition consumers into a small number of cohorts or consumer segments. We previously discussed creating consumer segments in detail in Chapters 2 and 5.

To augment the effectiveness of this segmentation approach, pay attention to how you partition the market. In our experience, segmentation frameworks anchored by consumer attitudes, needs, and motivations are highly predictive of their purchase patterns and spending. Demographics and behaviors do not predict consumer behavior as well but have the benefit of being more easily observed. Integrating these kinds of observable data into segments based on attitudes and motivations ensure that you'll be able to identify a consumer's segment membership in the broader population.

Once your segments are in place, you can apply analytical techniques to evaluate hypotheses on how to win with individual segments. There are several ways that you can integrate your segmentation framework into your qualitative research. Primary research, where representative samples of consumers are interviewed one on one, provide an in-depth look at the attitudes and motivations of consumers. Focus groups can provide a more free-form environment that can help with hypothesis generation. Other techniques, including psychological drawings, consumer diaries, and psychographic interviews, can further enrich your understanding. The insights generated through these qualitative interactions with consumers will generate many of the hypotheses that need to be tested and refined quantitatively.

Once you have generated hypotheses on locating and capturing demand, it is time to evaluate them. The first step in evaluating your hypotheses is to apply your segmentation framework onto professional consumer panel assets, the compilations of participants who are incentivized to report information over time and are representative of the market as a whole. Panels track consumer behavior over time, unlike most primary research methods. As a result, you can observe consumers as they try, consume, and repeatedly purchase products. This information can be analyzed in conjunction with your segmentation framework to gain a nuanced understanding of the way that different types of consumers interact with your product and category. This deeper understanding of your consumers is crucial for precisely identifying demand and realizing sales.

If your company has an internal CRM database, it can be used in identifying the segment membership of your customers and can provide you with another tool for improving your offerings. Combining your segmentation framework with a CRM database allows you to customize product offerings and can lead to improved customer satisfaction, loyalty, and retention. Depending on your product, you can apply a variety of predictive algorithms to help with targeted marketing efforts. For example, some algorithms can flag customers with a high risk of attrition, which enables companies to take preventative action. Others can estimate consumer satisfaction based on shopping and transaction patterns. Algorithms that predict lifetime customer value can also be used to help companies understand the value of investing in a customer relationship.

For a major grocery retailer, we divided the company's member database into shopper cohorts and then determined how common each of them was at individual retail outlets. Knowing the incidence of members of different segments at each store helped our client determine the optimal assortment, merchandising, and pricing for every retail outlet. In one case, we realized that many locations were dominated by a segment that loved experimenting with different varieties of beer. Their presence informed our strategies for improving the customer experience at these stores. Since these customers loved variety, we decided that certain stores should allow them to mix and match different brands of beer into six-packs rather than force them to buy 24 and 36 packs of the same beer. In addition, our primary research indicated that this segment consumed 80% of their beer within three hours of leaving the store, which meant that a large fraction of consumers would forego purchasing beer that hadn't been refrigerated. To encourage these customers to buy more beer at our client's stores, we introduced a section of refrigerated beer by reallocating some space from dairy products. Shortly after introducing these changes, beer sales increased by 18% on average at the locations where these new approaches were implemented. In addition, foot traffic in these same stores increased by 8%.

In addition to applying your segmentation framework to your CRM database, applying it to media panels helps with targeted messaging.

Knowing how segment membership varies among consumers of different media will allow you to optimize advertising and creative materials while also tailoring messages to individual consumer segments. This precise targeting, in turn, allows you to eliminate waste and realize savings in marketing budgets. For example, by airing segment-specific advertisements during certain times and television programs that resonate with targeted consumer groups, firms can increase their reach without increasing budgets. Alternatively, once media buying is appropriately optimized, it is possible to maintain the same reach with lower budgets. By increasing precision, your organization can realize substantial cost savings by reducing the number of advertisements that fail to reach their intended audience.

Significant cost savings can also be realized by projecting your segmentation onto all possible prospects and targeting your outbound offers only to consumers who are most likely to positively respond. To help our CPG and financial services clients find more customers, we have applied segmentations and predictive algorithms to all of the roughly 130 million households in the U.S. The segmentation has been used to generate algorithms producing the likelihood of response to offers for each prospect. Relying on this information, firms can design different advertisements and marketing strategies that appeal to members of select consumer groups they are targeting. To increase the efficiency of mailings, the cost of the outbound materials can be balanced against the incremental revenue expected to be generated. By knowing the probability of a person responding to a mailing, it is possible to send offers only to people who are sufficiently likely to respond. This selection process assures that the mailings sent out will be profitable, as measured by a sufficiently high response rate. This strategy ensures a higher response rate at a lower cost than the blanket mass-marketing approach that many firms use today for their outbound offers.

Precision-demand systems hold the potential to transform traditional go-to-market approaches and introduce numerous efficiencies within your organization. By understanding the variation of tastes, motivations, and benefits sought by different groups of consumers alongside broader trends, it is possible to streamline the allocation of resources through a rigorous process built on Big Data, segmentation frameworks, and predictive algorithms.

# Implementing a Precision-Demand System at Your Organization

In closing, we offer 10 tactical steps needed to build a precision-demand system at your company.

### Foster a culture of experimentation

It is imperative to foster a culture of experimentation within your organization that supports analytically driven decision-making. A successful go-to-market strategy that precisely identifies and captures consumer demand takes time to build and requires many iterations to perfect.

### Secure appropriate staffing and resources

Continuous learning about current customers and prospects in precision-demand systems requires strong senior sponsorship. Appropriate staffing and dedication of resources are prerequisites for building out necessary strategic and operational transformations at your company.

### Create a "sandbox" environment

A data-driven and consumer-focused system for capturing demand requires a sandbox environment, which is accessible to all departments within the organization and serves as a breeding ground for hypotheses. It is where predictive algorithms are constructed, testing takes place, and tactics are implemented prior to broad market rollouts with the results used to fine-tune the process at every iteration.

### Leverage all internal customer data

The core of this sandbox is the customer data available within a company. Make sure to leverage data from all departments in your company. These data serves as the sand from which hypotheses will be built and tested.

### Fill internal data gaps with third-party sources

Third-party data sources should be used to fill gaps left by your internal data. Thankfully, today, third-party data are rarely exclusive to a specific supplier. Instead, it is resold through multiple companies, making it much easier to procure.

### Construct a segmentation framework

Recognize that you cannot serve consumers in the marketplace without a differentiated strategy. Consider various groupings of your consumers anchored on distinct attitudes, motivations, and benefits they seek from the consumption of your products.

### Build predictive algorithms

In addition to enabling the generation and testing of hypotheses, the sandbox is also the place to construct statistically valid predictive algorithms. Those algorithms allow you to extrapolate learnings from small samples to larger populations and the general market.

### Generalize patterns and project outcomes

Algorithms enable users to generalize patterns and uncover relationships that are hidden deep within the data. These hidden insights can significantly improve your company's competitive position and share in the market.

### Apply algorithms to broader consumer populations

Algorithms allow you to project market outcomes on CRM databases, point of sale or panel assets, and even the entire U.S. population. Use estimated outcomes to produce simulations for scenario planning and tactical execution of your strategy.

### Construct a "feedback loop" between modeled and observed outcomes

Once algorithms are constructed and applied in the field, introduce a feedback loop where performance results are triangulated back to the algorithm outcomes. Feedback loops ensure continual refinement that leads to maximum efficacy. Keep algorithms current and robust by constantly linking predictions with observed outcomes and using those observations to tweak future versions of the algorithms.

## Questions for Monday Morning

1. How do you foster a culture of experimentation supporting analytically driven decision-making?
2. How do you build a sandbox environment incorporating all available data to serve hypothesis generation?

3. How do you construct statistically valid predictive algorithms and extrapolate learnings from small samples to the general market?

4. How do you design randomized control experiments and validate prediction results?

5. How do you continually refine algorithms and link modeled outcomes to observable metrics?

## Endnotes

1. Bradt, George. "Wanamaker Was Wrong – The Vast Majority of Advertising Is Wasted." *Forbes*. 14 September 2016. https://www.forbes.com/sites/georgebradt/2016/09/14/wanamaker-was-wrong-the-vast-majority-of-advertising-is-wasted/#b2386b8483b5. Accessed October 2017.

2. Lynch, Peter. "The Origins of Computer Weather Prediction and Climate Modeling." *Journal of Computational Physics*. 19 March 2007. http://www.rsmas.miami.edu/personal/miskandarani/Courses/MPO662/Lynch,Peter/OriginsCompWF.JCP227.pdf. Accessed via ScienceDirect in October 2017.

3. Ibid.

# Brand Economics: Unlock the Power of Your Brand

---

### The Big Ideas

- A brand is often the most valuable and enduring asset a company owns.
- Like any asset, the value of a brand can be managed and maximized or mismanaged and diminished.
- Understanding your target customer's demands and how the equities of your brand and your Brand Value Proposition (BVP) deliver on those demands is the key to increasing brand value.
- In many cases, brands can be improved and extended to new offers/categories to increase their value.

---

*"A brand is simply trust."*

—Steve Jobs, Apple[1]

*"Your brand is what people say about you when you are not in the room."*
                                                              —Jeff Bezos, Amazon[2]


*"A brand is the set of expectations, memories, stories, and relationships that, taken together, account for a consumer's decision to choose one product or service over another."*
                                     —Seth Godin, entrepreneur and best-selling author[3]


As you can see from the quotes, there are many different ways of describing and defining brands. While no two definitions are exactly the same, virtually all business leaders agree that brands have very real economic value. In fact, experts generally consider brands to be the most valuable and enduring assets that most companies own. As *The Economist* pointed out in 2014, "Brands are the most valuable assets many companies possess. But no one agrees on how much they are worth or why."[4] Like any asset, brands can be managed in ways that maximize value or mismanaged in ways that destroy value. Despite how ethereal brands can often feel, what's clear is that the real power of brands is their economic power. This is why we've developed an approach that we call "Brand Economics" to understand the drivers of brand value and how best to maximize brand value. Importantly, our approach focuses on identifying practical ways to make any brand more valuable rather than on calculating a theoretical dollar value for a given brand.


## What Is a Brand?

Take a moment to think of some of your favorite brands. They could be in any category: Toothpaste, apparel, cars, hotels, coffee, mobile phones, or anything you choose. Why are they your favorites? What do they provide that makes them different from and better than other brands in the same category? For most people, their favorite brands deliver a unique bundle of important benefits that no other brand can match. Those brands hold special meaning because they can be counted on to deliver the benefits being sought each and every time without fail. Simply put, the key to driving brand value is to understand the most valuable benefits sought by target customers and then consistently deliver those benefits in ways that target customers find meaningfully different from competitors.

According to *Forbes* magazine, the most valuable brand for 2017 was Apple with an estimated brand value of $170 billion and annual advertising spend of $1.8 billion.[5] Rounding out the top five most valuable brands for 2017 were Google, Microsoft, Facebook, and Coca-Cola, with values ranging from $101.8 billion for Google to $56.4 billion for Coca-Cola.[6] As you can see when you review the list from *Forbes*, the companies that own the top ten brands have invested over $28 billion dollars in company advertising, in part to build their brands. Also notable is how strongly technology brands are represented at the top of the list. Four of the top five brands (Apple, Google, Microsoft, and Facebook) and six of the top ten brands (add Amazon and Samsung to the previous list) are categorized by Forbes as being part of the technology industry.[7]

The critical benefits brands deliver typically reflect one of three types: Rational, emotional, or social benefits. Rational benefits include dimensions such as perceived quality, performance, size, taste, or value for the money. While these aspects may very well be subjective in nature, they are relatively tangible benefits. Emotional benefits, on the other hand, are the intangibles related to how the brand makes the buyer feel. These feelings can be elicited by the product itself, by the experience of using or consuming the product, or by both the product and the experience. For example, your favorite brand might make you feel certain emotions or several emotions, including feeling confident, happy, satisfied, or smart. Finally, most brands have a social dimension as well, which reflects how the buyer wants to be perceived by others or what the buyer hopes others will think of him or her because he or she chose this brand. Some of the benefits people seek from brands are conscious decisions while others are unconscious drivers the consumer may have difficulty articulating or even admitting to at all.

When someone chooses their favorite brand of soft drink, they might say it has a flavor they prefer, or a nostalgic flavor they grew up with. Or maybe they feel this drink is more refreshing than any other brand. Using this brand of soft drink might make this person feel more satisfied or happier than he or she would be by drinking any other brand. Finally, the logo and brand name on the can or bottle might "say something" positive about the user that he or she wants others to associate with him or her as well.

So with all of the possible definitions of brands and the various benefits of brands, how do we define a brand? We believe a brand is a promise that sets expectations about what will be delivered, how it will be delivered, and how it will make consumers feel. Like any promise, the brand promise can be delivered in full, partially fulfilled, or altogether broken. One of the reasons we think of this concept as a "brand promise" is due to the trust and the relationship implied in the term: Promises create an emotional bond between a buyer and a brand that can be trusted to deliver on its promises. One of the most famous examples of this type of promise comes from the B2B world and the well-known saying, "Nobody ever got fired for buying IBM."[8]

Based on our experience, we believe thinking of brands in terms of the promises they make and the expectations they set among customers is the most helpful way to assess brands and determine how to maximize their value. What are your target customers' most important expectations? What benefits will delight your most attractive customers and fulfill the promises made? Conversely, what missteps will break your promise and disappoint those customers so badly that they might never come back? Many businesses/brands invest significantly to win a customer for the first time only to break their promise to that customer and immediately lose them. Having a clear understanding of your customers' expectations and how your brand promise will consistently deliver on those expectations is the starting point for enhancing brand value.

## Driving Brand Value

As we have noted, the real power of brands is their economic power. One reason brands are so important and why both B2C and B2B companies spend huge amounts of money building and protecting their brands is due to a brand's potential impact on customer purchasing decisions. A strong brand can move right to the top of a customer's consideration set or even become the only choice that the customer will consider. In addition, some brands are so strong and so highly differentiated that they command a price premium versus their competitors. As *The Economist* noted, "Everyone knows that a Ralph Lauren Polo shirt costs more than a polo shirt; Coke without the logo is just cola."[9] Investments made to strengthen a brand can pay off in two ways: By moving the brand to the top of the customer's consideration set and by earning a price premium.

One of the first exercises to conduct in order to increase brand value is to create a ledger of what we call your brand's "drivers" and "drags."

These are the equities or associations that your brand has among customers that are either positive drivers of choice, negative drags on choice, or simply neutral aspects of the brand that do not really influence choice. These brand equities will reflect the rational, emotional, or social benefits sought that ultimately influence brand choice positively or negatively.

Having conducted these types of assessments both qualitatively and quantitatively with some of the most valuable brands in the world, there are almost always surprises, many of which are related to negative perceptions of the brand that the internal team had never noticed but are raised by highly valuable customers. In some cases, brand equities that the internal team considered positives are actually seen as negatives by target customers. For example, a brand that enjoys a reputation for being "exclusive" or for "discerning buyers" might actually be seen as off-putting, arrogant, or something that is "not for someone like me" by significant numbers of target customers. As a result, that brand might work to erase the arrogant image and be seen as more accessible by target customers while maintaining its reputation for quality.

The most important part of this drivers and drags assessment is to understand perceptions among your most valuable customers. Other points of view are useful, but ultimately this analysis is about leveraging your brand to win with your target. It is not about what your internal team thinks of your brand. It is not an assessment of what all customers think about your brand because everyone is not equally valuable to your brand. However, one important source for identifying the equities that drag your brand down is to talk to lapsed customers or non-customers. Remember, for this exercise, perceptions are reality. Do not cut customers off and try to correct them. Let them have their say. Learn from what Jeff Bezos might call "the things people say about your brand when you are not in the room."[10]

We've discussed our work helping to create Bud Light Lime along with our client friends at Anheuser Busch. At the time, the internal team at AB was rightfully concerned about the potential impact that introducing the new Bud Light Lime offer might have on the existing Bud Light brand. After all, Bud Light was the best-selling brand of beer in the world and the flagship for AB. Trying to stretch the equities of the Bud Light brand to encompass this very different new beer could damage AB's biggest franchise by alienating Bud Light's core consumers.

As you know, we found that introducing Bud Light Lime would significantly help enhance perceptions of Bud Light. Bud Light Lime's Mexican beach beer vibe, active outdoor feel, slightly sweeter taste, and zest for fun all helped make Bud Light itself feel younger and hipper by association. Bud Light Lime also appealed to consumers who were younger, more diverse, and more often to be female than the typical Bud Light fan. The introduction of Bud Light Lime also brought some interesting new news to the beer category and to Bud Light specifically. All of these factors proved to be positives that helped energize and contemporize the more traditional Bud Light brand.

Finally, we also learned that the Bud Light brand could be extended even further beyond just Bud Light Lime. Bud Light was able to accommodate other successful new offers within the growing Bud Light family including Bud Light Platinum, Bud Light Chelada, Bud Light Lime-a-Rita, and a series of other new "Rita" beverages. While there is often a desire to protect brands and avoid the risk of extending and potentially diluting a powerful brand, brand extension opportunities should be explored and, if validated, pursued. It is typically much more cost effective to extend an existing brand than it is to build an entirely new brand from scratch. And, it's quite possible that extending a brand will pay significant dividends while also creating a broader set of potential extensions in the future as was found for Bud Light.

## The Brand Value Proposition

That bundle of benefits your brand promises to deliver is called the "Brand Value Proposition" (BVP). Essentially, the BVP is the set of promises your brand makes to your customers. Those individual promises are like the planks in a political campaign that represent the values and ideas for which a particular candidate or political party stands for. Aligning your BVP to the most important demands of your target customers provides the roadmap or strategy for enhancing brand value. Of course, making BVP promises is much less important than consistently delivering on these promises.

We think of the BVP as having three key components: The demands target customers want fulfilled, the way the brand intends to fulfill them, and how this is intended to make the customer feel. A strong BVP will generally have between four and seven different planks or promises that it makes to its customers, largely because these promises should reflect the most important demands and decision drivers among target customers rather than an endless laundry list of ideas and basic table stakes for participating in the category. It is also due to the fact that target customers should be able to stand back and see these individual promises as an integrated whole that is motivating to the customer and also "feels right" for the brand. Finally, the promises or planks that make up the BVP should highlight at least one promise that differentiates the brand from its competitors.

To bring the idea alive, Figure 7.1 is an illustrative example of what the BVP for a global information technology provider serving B2B customers we worked with might look like.

From left to right, the three major aspects of the BVP include the "Target Customer Demand," the "Brand Value Proposition," and the "Desired Customer Belief." Basically, the Target Customer Demand, in this case among chief information officers or other IT decision makers, leads to a response or a promise from the IT firm in the form of a BVP plank. That plank then creates an intended reaction in the target customer's mind, which is the Customer Belief System. The IT firm has five promises or planks in its BVP that help guide the brand's actions. At the foundation on the bottom of the chart, the plank promises "A Loyal Partner."

| Target Customer Demand | Brand Value Proposition | Desired Customer Belief |
|---|---|---|
| • Listens to our needs; works with us<br>• Capability to develop optimal solutions<br>• Not pushing products | Developing the Best Solutions | • Greatest breadth and depth of business know-how<br>• Best end to end IT breadth |
| • Share information across any systems<br>• Information any time; any place | Creating Seamless Systems | • Flexible/scaleable/inter-operable<br>• Setting the IT agenda<br>• Leverages current investments |
| • Reliable and secure<br>• Internal and external customers can depend on us | Unsurpassed Reliability and Security | • Most reliable products and people<br>• Lets us focus on the business<br>• Leaders in IT Security |
| • Respond with a sense of urgency<br>• Expertise to fix it right the first time | Superior Customer Service | • Minimizes downtime<br>• Fix it right the first time<br>• Empathy and urgency |
| • Don't want to be a beta site<br>• Innovator who can impact our business in a timely fashion | Innovative Approaches | • A leader with dynamic, success future<br>• Customer focused<br>• Innovative and agile |
| • An advisor for our most important IT issues<br>• Someone we can count on<br>• Easy to do business with | A Loyal Partner | • Trust<br>• Experience<br>• Staying power<br>• Accessible and helpful |

**Figure 7.1  Illustrative Brand Value Proposition for global IT firm.**

This plank notes the demands customers have for an IT advisor who can be counted on to tackle tough issues but is also easy to work with. Among the planks that are truly differentiating for this IT firm are their promises to deliver "Superior Customer Service" and "Unsurpassed Reliability and Security." These promises reflect issues that were top concerns among target customers that this IT firm was also uniquely advantaged to deliver on versus competitors.

## A Brand Turnaround: The Samsung Story

Perhaps we are dating ourselves here, but it does not seem like all that long ago that Sony was the "big kid on the electronics block." Throughout the average consumers' day, Sony had multiple touch points – Sony clock radio, Sony Walkman, Sony entertainment systems, and so on – and Sony delivered quite well on the expectations of electronics consumers across all these touch points. Sony had enjoyed years of growth and appeared positioned to enjoy several more years of uninterrupted growth. That is, until Samsung developed some new aspirations.

In 1993, Samsung chairman Lee Kun-hee famously took a trip around the world to take a pulse check on Samsung Electronics' brand health. Lee Kun-hee was not pleased. He convened a meeting of his top executives and made it clear that things had to change, and quickly. He aligned his team behind a strong value proposition to fundamentally change the trajectory of Samsung. Three of the most critical planks of Samsung's new value proposition revolved around quality, design, and price. Samsung already had a strong position with regard to quality, but the firm saw an opportunity to further solidify its position in this area by repositioning itself as a premium brand. It was on the design front, however, that Samsung really fundamentally changed the game, investing in incremental designers and innovating behind design. Put differently, while Samsung's products had functionally delivered through product quality for some time, the team now also worked tirelessly to ensure that the aesthetics of their products outpaced Sony. The team believed that quality was delivered not only in product functionality, but also in the quality appearance and quality "feel" of the product in the hands of the consumer. Connecting back to our earlier points around brand, Samsung recognized that conveying premium quality to consumers relied not just on functional delivery, but also sensory and emotional characteristics as well. Finally, Samsung chose competitive

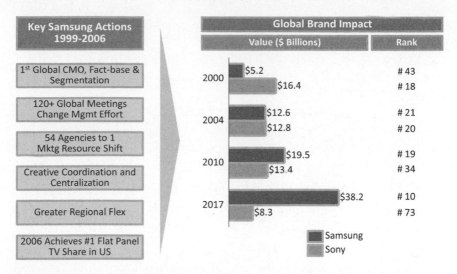

**Figure 7.2** **In 1999, Samsung set an aggressive goal to build a brand rivaling Sony in five years.**

*Source: Businessweek*, Forbes, Brand Finance; TCG analysis

price points versus their top rival, Sony, to support brand and volume growth. It is a value proposition that the team aligned behind in the 1990s, and still tirelessly delivers against today.[11]

And it has paid clear dividends for Samsung (Figure 7.2). According to the *Forbes* Ranking of the World's Most Valuable Brands in 2017, the Samsung brand value reached an impressive $38.2 billion in 2017. To underscore this feat, this performance earned Samsung the number 10 spot in the 2017 list. Sony earned a position of number 73 on the same list, with an estimated brand value of $8.3 billion.[12] Of note is Samsung's simultaneous persistence and patience in attaining and maintaining this goal of surpassing key competitor Sony. And at the heart of all of it, Samsung remains a solid adherence to a meaningful yet differentiated value proposition.

## Characteristics That Set Great Brands Apart

What really separates great brands from others is this ability to consistently deliver on their target customers' most critical rational, emotional, and social expectations. Over the past four decades we've had the privilege of working with some of the most highly recognized and valuable B2B and B2C brands globally across a variety of categories. All of that experience has enabled us to identify several characteristics of great brands regarding what they stand for, what they deliver, and how they deliver. These include:

**A focus on the demands of their most profitable customers**
Great brands are constantly monitoring and developing a deeper understanding of what their most attractive customers are looking for and how best to deliver.

**Establishing the brand as *the* source of something highly meaningful**
These brands have often transcended the category and become a source of something highly motivating to the target customer, such as freedom, possibilities, or fun.

**Leveraging the brand as a platform for innovation**
One role brands can play when it comes to innovation is often referred to as "brand elasticity." The notion is to understand how the equities of a brand can be stretched to introduce new products in the same category or to enter entirely new categories. Beyond the offers themselves, brand-led innovation can also focus on the customer experience, a new business model, or innovative marketing and sales approaches.

**Differentiating the brand from competitors in meaningful ways**
These brands have determined what matters most to target customers and how to uniquely deliver on those benefits.

**Aligning all actions and communications to the brand promise**
Everything these brands say and do reflects a clear commitment to the brand promise to ensure that target customers are never disappointed.

**Earning customer loyalty by being loyal to customers**
By striving to deliver on the brand promise each and every time, these brands earn their customers' loyalty. Those investments in loyalty pay significant dividends in ongoing purchases and in goodwill in the event a customer is ever disappointed, despite all of the steps taken to deliver on the brand promise.

# Brand Economics at Facebook

When we started working with Facebook in 2014, the platform already had over a billion users and was expanding around the Internet-using world. In the preceding year, founder Mark Zuckerberg described the platform's objective of becoming a ubiquitous utility. He also said that he did not care if Facebook was perceived as "cool": "Maybe electricity was cool when it first came out, but pretty quickly people stopped talking about it because it's not the new thing; the real question you want to track at that point is are fewer people turning on their lights because it's less cool?"[13]

He has a point – utilities, by their very nature, need ubiquity more than positive perceptions of their brands. They are essential to modern life and therefore users have to have them. Chris Cox, Facebook's chief product officer, had a similar take: "We talk a lot about Facebook being a medium. And the idea is just that a good medium doesn't interfere with the message. It provides a container that's transparent, easy to use, reliable, fast, and honors the message of the sender."[14]

This philosophy had been built in to Facebook from its early days when the site's browser title bar said, "Facebook—A Social Utility." Even new "products" on Facebook followed a simple formula of generic branding that tried to stay out of the way of users and their content. For example, the messaging function was called "Messages," the news feed was branded "News Feed," events were titled "Events," and interest groups were boldly named "Groups." With this approach, Facebook had won users in most of the developed world and continued to best the expectations of Wall Street analysts.

But Facebook's first-ever chief marketing officer, Gary Briggs, and his team were seeing something concerning: Negative opinions of Facebook, among users and non-users, were growing. These feelings were especially true in countries where Facebook was not widely used or had a strong, local competitor. Even in the U.S. where everyone, it seemed, was on Facebook, consumers viewed Facebook less favorably over time.

Some of this could be blamed on the 2010 movie *The Social Network*. The movie grossed an estimated $225 million USD and won substantial critical acclaim including the Golden Globes for Best Drama, Best Screenplay, and Best Director.[15] It also portrayed Mark Zuckerberg unfavorably, to say the least. Zuckerberg himself has said the film "made up stuff that was hurtful."[16]

Other negative sentiments found in Facebook's own research could be blamed on the product itself. Users often complained when the product changed, having become accustomed to it after so many years. They also started to see users scrolling through News Feed as a "time filler" and that not all users thought their time on Facebook was satisfying or "time well-spent." Some people even reported feeling like they were wasting time on Facebook.

Gary Briggs and many others within Facebook were concerned – declining sentiment and outsized growth in users were two metrics that were at odds. Would people continue to sign up for Facebook and increase their usage if they started feeling worse about using it? Probably not: Either people's feelings about Facebook would improve or growth would have to slow, both in the number of users added every month and in user engagement.

Complicating matters were differing views from management. On one hand, Facebook did not need to be "cool" or even liked for explosive growth, as proven by strong recent performance in the face of declining user sentiment. What appeared to matter was what people did on Facebook, not how they felt about it. On the other hand, it just did not feel right knowing these negative feelings about the brand were festering among both current and potential users of the platform. How would this apparent conflict be resolved?

It turned out that both sides could be "right" and that this conflict could be resolved to the satisfaction of everyone, especially the users. The solution was theorized by Lufi Paris, a researcher working with the marketing team at Facebook: A model for improving people's feelings about Facebook needed to be directly and observably connected to their behaviors.[17] This was the birth of Brand Economics—the idea that a brand marketing effort should be linked to and aimed at winning with consumers (Figure 7.3). For Facebook, this created the possibility for a

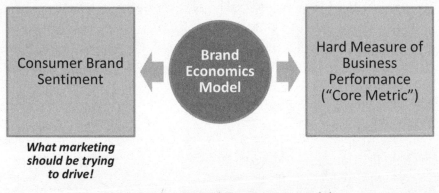

Figure 7.3    Brand Economics model.

significant win-win: If people's sentiments about Facebook improved and, in part because of these sentiments, their use of Facebook also increased, everyone would win.

Organizationally, this idea was incredibly important to the marketing team and to Mark Zuckerberg. For marketing, there would have to be some justification for making a long-term investment in improving the public's sentiments about Facebook. And, perhaps more critically, they would have to possess a clear rationale for *which* sentiments should be enhanced. In marketing speak, if one is going to invest to build brand equity, it helps enormously to know *why* this will matter to the business and *which* equities exactly are most important to the business. For Zuckerberg and the leadership team, this model would provide confidence in their substantial marketing investment and in the team driving it. If the model worked, the equities on which marketing was focused should predictably drive growth!

The process of creating this link between consumer sentiment and hard measures of the business had four key pieces:

1. Identifying the brand sentiments that have the greatest impact on hard measures of the business.
2. Establishing the true brand value equation that consumers use to make purchase decisions.
3. Identifying which consumers have favorable or "costly" value equations.
4. Providing a clear link to key segments, products, and consumer behaviors for actionability.

To evaluate each of these, we analyzed anonymous data (any personally identifying information was stripped out by a third party before the data were analyzed) for thousands of users and non-users of Facebook in several countries around the world. We gathered data on their feelings about Facebook, competitors, and their time online. We also gathered anonymous data about their use of Facebook and assessed how usage and behaviors shifted with sentiment.

What we learned surprised us: Consumers did not have exclusively positive or negative perceptions of Facebook; instead, they all possessed both in varying measures. These people were consciously and often unconsciously making cost-benefit trade-offs in choosing whether to become more or less engaged in the platform, which is a very similar decision-making process to making purchases on a given day. The key was

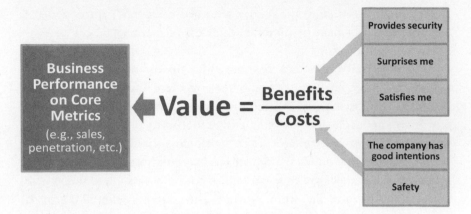

Figure 7.4   Cost-benefit trade-offs among Facebook users.

to figure out which trade-offs were being made and what the thresholds were for improving the business metrics (Figure 7.4).

In the simplest terms, we found that people expected Facebook to enhance their relationships and to be fun. However, they were wary of Facebook's privacy policies: Despite how seriously Facebook takes privacy and the lengths it goes to in order to protect privacy, consumers did not always trust Facebook to properly handle their personal information. This safety concern acted as a sort of speed limit on how engaged people could be in Facebook and whether or not they would sign up for it. One immediate solve was to introduce Privacy Basics – a tool on Facebook that massively clarified and simplified privacy settings and immediately helped with sentiment. Combined with the marketing team's other efforts, the findings from the Brand Economics model began to reverse the tide of negative consumer sentiment, and Facebook's core equities began to improve, according to Facebook's ongoing research.

Other changes took place as well. Marketing began to measure and try to affect the brand equities that impacted the business by developing higher-impact messages based on the value equation consumers actually used in changing their behaviors. This new structure enabled more effective communication with target consumers in growth markets, and "at-risk" users could be identified and helped with better tools like Privacy Basics. Of course, in the years that followed, not only did Facebook's brand equities improve, but also the business performance, across all metrics, continued its historic trend of year-on-year growth.

The model also changed the way Zuckerberg talked about the platform: "Our mission is to make the world more open and connected. For the past few years, this had mostly meant building mobile apps that help you share with the people you care about. We have a lot more to do on mobile, but at this point we feel we're in a position where we can start focusing on what platforms will come next to *enable more useful, entertaining, and personal experiences*."[18]

The link between the hard economics of Facebook's business and its brand's equities made for easy alignment on brand marketing objectives. Executing these objectives became easier too: The team now knew what to test for with a new branded message or product! The Brand Economics model also made the outcomes predictable – as key equities improved, so would consumer behaviors and business performance. Facebook marketing had transformed its role from stewards of the Facebook brand to activators of the business through the power of the brand.

## Take the Brand Challenge

While they may often seem ethereal, brands clearly have real, enduring value and play an important role in customers' decision-making processes. And, the value of a brand can be managed and increased even over relatively short periods of time. Importantly, developing a more precise understanding of what drives your brand's value and then effectively enhancing it can pay significant dividends by increasing choice and earning price premiums. A strong brand value proposition articulates a compelling set of promises for the brand's most valuable customers that describe what will be delivered and how it will be delivered. In essence, a powerful BVP reflects the who, what, and how of strategy, which is why we often say that your brand is really the name you put on your business strategy.

These are challenging times for many established brands across industries as diverse as food, cars, retailing, and banking. Many customers have migrated to new benefits, new experiences, and the cachet that newer, nontraditional brands offer. In some cases, more traditional brands don't seem as authentic to consumers, or they are not as trusted by consumers. All of these obstacles make successful approaches to analyzing and managing brand value increasingly important.

Going forward, it will also become increasingly critical to understand how your brand shows up in customers' digital decision processes.

Specifically, your firm should carefully track customer reviews about your brand, the promises the brand makes, the overall experience it provides, and how well those brand promises are delivered. Monitoring customer reviews and applying various analytical approaches that leverage Big Data to understand the information can provide an invaluable source of ongoing, virtually "real-time" customer input. With this information stream, managers can determine where their brand lives up to its promise, where it falls short, and how to address any issues. Similar data for major competitors can also provide a scorecard that shows how your brand is faring versus the competition. More importantly, the data can often highlight the areas to focus on to enhance the value of your brand.

## Questions for Monday Morning

1. What are the key equities your target customers would associate with your brand today?
   a. Which equities are the positive "drivers" of your brand's value?
   b. Which equities are potential negatives that create a "drag" on your brand's value?
2. How can you strengthen positive drivers or limit negative drags to increase brand value?
3. What are the key promises your brand makes today?
   a. Are these the right promises to make?
   b. Do they align with the most important demands of your most valuable target customers?
4. What are your customers' most important demands?
5. How does your brand value proposition (BVP) deliver on those demands?
6. What differentiates your brand today?
   a. What could differentiate it going forward?
7. How can your brand's BVP be improved going forward to enhance customer success and brand value?

# Endnotes

1. "A brand is simply trust." http://www.azquotes.com/quote/1417040. Accessed August 2017.
2. "Your brand is what other people say about you." http://startupquotes .startupvitamins.com/post/77385350314/your-brand-is-what-other-people-say-about-you. Accessed August 2017.
3. "Define: Brand." http://sethgodin.typepad.com/seths_blog/2009/12/define-brand.html. Accessed August 2017.
4. "What Are Brands For?" *The Economist.* 30 August 2014. https:// www.economist.com/news/business/21614150-brands-are-most-valuable-assets-many-companies-possess-no-one-agrees-how-much-they. Accessed August 2017.
5. Badenhausen, Kurt. "The World's Most Valuable Brands 2017: By the Numbers." *Forbes.* 23 May 2017. https://www.forbes.com/sites/ kurtbadenhausen/2017/05/23/the-worlds-most-valuable-brands-2017-by-the-numbers/#6ad1d23d303d. Accessed August 2017.
6. Ibid.
7. "The World's Most Valuable Brands." *Forbes.* https://www.forbes .com/powerful-brands/list/2/#tab:rank. Accessed August 2017.
8. Vaughan, Jack. "The PC: Personal Computing Comes of Age." 10 December 2004. http://www-03.ibm.com/ibm/history/ibm100/ us/en/icons/personalcomputer/words/. Accessed August 2017.
9. "What Are Brands For?" *The Economist.* 30 August 2014. https:// www.economist.com/news/business/21614150-brands-are-most-valuable-assets-many-companies-possess-no-one-agrees-how-much-they. Accessed August 2017.
10. "Your brand is what other people say about you." http://startupquotes .startupvitamins.com/post/77385350314/your-brand-is-what-other-people-say-about-you. Accessed August 2017.
11. Velazco, Chris. "How Samsung Got Big." *Tech Crunch.* 1 June 2013. https://techcrunch.com/2013/06/01/how-samsung-got-big/. Accessed August 2017.
12. "The World's Most Valuable Brands." *Forbes.* https://www.forbes .com/powerful-brands/list/2/#tab:rank. Accessed August 2017.
13. Constine, Josh. "Facebook doesn't want to be cool, it wants to be electricity." *TechCrunch.* 18 September 2013. https://techcrunch .com/2013/09/18/facebook-doesnt-want-to-be-cool/. Accessed August 2013.

14. University of California Television. "Mapping the Future of Networks with Facebook's Chris Cox: The Atlantic Meets the Pacific." YouTube. 30 October 2012. https://www.youtube.com/watch?v=SVPran908cY. Accessed August 2017.

15. Germain, David. "'The Social Network' Has Lead at Globes with 3 Prizes." San Diego Union Tribune. 16 January 2011. http://www.sandiegouniontribune.com/sdut-social-network-has-lead-at-globes-with-3-prizes-2011jan16-story.html. Accessed August 2017.

16. "The Social Network 'made up stuff that was hurtful,' says Mark Zuckerberg." The Guardian. 8 November 2014. https://www.theguardian.com/technology/2014/nov/08/mark-zuckerberg-social-network-made-stuff-up-hurtful. Accessed August 2017.

17. Client interviews.

18. Hof, Robert. "Why Is Facebook Acquiring The Maker Of A Virtual Reality Headset You Can't Even Buy Yet?" Forbes. 25 March 2014. https://www.forbes.com/sites/roberthof/2014/03/25/why-is-facebook-buying-the-maker-of-a-nonexistent-virtual-reality-headset/#7f32e9d73baa. Accessed August 2017.

# CHAPTER 8

# Pricing with Precision

---

### The Big Ideas

- An optimized pricing strategy is one of the most effective ways to increase profits for almost any business.
- Meaningful differentiation is the fundamental driver of pricing power.
- To optimize pricing, start by understanding the pricing opportunities within distinct customer segments rather than across broad markets.
- The value equation for your offers needs to be understood in detail and managed on an ongoing basis by assessing value drivers, price points, and trade-offs.
- A compelling "good, better, best" trade-up architecture helps guide customers to the right offer for their needs while motivating more sales at premium price points.
- One of the most common pricing pitfalls to avoid is operating with a commodity mindset rather than a pricing power mindset.

---

*"Price is what you pay. Value is what you get."*

—Warren Buffett[1]

For most businesses, pricing offers the most effective, lowest-risk opportunity for improving profits. Multiple analyses have shown that pricing is the strategic lever with the single greatest potential impact on profitability. Raising prices by 1 percent typically has a much greater impact on the bottom line than increasing sales by 1 percent or reducing costs by 1 percent. In fact, assessments of businesses across industries have shown that bringing prices up by 1 percent, as long as sales volumes remain constant, increases operating profits by about 8 percent on average. Meanwhile, a 1 percent change in the form of lower variable costs produces only about a 4 percent increase in operating profits, while increasing volume by 1 percent generates only about a 2.5 percent improvement in operating profits.[2] These metrics highlight why precision is critically important when it comes to pricing decisions: Just a 1 percent price increase can have a huge impact on the performance of any business.

## Driving for Differentiation

The ultimate driver of pricing power, other than having a monopoly, is truly meaningful differentiation. There are many ways to drive meaningful differentiation, but one of the biggest barriers to achieving differentiation that we come across in client work is the "commodity mindset." Senior managers often believe their business is stuck in a commodity category with commoditized offers that take whatever price the market will bear. The truth is that nothing *has* to be a commodity. Companies we have worked with that once felt like they were in commodity categories – including beef, motor oil, socks, paper products, car insurance, and others – have successfully gained pricing power by leveraging the right strategies and driving greater differentiation.

Strategically, there are really only two options for a business to be successful: Compete on price or compete on value. The most successful price-based competitor will be the lowest-cost producer in the industry, and, for most industries, there can be only one "lowest" cost producer. However, remaining the lowest-cost producer in an industry is rarely easy and it requires sustained effort over time. Given these challenges, most industries have only one or maybe a small handful of companies that can successfully compete on price by keeping costs as low as possible.

Competing on value means identifying opportunities to successfully differentiate your offers from those of competitors and thereby earn a price premium. As Michael Porter of the Harvard Business School observed in his book *Competitive Advantage*, "In a differentiation strategy, a firm seeks to be unique in its industry along some dimensions that are widely valued by buyers.... It is rewarded for its uniqueness with a premium price."[3] Even if that price premium is only an additional 1 percent, it can have a huge impact on profitability.

Porter also noted that, "The means for differentiation are peculiar to each industry. Differentiation can be based on the product itself, the delivery system by which it is sold, the marketing approach, and a broad range of other factors."[4] While there are many potential paths to driving differentiation, they all begin with your target customers. At the end of the day, it does not matter if your team thinks your offers are highly differentiated or if your distributors or retail partners think your offers are unique: Successful differentiation is in the eye of your target consumer.

Finding the right path to successful differentiation is well worth the payoff it creates in the form of pricing power. In fact, Warren Buffett says pricing power is the "single-most important decision in evaluating a business."[5] As alluded to in Chapter 1, Buffett places more emphasis on a company's ability to successfully raise prices than on any other metric of its performance because it indicates a healthy business with differentiated offers and attractive, ongoing growth prospects.

## Price to Customer Segments, Not Markets

The foundation of any successful pricing strategy is to price to distinct customer segments rather than to the entire market. No two customers – and no two customer needs – are exactly alike. Each customer has a different level of interest in your category, is seeking a different set of benefits, and has a different level of price sensitivity. As a result, the most successful approaches price to specific customer segments, sometimes focusing on customers in certain situations rather than to broad "mass markets."

Why price to specific segments? Businesses almost always leave money on the table when products and services are priced to broad markets instead of to specific segments. The fact is that pricing to the "average" customer means that some segments of customers, or some segments of customers in certain situations, would have gladly paid more for benefits that are currently being "given away." As we have seen, even a relatively modest 1 percent increase in the price paid can have an enormous impact on your profits. On the other hand, the average price that was set for the offer is probably too high for some customers and they won't purchase at all. This dichotomy is why precision is so important when it comes to pricing decisions: To optimize sales and profits, you can't stop with an understanding of the market broadly. What is needed is an understanding of how the benefits offered and the price points charged influence purchase decisions for major customer groups.

Revisiting Allstate's introduction of "Your Choice" auto and home policies from a pricing perspective helps illustrate the point. Recall that in the insurance market, some segments of customers would pay only the lowest possible price for auto or home insurance policies that would cover only the bare minimum. At the other end of the spectrum, Allstate identified segments of customers who were willing to pay a premium price for additional benefits such as "Accident Forgiveness." Given Allstate's network of insurance agents and the personalized customer service those agents could provide, Allstate focused on winning with customers who were willing to pay a premium for additional, value-added benefits.

But, even that level of segmentation did not optimize the opportunity for Allstate. Customers in the market could be further segmented and offered "Standard," "Gold," and "Platinum" versions of Your Choice policies. As the names imply, each version of Your Choice, from Standard to Platinum, provided greater benefits at a higher price premium. These successful price tiers reflected distinctly different demands and opportunities in the market that a single price point would not have addressed. Had Allstate offered only the "average" price, as represented by its Gold price tier, it would have priced many consumers out of the market. At the same time, Allstate would have foregone the opportunity to charge higher prices for the additional benefits their Platinum offer provided to other segments of customers.

Another successful means of segmenting customers in order to better understand pricing opportunities is to develop a clear sense of the situation the customer is experiencing. One somewhat infamous example of this type of model is Uber's ability to enact "surge pricing" when demand for transportation spikes. Through an approach called "dynamic pricing," Uber can charge more when demand for its car service increases due to a rain storm or because of an issue impacting public transportation. This pricing model allows Uber to be even more competitive with traditional taxis, which charge a fixed rate no matter how much or how little demand there is at a given time. Dynamic pricing can also be used to lower prices in order to increase sales when demand falls. Last-minute fares on plane tickets when the flight is not full or discounted hotel rooms after the peak travel season ends are two examples of dynamically lowering prices in order to motivate purchases in periods of weak demand.

One other well-known example of pricing to specific situations is the need across many aspects of our personal and work lives for "rush orders." Paying extra to have an important package sent overnight by FedEx, paying for Prime membership on Amazon for faster deliveries, or paying extra to have dry cleaning done in an hour are all familiar examples.

## Differentiation in Commercial Printing

Years ago, the idea of rush orders was an important way of improving performance for a commercial printer with whom we were working. The printer was in danger of being shut down by its parent company because it was losing money in an industry that was awash in too much printing capacity. The industry over-capacity allowed potential customers to pit printers against one another to see who could complete any given print job for the absolute lowest price. To keep the presses running, many companies, including our client, often took jobs with little or no profit margin. As we understood the situation in greater detail, we saw that one of the few bright spots for our client was expedited orders for which our client could charge a premium. In addition, our client was well suited to handling rush orders because it had a national network of printing plants and other capabilities that allowed it to get a catalogue printed and mailed throughout the U.S. faster than almost any other printer.

Our client agreed that expedited orders were attractive, but it quickly pointed out that it had only a few customers who occasionally ran into time crunches. As we interviewed customers and began to understand their demands, we realized that there was a segment of print customers who routinely ran into time crunches and would pay a premium for expedited printing. These customers were characterized by centrally controlled decision-making that slowed their approval processes down. Imagine a fashion catalogue with a distinctive look and feel that was tightly controlled by a corporate creative or design team, or a bank or retailer that needs to send out mailers to announce a new branch or store opening but has multiple layers of approval that slow the process down. Customers like these would try to meet deadlines, but somehow their decision-making processes always got in the way. Moreover, their need for expedited help was fairly predictable throughout the year, with focuses on holidays and new store openings, to name a couple of examples.

Our client had significant advantages in delivering on rush orders, and, once they understood this demand more fully, they developed additional capabilities to improve their ability to do so. Importantly, we also discovered a better means of predicting who would need rush orders and when. Our client's sales teams began calling on the advertising agencies that worked with their printing customers, in addition to calling on the customers themselves. One visit to an ad agency could put the printer's sales force in front of key decision influencers for half a dozen or more important printing customers while also providing information about their print schedules. Over time, our client developed a reputation for being the one printer to trust with expedited orders. Ultimately, focusing on demand for expedited orders turned our client's performance around, bringing them back to healthy profits.

## Managing the Value Equation

As the quote from Warren Buffett at the start of this chapter points out, pricing is really about value: The value perceived by each group of customers, the value your business creates for them, and what your business can charge for that value. That is why one of the most fundamental aspects of pricing to understand is the "value equation" and how it varies by customer segment.

The value equation for any offer is calculated simply as benefits divided by price. For some offers, especially durable goods like cars, consumer electronics, or appliances, it is generally more accurate to think of price as "total cost of ownership" (TCO). This TCO approach factors in the initial purchase price paid, the ongoing costs of operating and maintaining the item, any potential disposal costs, and any residual value for which the used item can be sold in the future.

As you can see from the value equation, overall value will go up if the benefits in the "numerator" are increased or if the price in the "denominator" is decreased, thus making benefits and price the critical levers to work with in order to manage perceptions of value on an ongoing basis. It is important to note that the "benefits" include any and all potential benefits that different customer segments might perceive, including obvious rational benefits as well as *emotional* ("how it makes me feel") and *social* ("how others will feel about me") benefits. This structure relates directly to our previous discussion of the functional, emotional, and social benefits of brands, and the notion that the "real" power of a brand is its "economic" power. The key, as far as pricing is concerned, is to understand what your most attractive customers value most and then make adjustments to deliver more of those benefits at a price premium.

For example, an office products company with which we worked had determined that its products were becoming commoditized. Without a complete understanding of what benefits consumers were seeking in the category, the company wasn't able to clearly communicate the benefits of its products in a really compelling way. The company also did not have a very good track record of introducing new product innovations to meet consumer needs. The result? Over time, consumers struggled to see the difference between our client's higher-priced brand name products and their private label counterparts, which sold at much lower price points. Our client had to keep taking price cuts as competition with lower-cost private-label offerings intensified.

In response, our client tried to add new benefits that would justify their price premium and bring the value equation back in line. Their engineering department created several features that made the products easier to use, and marketing focused on these features in messaging designed to win with consumers. However, these efforts had little effect. Why? Consumers were actually looking for a different value proposition. In reality, they wanted to feel more confident about the reliability of these products and about the actual documents and work products they helped produce. Ease of use was only one aspect of getting paperwork done efficiently, and being confident that these office products could be counted on as a critical deadline approached was an even more compelling benefit.

Once we understood that reliability was the key and that it had both functional and emotional aspects to it, we were able to find several existing features in the product that target consumers believed were important ways to deliver on this promise. By shifting the messaging and point-of-sale materials to clearly highlight this new range of applications and benefits, consumers quickly recognized the key trade-off between our client's offers and private label offers. Consumers were motivated to trade up to products that more clearly addressed their needs for reliability, speed, and confidence. Focusing on these new benefits also redefined ease of use as table stakes for these office products rather than as important differentiators.

With this strategy, the company was able to reverse the price declines it had been experiencing, all while increasing sales and motivating trade-up, which made our client's offers much more attractive to their retail partners. At the end of the day, the new pricing strategy created a win-win-win for consumers, retailers, and our client.

## Good, Better, Best

One approach from which both Allstate and the office products client benefited was creating a clear and compelling "good, better, best" trade-up architecture to guide consumers to the right offer for their needs. A strong good, better, best pricing architecture essentially highlights different benefit and price tiers along the value equation. If you imagine the value equation as a graph (see Figure 8.1) with price along the vertical axis and benefits along the horizontal axis, there is a positively sloped best-fit line that describes the points at each increasing price tier where more benefits

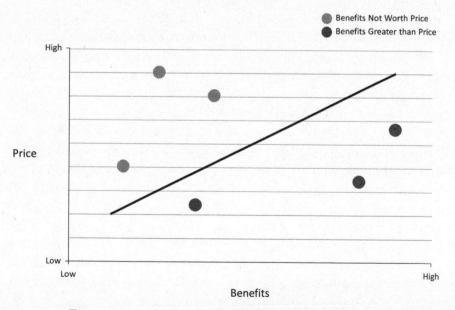

Figure 8.1    Theoretical value equation alignment.

perfectly match price increases. In effect, points above this vertical line break the value equation by charging too much for the benefits delivered. At the same time, points below this theoretical vertical line are giving away benefits by charging a price that is too low. A "good, better, best" pricing approach is like a set of stairsteps moving up the vertical line of the value equation while making sure the benefits gained are worth the price paid.

Getting "good, better, best" pricing tiers right can have a profound impact on sales and trade-up. We had a client in the oral care industry that offered a wide array of manual, battery-powered, and electric rechargeable toothbrushes. The firm's sales had stalled out, and nobody could figure out why. If anything, they had added more and more new toothbrushes, allowing consumers a wide variety of choices to find just the right tooth-brush for their specific needs at any number of price points. In addition, our client had great relationships with dentists who recommended their brand of toothbrushes and sent consumers to the store with our client's brand at the top of their consideration set.

So what was the disconnect? The problem was happening at the store shelf. Consumers stood in front of a dizzying array of potential toothbrushes from our client and from competitors and became totally overwhelmed. Across our clients' offers alone, there was no clear "good, better, best" pricing architecture, which made it almost impossible to determine which toothbrush across manual, battery-powered, and electric rechargeable options to buy. Facing this jumble of overlapping price points and benefits was paralyzing for most consumers in large part because they only bought toothbrushes infrequently. Without clear price tiers to guide them, most consumers went with cheap manual toothbrushes and often bought competitors' offers despite the recommendation of their dentist. The clutter and confusion at shelf derailed the buying process and actually inhibited sales of our client's top-of-the-line offers.

Fortunately, once we understood how the lack of a "good, better, best" trade-up architecture was impacting sales, we were able to work with our client and its retail partners to reverse the situation. Organizing the prod-uct assortment at shelf around a clear "good, better, best" trade-up archi-tecture for each type of product, from manual to battery-powered to the high-end electric rechargeable offers, had an almost immediate positive impact on sales. Consumers were no longer stymied by the myriad choices in a category that they did not shop very often. Additionally, they had clear and compelling reasons for trading up to gain more benefits at prices that made those premium products a good value. As a result, our client's sales, especially at the higher end, increased dramatically.

## Pricing Reference Points

One of our client friends at the toothbrush company likened the impact of the new "good, better, best" trade-up architecture to the way a good wine list works at a restaurant. As he noted, "A good wine list always has a few amazing bottles of red and of white across varietals that are really expensive. Those bottles, at those prices, actually pull the average price per bottle of wine purchased up across the menu. People tend to move up from the least expensive wines to a bottle of their favorite type of wine at higher prices. Without the expensive wines as a comparison, that trade-up does not happen."[6] He was absolutely right. Reference points, like his wine example, play an important role in the psychology of pricing.

Purchase decisions do not take place in a vacuum. Your customer is comparing your offer and the value equation it represents to other potential substitutes. Today, those comparisons are enabled by smartphones and can take place in just a few seconds right at the store shelf, from the comfort of home, or anywhere in between. All of this makes it increasingly important to understand the value equation for your offers and how they compare to potential substitutes, especially any substitutes that may serve as a reference price like the most expensive wines on the wine list.

The price points consumers refer to in order to assess the value of a potential purchase are typically prices for the most similar product substitutes. These alternatives are generally sold in the same section of the store or come up under the same search online. Typically, consumers will look at the lowest-cost and highest-cost options to get a sense of the pricing spectrum for that category of products. The more familiar consumers are with a given product and what it "should" cost, the less likely they are to do any research on reference prices. What is important is to understand what your target customers use as reference prices and how the value equation for your offer stacks up. Do the perceived benefits of your offers compare favorably to the benefits offered by those substitutes used for reference pricing or not? Can you work with retail partners to add your own version of a premium wine to the product mix to reset price perceptions in ways that benefit both your offers and the retailer?

Are there ways to meaningfully differentiate your offers such that they earn a price premium and have no viable substitutes?

## Developing a Pricing Power Mindset

The new CMO of an appliance maker we worked with was tired of hearing the same refrain from her new colleagues. Across the company from marketing to sales to engineering, the entire organization talked about the commodity market they were competing in and how difficult it was to maintain prices in the face of stiff competition and discount retailers. Our friend the CMO liked to point out that "nothing has to be a commodity unless commodity managers allow it to be."[7] She asked for our help on the company's most challenging category: Dishwashers.

For starters, the internal team did not think consumers cared much about dishwashers. The conventional wisdom was that consumers thought all dishwashers were pretty much the same: Nothing more than a basic convenience item. While someone who really enjoys cooking might spend more for a commercial grade oven, a great stove, or the latest kitchen gadgets, the thinking went, nobody really cares about the cleanup afterward. All anyone needs is a basic dishwasher that can get the job done, so lowest price wins.

We tested this hypothesis, as well as many others, with appliance consumers, and we found that there were at least two segments of consumers who cared quite a bit about their dishwashers and how they performed. One group, the "kitchen connoisseurs," wanted all of the equipment in their kitchen to be top notch. For them, a dishwasher that did not perform created an annoying hassle because the pots, pans, and utensils they wanted to use right now might need additional scrubbing even after going through the dishwasher once. Another segment, the "home entertainers," enjoyed hosting others at home, where somehow the party always ended up in the kitchen. For these consumers, the kitchen was also the center of their busy family life. Because they spent a lot of time in their kitchen with both friends and family, they wanted it to be an enjoyable, comfortable place for everyone. Both of these segments cared more than the average consumer about their kitchens overall and about their dishwashers specifically.

The other insight we soon discovered about these consumers is that they were not very satisfied with the performance of most dishwashers on the market. For the most part, companies making dishwashers had been locked in a battle over cleaning power and speed. As our client told us, the industry had been focused on improvements to both cleaning power and speed for decades and further enhancements were unlikely to generate any breakthroughs. As they noted, "We are on the two yard line of innovation. There just isn't much room left for improvement."[8] More importantly, consumers were already pretty happy with how well their dishes were cleaned and how quickly they were washed. What they were increasingly unhappy with was how loud their dishwashers were as they cleaned.

At the time we did this work, many aspects of American culture were in the process of becoming much less formal. Casual Fridays had extended into casual dress codes for the entire workweek. Formal titles went on a first-name basis. Traditional sit-down dinners were being replaced by snacking, grab-and-go meals, and even "dashboard dining" in the car. All of this translated into home designs, as the formal floorplans of most traditional homes morphed into highly coveted open floorplans.

As homes changed, the kitchen went from being a relatively small, private part of the house to the center of a new great room that combined the kitchen, the family room, and a casual eating area. To accommodate the new great rooms, the old living rooms, which were usually large, seldom-used formal spaces, were recast as small sitting rooms. Now that people were spending most of their waking hours in their kitchen/family room, they really noticed how loud the dishwasher was. The racket made by the dishwasher drowned out the TV and meant you had to shout to have a conversation. But, the industry had not identified those changes yet and remained focused on greater cleaning power and speed, which often exacerbated the noise issue.

With new insights into consumers' demand for quieter dishwashers, especially among the two most attractive consumer segments, the client team got to work designing a new dishwasher that provided excellent cleaning power and washed dishes quickly yet quietly. Our quantitative testing with consumers showed just how much they valued any trade-offs in order to get a quieter dishwasher and how much more they would be willing to spend in order to have the peace and quiet they wanted to enjoy in their homes. With the same quantitative work, we also identified the most compelling messages for advertising and point-of-sale materials about the new dishwashers. We also found naming and sub-branding options and product design elements that were extremely effective at communicating the new benefits of a quieter wash cycle while providing reasons to believe that the new dishwasher really delivered.

Sales of the new dishwasher exceeded expectations despite the price premium being charged. Understanding specific customer segments and identifying their unmet needs had allowed the appliance maker to differentiate its dishwashers on a benefit that really mattered to their most attractive customers. Successfully delivering on this new benefit created the differentiation that allowed the company to command a price premium while maintaining a strong value equation. The cost of adding the new quieting benefits were more than recouped by the premium prices charged, which made the new line of dishwashers the most profitable products the company had ever produced. The CMO and her team had successfully taken a pricing power mindset and broken out of what had long been considered an unattractive commodity market.

## Conclusions

Ultimately, pricing power is the tangible outcome of an effective strategy – one that differentiates businesses from their competitors and creates something that is more valuable to consumers. In contrast, undifferentiated commodities that lack pricing power must simply accept the level of pricing the market will bear. And yet, while pricing strategy should play a critical role in the success of any business, managers often feel their approach to pricing is suboptimal. In most cases, this lack of confidence about their own ability to optimize pricing is driven by a lack of the necessary insights into consumer demand. As a result, managers are often left wondering if their current pricing strategy is leaving money on the table because prices are too low or if a significant amount of business is being lost because prices are too high.

Fortunately, the principles we have discussed here can help your firm assess its current approaches and harness the potential of pricing power. Done correctly, a more precise and comprehensive pricing strategy should increase both sales and profits. The right pricing strategies can be used to communicate significant value, to motivate purchasing, and to drive trade-up to more expensive options. The tools and approaches of pricing strategy also highlight a potentially significant opportunity to enhance performance for any business that has not yet optimized its approach to pricing.

## Questions for Monday Morning

1. Who are your most valuable customers, and with whom are you trying to win?
   a. How can you segment them?
   b. Can they be segmented by benefits sought?
   c. By price sensitivity?
   d. Can they be segmented by specific situations they experience?
2. What differentiates your products/offers today?
3. What would your most valuable customers say is most unique about your offers?
4. Are there opportunities to drive meaningful differentiation versus competitors?
   a. Increased performance for current benefits?
   b. Adding a new benefit?
   c. Communicating an existing benefit that has been overlooked?
   d. Enhancing the experience rather than the product?
5. How can you rethink the value equation for your products or services?
   a. Can new rational benefits be added that align more closely with customers' major decision drivers?
   b. Are there key emotive benefits that can be highlighted and clearly communicated?
   c. Are there aspects of the offer that can be stripped out because they add cost but add little value to target customers? Can total cost of ownership (TCO) be reduced in some manner?

6. What reference price points do customers use to evaluate the value equation for your offers? How do they determine if your offer is worth the price being charged?

7. How can you challenge the commodity mindset?

   a. Could a cross-functional view of pricing strategies help break out of the commodity pricing approach?

8. Can you enact a price increase of 1 percent or more without losing customers or market share to competitors?

   a. If not, what would have to be true in order to do so?

## Endnotes

1. "Warren Buffet Quotes." https://www.brainyquote.com/quotes/quotes/w/warrenbuff149692.html. Accessed September 2017.

2. Maryn, Michael, Eric Roegner, and Craig Zawada. "The Power of Pricing." *McKinsey Quarterly*. February 2003. http://www.mckinsey.com/business-functions/marketing-and-sales/our-insights/the-power-of-pricing. Accessed September 2017.

3. Porter, Michael. *Competitive Advantage*. New York: Simon and Schuster, 1985.

4. Ibid.

5. Frye, Andrew and Dakin Campbell, "Buffett Says Pricing Power More Important Than Good Management." *Bloomberg*. 17 February 2011. https://www.bloomberg.com/news/articles/2011-02-18/buffett-says-pricing-power-more-important-than-good-management. Accessed September 2017.

6. Interview with client.

7. Interview with client.

8. Interview with client.

# Moving to a Demand-Driven Business System: The Big Data Advantage

# CHAPTER 9

# Innovation That Works

---

### The Big Ideas

- Successful innovation is possible in virtually every category, including commodity categories.

- A clear innovation strategy, senior management commitment, and a robust innovation process are all foundational for innovation success.

- Innovation opportunities can be identified across a wide portfolio of innovation types, from small improvements to existing products to entirely new business models.

- Identifying the right innovation "drill sites" as inputs to the process is critical.

- Approaches for identifying potential innovation drill sites include "Demand Profit Pools," breaking compromises, reassessing category intersections, and "Jobs-To-Be-Done," among others.

- Big Data, including digital learnings, can be used to find target customers in geographic markets and online to understand the digital shopping journey, and to optimize offers and launch activities.

---

*"Above all, innovation is work rather than genius. It requires knowledge.
It often requires ingenuity. And it requires focus."*

—Peter Drucker[1]

We have helped clients across industries develop some of their most successful innovations for over forty years. Sometimes those innovative new offers were new to the industry, like Allstate's "Your Choice" insurance policies. Sometimes they were meaningful improvements to existing offers, like Bud Light Lime. At times, the innovation that drove significant growth was not related to the product at all, but instead consisted of innovative go-to-market approaches or a new business model. Across all of these experiences we have learned several important lessons about what drives innovation success and what makes innovation efforts fail.

First, we have learned that innovation is possible in virtually every category imaginable, even in those that are considered commodities. In addition, innovation can take many forms including the product's features, construction process, or sales method, as well as the associated customer experience or the producing firm's business model. And, based on four decades of experience across hundreds of innovation efforts, we have honed a repeatable process for identifying customer demand, sizing opportunities, developing solutions, and determining how to launch those new offers. We have also learned that one of the most difficult aspects of innovation is determining *where* to look for inspiring new ideas. All of this has taught us that Peter Drucker was right. Innovation is work. And, it does require knowledge, focus, and some ingenuity as well.

We have also learned a lot about why individual innovations and entire innovation efforts fail. Most of the time the failures stem from missteps conducted at the start of the process or what former senior partner at The Cambridge Group, Kevin Bowen, calls the "fuzzy front end of innovation."[2] What Kevin is describing is a hazy innovation strategy, unclear commitment from senior management, and a faulty innovation process that fails to identify high-potential innovation opportunities at the outset. When these "front end" conditions are fuzzy at best, no amount of ingenuity can make up for them. What is needed instead is a solid foundation to serve as a platform for successful innovation.

## Building the Right Foundation

In our experience, the right foundation for successful innovation has three major components. The first is to ensure alignment about what you are trying to achieve through innovation. What is the strategy? Where will innovation efforts be focused? What will success look like? In far too many situations there is no innovation strategy in place to guide efforts. Rather than developing a true innovation strategy, many organizations operate from an amorphous decree to "drive innovation" or "create more innovative offers."

A thoughtful innovation strategy should be developed with perspective and input from a team of people representing the key functions across the organization. It should not be developed by any one function, such as R&D or marketing, alone. Gaining cross-functional input makes for a much richer, more realistic, and more thorough innovation strategy. For example, while sales or marketing might want to invest in innovation in one specific area, further examination by the finance team or the supply chain team might reveal the fact that it is economically unattractive or that there is not enough manufacturing capacity to support it. Without cross-functional input at the outset, companies often waste time chasing the wrong opportunities. Finally, developing the innovation strategy is not a one-time event: This process should be revisited and discussed on a regular basis to determine what progress is being made and what, if anything, needs to change.

One of the first decisions to make is to determine which business units (BU) or brands should invest in innovation at all. Remember, innovation is one means of driving growth, but as we have shown, it is not the only means. The right solution for driving growth for some BUs and brands might stem from a new pricing strategy, from investing to build better relationships with channel partners, or by rebuilding the brand to make it stand out from the competition.

Broadly speaking, innovation efforts and the resources required to fuel them should be focused on only two types of BUs or brands: Those that are core to the business today and those judged to have the greatest growth and profit potential going forward. While the latter situation may be straightforward, it is important to clearly define what we mean by "core to the business." These are the key offers that drive the overall health of the business and generate the profits that allow for further investment. These BUs and brands are very different from the "cash cows" that are being milked by the business or those BUs and brands that the business plans to divest. These BUs and brands need to continue to perform while also being protected from both traditional competitors and potential industry disruptors.

Once the right BUs and brands have been identified for innovation investments, the organization must then identify the specific innovation charter for each of the BUs and brands and how each of these charters fit into the innovation strategy overall. The charter is meant to clarify objectives, roles, resources, and time lines for that specific innovation effort. Clear objectives will help guide efforts and help determine if the right types and amounts of resources have been committed to achieve the innovation objectives over the time line required. A critical aspect of the innovation charter is determining who will contribute to the effort and in what specific roles. We have found that four major roles help drive innovation success: A steering committee to guide efforts broadly and conduct periodic reviews, a team leader to manage the details, working team members to conduct the work from day to day, and subject matter experts to provide specialized knowledge as needed. Beyond this optimal structure, we have never seen any one way of structuring innovation efforts that is the single best approach. In fact, the exact structure of a successful innovation team differs based on the specific situation, the innovation objectives, and the culture of the firm.

Another major driver of successful innovation is strong, visible senior management support starting from the CEO. Without support from senior management, the odds of successfully introducing new innovations are significantly diminished, while the ability to build a true culture of ongoing innovation is virtually impossible. Senior managers need to make innovation a key priority and recognize innovation efforts, including those that fail. Depending on the industry, studies have estimated that innovation efforts fail as much as 80% of the time or more.[3] The way failures are handled and the learnings developed from innovation failures have a huge impact on ongoing innovation efforts. A true culture of innovation can't be developed if the organization is too afraid of failure to get involved.

# A More Robust Innovation Process

The last foundational element that must be in place is a robust, repeatable innovation process. That process has to identify and size potential innovation areas while also developing solutions to be evaluated further. The process we have developed over the years has five major steps:

### 1. Build the strategic foundation
This initial step is focused on identifying inputs into the innovation effort. What "forces" and "factors" are shaping category demand today? What are smaller companies and start-ups doing in this space, or adjacent spaces? What can we learn from them? Will the category change dramatically, similar to the way the beer market shifted to the sweeter taste many Millennial consumers preferred? What can existing data tell you about the current market? How do consumers make purchase decisions? What do they think of the different brands available, and why? Where are customers dissatisfied, and why? If an Enhanced Demand Landscape was developed, it can be used as a significant source of insights. All of this analysis is aimed at creating hypotheses for potential innovation opportunities to explore going forward.

### 2. Identify and prioritize opportunities
In this step, additional qualitative research with customers helps provide answers to the hypotheses developed in Step 1. Doing so identifies priorities among potential opportunity areas or "Jobs-To-Be-Done," as Clay Christensen and our colleague Taddy Hall, a former Principal at The Cambridge Group, call them.[4] Potential Jobs-To-Be-Done, or "drill sites," are typically prioritized based on market size/attractiveness, profitability, ease of execution, competitive dynamics, and fit with the brand, among other possible metrics. High-priority drill sites are explored further in subsequent steps. Those that do not make the cut to move forward are banked to potentially be assessed at a later date.

### 3. Explore solutions
With a list of high-priority drill sites or Jobs-To-Be-Done, the task is now to develop ideas for how to address each opportunity. The cross-functional

team should be involved in a structured idea-generation process that is typically conducted over one or two days. With Jobs-To-Be-Done/drill sites as inputs, the team works through structured ideation exercises to determine how to solve for each potential "job." For example, for Bud Light we had determined that there was a high-potential opportunity for a slightly sweeter beer – specifically, in situations when consumers felt a beer was appropriate, but sought a product that was sweeter as opposed to the more standard "bitter" taste of beer. With that input, the cross-functional team was able to develop a range of potential solutions. Ideas for a slightly sweeter beer might have included brewing with fewer hops, using a different type of hops, brewing with different malt grains, or adding flavoring, such as orange, strawberry, or lime, or even adding spices such as cinnamon or coriander. With a broad set of brainstormed ideas, the team could then prioritize the ideas with the highest potential to bring forward to the next step.

### 4. Develop innovation concepts

Ideas are now developed into concepts to be tested qualitatively with target consumers/customers. The concept should provide a brief written description of the new innovation and its key benefits and might include an illustration or image of the new offer or even an actual physical prototype of the offer. The concept might also provide a brand name and an expected price point. In some cases these details are intentionally left out in order to assess the merits of the idea alone, without the additional impact of images, prototypes, branding, or pricing. While the format can vary, the description of the potential new offer must be as accurate as possible so consumers/customers can evaluate it and provide feedback. The goal is to understand why the concept is or is not interesting to customers. Learnings from each such discussion are used to revise and improve the concept in an iterative fashion. Concepts are revised and then finalized for the quantitative testing that is crucial to the final step. This concept testing process is likely to identify some concepts that seemed to have promise initially but do not generate much interest among customers. As a result, some concepts are de-prioritized or even discarded. It is much better and much, much less costly to kill these ideas at this point than it is to devote resources to a concept and launch it only to see it fail in the market. Ideally, concepts that move forward have the potential to serve as broad innovation platforms rather than just individual offers. We think of platforms as innovative ideas that can be applied across multiple offers. For example, Allstate's "Your Choice" offers were originally designed and tested for auto insurance, but the approach became a platform that could be applied to homeowners and motorcycle insurance as well.

**5. Optimize and size innovation concepts**

Once concepts have been optimized with customer feedback, the final step is to assess each concept quantitatively. Qualitative testing alone will not result in a statistically valid means of optimizing concepts or of sizing the economic opportunity for each idea. The quantitative testing is often done in two steps: Optimizing the offer and then assessing its economic potential. The approach we have developed for optimizing and sizing concepts is called "Customer Demand Analysis" (CDA). CDA is a form of discrete choice research that helps determine exactly what aspects of the potential offer maximize revenues across customers, including target customers. The aspects of the offer tested mirror real-world choices and include specific benefits, brands, and price points. The approach also provides an initial estimate of sales volume and market share while also determining from which competitors the new offer will source volume. If the offer is a consumer product, like candy, dog food, or toothbrushes, we typically recommend further assessment using Nielsen's BASES testing as a second step. BASES has a longitudinal database of new product introductions used to develop accurate projections of expected sales from new offers by comparing them to the in-market performance of prior new product introductions.

As you can see from the process we have described, the inputs feeding into the process in the very first step are absolutely critical. The process is designed to identify, refine, and prioritize potential innovation opportunities or drill sites. Nothing happens without high-quality inputs at the outset. Additionally, the odds of success drop dramatically if the "fuzzy front end" of the process results in a pool of low potential, unattractive opportunity areas as inputs. As Peter Drucker observed, "Purposeful, systematic innovation begins with the analysis of the sources of new opportunities."[5] So, the question ultimately becomes: Where should your firm look for potential sources of successful innovation?

# An Innovation Portfolio

Successful innovation opportunities can be identified in areas that are as broad as moving to an entirely new business model or as narrow as making an incremental change to an existing product: It should not be thought of in the narrow scope of new product development. At the highest level, we have found that innovation opportunities can be identified across a portfolio of six distinct areas. We think of this portfolio of opportunities in two broad buckets: Product-oriented opportunities and business model opportunities. Each of these can cover a spectrum from smaller-scale opportunities that align with current demand to "big bets" that align more closely with latent demand. These six areas are described in Figure 9.1.

A well-structured innovation strategy should place bets across different types of innovation for three important reasons. First, as we have mentioned, not every innovation effort is going to succeed. Applying the learnings we have developed and following the process we have honed over the years will help increase the odds of success. However, placing one big, "all or nothing" bet is just as risky when applied to innovation as it is with any other type of investment. Risk can be mitigated by spreading efforts across multiple types of innovation to help increase the odds of organizational success.

The second reason for diversifying across types of innovation is that even small-scale product enhancements that are incremental improvements to existing offers are valuable. Done correctly, they create real value

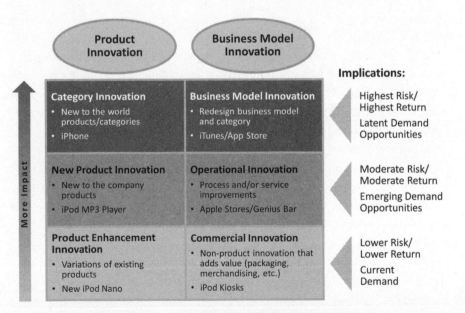

Figure 9.1    Portfolio of innovation types.

for target customers while refreshing your firm's offer and creating buzz in the market. These smaller innovations are also important for the internal team, for successfully introducing incremental innovations helps the team gain experience, confidence, and momentum.

Finally, thinking about innovation opportunities across your firm's portfolio can help highlight the potential for breakthrough products or disruptive new business models. These could create opportunities for your business, or they could pose threats to your existing business. In either case, identifying these potential disruptors is important both for offense and for defense. Identifying potential disruptors could lead to important new opportunities. They could also help you anticipate and defend against disruption from competitors. The reality is that identifying innovation opportunities grounded only in data and observations in current solutions can't get you to the breakthroughs you need to anticipate and defend against disruption. To achieve that, brands and companies, as it were, need to get "into the shoes" of the consumer and think outside the typical boundaries of what consumers are truly trying to accomplish.

# Finding Innovation Drill Sites

## Demand Profit Pools

In our discussion of the Enhanced Demand Landscape, we pointed out the need to understand both *who* is or is not buying your products as well as *why* they purchase the products they buy. Determining who buys your products and who does not is only part of the story: The other half of the equation is to understand *why* they are or are not buying. As you will recall, the *why* is the need state or occasion experienced that drives the purchase. Consumers experience a wide range of need states that can vary in both frequency of occurrence and the specificity of the occasion. We call this intersection of *who* and *why* within the Demand Landscape a "Demand Profit Pool."

Demand Profit Pools are one of the most powerful tools we have ever used in identifying where to find innovation opportunities. Done correctly, each Demand Profit Pool not only answers *who* and *why* but also sizes the economic opportunity and highlights the current solutions consumers or customers use, if any. Some Demand Profit Pools represent true "white space" in the market because there is no solution that is currently available to the consumer or customer. Many of the most successful innovations we have helped our clients introduce over the past forty years, from new products to new business models, were identified using Demand Profit Pools.

## Breaking Compromises

At one point, pet parents had to choose between healthy foods that were good for their pet or the indulgent foods that their pets loved. Recall from Chapter 4 that solving for that fundamental compromise led to one of the most successful pet food launches in the industry while making millions of pet parents happy at the same time. The compromises consumers faced in the pet food category are not unusual: Choosing between great taste and healthiness, convenience and quality, or high performance and an affordable price are some examples of the trade-offs people make every day.

What critical compromises are your consumers or customers being forced to make? Do the trade-offs they are forced to make in your category create significant dissatisfaction? If so, will a solution for these compromises create attractive opportunities for your business? Understanding the compromises consumers or customers are forced to make and breaking them has often led to new breakthroughs.

## Reassess Intersections

One often overlooked way to drive innovation is to explore the intersections that separate categories or define category boundaries. Famously, the intersection of what he termed "technology and liberal arts" was a constant source of inspiration for Steve Jobs.[6] According to Jobs' biographer, Walter Isaacson, Jobs was taken with an insight Edwin Land shared with him: "Those people who can stand at the intersection of the humanities and science, the liberal arts and technology, that intersection, are the people who can change the world." Reexamining the accepted intersections that define category boundaries has proven to be a powerful source of new insight and new opportunities.

Before the introduction of Spinbrush, the toothbrush market essentially consisted of two separate categories: lower-priced, manual toothbrushes and relatively expensive, rechargeable electric toothbrushes. Rather than accepting these traditional category definitions, Spinbrush decided to stand at the intersection of these offers and found a way to erase the boundary between manual and electric toothbrushes. Specifically, the firm created a new category of low-cost, battery-powered toothbrushes that imported several attractive benefits from powered toothbrushes and incorporated them into manual brushes to develop an innovative new category.

A good starting point is to map the traditional definitions and boundaries between your category and neighboring categories or major substitutes for your offer and challenge them. List the most important benefits your offer provides and then determine what types of benefits the offers in other categories provide. Take a comprehensive view of benefits from your offers and from others by including the rational/tangible benefits delivered, such as great taste and high performance, as well as the emotional benefits provided (how it makes me feel) and the social benefits delivered (how others will feel about me). To unlock potential areas of innovation, review the benefits identified and determine which ones might be imported in ways that would enhance your offers.

## Jobs-To-Be-Done

Understanding consumers' Jobs-To-Be-Done is another valuable source for identifying new opportunities across the six different types of innovation we have discussed. The Jobs-To-Be-Done framework is part of a broader approach called "Jobs Theory," which points out the fact that all consumers and B2B customers have a wide array of "jobs" that they "hire" different products and services to perform.[7] Of note, Jobs Theory draws from Design Thinking, for those familiar with that concept, and really focuses on getting deep into the mind of the consumer, and how they live, make choices, and so forth. Successfully hiring for a Job-To-Be-Done helps the consumer or customer make progress by resolving a struggle or fulfilling an aspiration. A true differentiating point of "Jobs Theory" rests in that fact that Jobs-To-Be-Done always starts with a consumer circumstance. Looking for breakthrough innovation at a more general level is far less insightful, but when grounded in circumstances of daily life this approach is far more likely to bear fruit.

Potential jobs can be identified across a wide array of circumstances. They can be found in the struggle parents had in trying to get their kids to brush their teeth long enough and well enough prior to the introduction of Spinbrush, or in the compromise or trade-off among pet parents who wished that their dogs would eat healthier foods but fed them the indulgent foods they loved instead. Perhaps one of the most interesting hunting grounds for jobs is to assess non-consumption, or the "why nots" instead of the "whys." Why weren't younger 21- to 30-year-olds, especially Millennials, drinking as much beer as prior generations of young adults? Answering that question about non-consumption led to the introduction of Bud Light Lime.

Consumers have "hiring specs" for each job they want to fill that consist of the functional, emotional, and social benefits they are seeking at a given price (or salary). In addition to the hiring criteria, consumers have firing criteria for products and services that do not meet their expectations. Importantly, hiring a new product or service often means firing a product or service that used to perform that job. Replacing an incumbent product or service by overcoming the inertia and the risks involved with switching are potentially significant barriers to innovation. Any potential new innovation should have a clear answer as to exactly how it will overcome both incumbents and inertia.

## The Role of Big Data

Big Data can be used to enrich innovation insights and opportunities throughout the innovation process. However, Big Data should never be viewed as a replacement for the innovation process. Insights from analyzing Big Data sets, including digital learnings, can help inform the hypotheses at the outset of the innovation process that are then tested qualitatively and quantitatively throughout the process. For example, analysis of data sets might identify what is selling and what is not selling among different consumer or customer groups and in which geographic markets. Additional analysis might help define the key metrics of the digital shopper journey, including the sites consumers shop, how many they visit, what they buy, and where they buy. All of this information is potentially valuable for generating possible innovation drill sites to assess further. However, none of this is likely to tell you why customers buy or to provide causal relationships for making conclusions.

One valuable way that Big Data, including digital data, can be used is to create a more precise launch strategy for new offers. Analysis of these data sets can help pinpoint where to find your target customers at the local market, store, and household level. It can also help determine where to find the most attractive customers online and throughout the digital shopping process. Online purchasing is growing across categories and is increasingly moving to mobile devices, especially for consumer goods. Even if customers do not make their purchases online, they are increasingly conducting research and being influenced by reviews and ratings online prior to buying in-store. Analysis of these data can help with advertising and promotion by identifying which online sites and social media target customers find most engaging. In addition, analysis of Big Data sets can help drive acquisition of target customers by building "look-alike" models to find and reach more customers who look like the target.

Big Data can also provide virtually real-time insights for tracking customer reaction to the launch of new offers from products to business models. Sales, customer reviews, posts, likes, and comments can all provide important metrics about what is and is not working related to the launch. Importantly, the data can be used to quickly optimize key elements of the launch such as channels, messaging, and media mix. As needed, it can also be used to improve critical aspects of the offer itself.

## Stepping Up to the Plate

How is this for an innovation challenge? "How do you make a better paper plate? Specifically, how can paper plates be differentiated to drive growth?" This was the challenge our client's branded paper-plate business was facing when the president of the division asked us to help. Internally, their team had tried a number of approaches, but nothing seemed to work. While paper plates did not seem like an obvious area for innovation investments, the products were critical to the overall health of the division and sales had stagnated.

For context, this challenge was taking place in a category that had brand name and private label disposable plates made from paper, foam, and plastic. The cheapest of the thin, white, private-label plates were so inexpensive that they were often called "penny plates" by consumers. Imagine competing in a category with reference pricing set by penny plates!

We started by assessing the "forces and factors" shaping demand for the category, which highlighted a number of drivers that indicated strong ongoing demand for disposable plates, including a desire for greater convenience. Consumers were more time-pressed than ever, and every little shortcut for saving time helped. Moms in particular struggled to juggle all of their work and family commitments, yet they were usually in charge of meals. As a result, cooking had declined while bringing home prepared foods and takeout for dinner had grown in popularity (note that meal ingredient kits like Blue Apron did not exist yet). Disposable plates helped save time because there were no dishes to wash after a meal.

There were also important emotional and social benefits from disposable plates that went beyond convenience. With no dirty pots and pans from cooking a meal and no dishes to wash, mom could spend more time enjoying the meal with the rest of the family and less time stuck in the kitchen. The time that would have been spent preparing dinner and cleaning up afterward could now be spent connecting with family. These benefits were especially valuable as shared meals became less frequent. Increasingly busy schedules, especially as kids got older and had activities after school, often meant fewer meals together. It also meant more snacks and meal occasions taking place without mom being there. Having disposable plates on hand meant mom would not come home to a sink full of dirty dishes that had to be cleaned up.

At the same time, many of these busy consumers wanted to entertain at home more often. Most of the time, these events were just casual get-togethers like a backyard barbecue, sharing a potluck dinner, or getting together with friends and neighbors to watch the big game on TV. Once again, disposable plates were a much better solution for entertaining than traditional dishes: With no mess to worry about, everyone could relax. Plus, disposable plates can match the theme or décor of the event, whether it is a birthday, the Fourth of July, or just tuning in for that week's football game.

As we developed the Demand Landscape, we found that there were two segments of consumers who were particularly attractive buyers of paper plates. Together they represented over 60% of total paper plate spend in the category, in part because they preferred the more expensive branded plates to the lower-cost penny plates. Moreover, unlike other consumers who preferred foam or plastic plates or switched around among types of plates, the two most attractive segments strongly preferred paper plates over any other type. While both of these segments wanted convenience, one of them was more driven by the aesthetics of the plates while the other was more focused on the plate's performance.

As we spent time understanding these two segments and their needs in greater detail, we were surprised to learn that they had some significant issues with paper plates that caused them to be unsatisfied. They told us that they grouped paper plates into four distinctly different types based on their needs: Everyday plates for meals at home, party plates, heavy cardboard plates for special occasions, and penny plates. For the most part, they loved their go-to everyday paper plates. But, they often felt that they had to compromise because their everyday paper plates could not handle some of their favorite foods.

One of the issues was the fact that everyday plates couldn't handle favorites that were messy and/or a bit greasy, like fried chicken, pizza, or tacos. Some of those meals would soak right through the plate, creating a real mess on everything from the table to clothes. Moreover, the everyday plates were not strong enough to handle some heavier meals like spaghetti or sloppy joes. Consumers wanted to use their everyday paper plates, not the more expensive, heavy cardboard plates, for these meals. Simply put, target consumers wanted an everyday paper plate that performed more like traditional, permanent dishes.

The work had uncovered a potentially attractive drill site for innovation. The Demand Profit Pool we were focused on developing was an everyday plate that could stand up to consumers' favorite foods, no matter how greasy, messy, or heavy those foods might be. Importantly, our quantitative assessment gave us an estimate of the economic upside, from the opportunity and the type of price premium we might be able to charge for this new plate. Given all of these details, our client team and their technical folks came up with a brilliant solution that had never occurred to them before: Adding a special coating to the plate.

The coating solved for consumers' major issues with everyday paper plates. First, the very thin coating applied to the top of the plate created a barrier that prevented even the greasiest, messiest foods from leaking through the plate. Additionally, the coating actually strengthened the plate, allowing it to handle the heaviest foods consumers could dish out. Further, the coating helped plates stand up to cutting food with a fork and knife, which tended to be less of a concern among consumers but created yet another valuable benefit. Overall, the new coating created an everyday disposable that performed more like permanent dishes. Now consumers could confidently serve all of their favorite foods on an everyday plate without compromising.

The new coating had another important benefit. It differentiated our client's offers with an attractive shine that was visible to consumers and made other plates look dull. The shiny new coating was very noticeable at the store shelf, and the client's marketing team took advantage of this visible improvement and added a claim to the packaging, promising a new "leak proof barrier." That new promise was highly compelling to consumers, as the shiny coating gave them reason to believe that the new plate really delivered on its promise. The coating was also a "platform" solution that could be applied to everyday plates, a new line of party plates, and cups for coffee and other hot beverages.

Finally, adding the new coating actually lowered the cost of producing plates, because the coating made the plates stronger while using less paper in the plate itself. Further, using less paper in the plates also increased throughput on the manufacturing lines, which turned out to be significant as sales jumped by double-digits. While sales climbed, profits soared even higher based on the cost-efficient new plate and the price premium it earned for the new benefits it provided. You could say that with this innovation the team stepped up to the "plate" and hit a home run.

## Conclusions

Is a new paper plate really an innovation? In hindsight, the solution seems so obvious. Once again, Peter Drucker has the answer: "Indeed, the greatest praise an innovation can receive is for people to say, 'This is obvious! Why didn't I think of it? It's so simple!' "[8] This quote has proven to be true across almost all of the most successful innovations we have helped our clients develop.

What is also true is that if successful innovation can be found for paper plates, including how to market them and how to make them, we believe innovation opportunities can be identified in almost every category. In this case, innovative new solutions were found for the product itself, for how to position and market it, and for the manufacturing process. With all of these elements working together, sales went up despite charging a premium price while manufacturing costs dropped and profits jumped. And all of it was based on a systematic, repeatable process for innovation rooted in understanding demand.

# Questions for Monday Morning

1. What has been the difference between innovation successes and failures for your business over the past three to five years? How did each of the following drive success or failure?

    a. Focus: Today vs. tomorrow, inward or customer-centric

    b. Attitude: Support across the organization, including senior management

    c. Risk: Tolerance for appropriate level of risk

    d. Bureaucracy: Is the innovation process helping or hindering efforts?

2. What are your objectives for innovation?

    a. Percent of revenue from innovation introduced in past three years

    b. Innovation portfolio objectives by type, from incremental product improvements to new business models

3. Where will you drive innovation across your business system?

4. What are your expectations for who is involved and what roles they will play in the innovation process?

5. How will you monitor and measure success against your objectives?

    a. What are the right metrics and milestones?

    b. When should they be assessed?

    c. Are you prepared to take corrective actions as needed?

6. How will you gain and maintain senior management commitment?

7. Who is the right cross-functional team in order to drive success?

    a. What functions are represented?

    b. At what level?

    c. What is the role of the team?

8. How can you build a more supportive innovation culture?

9. What are the current strengths and weaknesses of the innovation culture?

10. Do you have the right process for driving innovation success?

    a. How does your process compare to best practices?

    b. By assessing past performance, what process weaknesses are identified?

    c. How can those weaknesses be addressed?

11. What are the critical "forces and factors" shaping current, emerging, and latent demand for your category?

    a. Demographic shifts, cultural trends, technology breakthroughs, legislative changes, retail changes, competitive landscape, and so on.

    b. What can you learn from analogous categories outside your own?

    c. What can you learn from other geographic markets beyond your own?

12. What do you know about the demand of your most profitable customers that your competitors do not know?

    a. Who are they?

    b. Why do they buy?

13. Never underestimate the power of your heavy users, heavy needers, or the "power users" at the leading edge.

    a. What can you learn from the ways they use your product/service?

    b. What can you learn from the ways they work around the pain points related to your product or the holistic product experience?

    c. What "need states" do they experience, and which are most valuable to serve?

# Endnotes

1. Drucker, Peter F. "The Discipline of Innovation." *Harvard Business Review*. August 2002. https://hbr.org/2002/08/the-discipline-of-innovation. Accessed September 2017.
2. Kevin Bowen interview.
3. Schneider, Joan and Julie Hall. "Why Most Product Launches Fail." *Harvard Business Review*. April 2011. https://hbr.org/2011/04/why-most-product-launches-fail. Accessed September 2017.
4. Christensen, Clayton M., Taddy Hall, Karen Dillon, and David S. Duncan. *Competing Against Luck*. HarperBusiness: 2016.
5. Drucker, Peter F. "The Discipline of Innovation." *Harvard Business Review*. August 2002. https://hbr.org/2002/08/the-discipline-of-innovation. Accessed September 2017.
6. Lehrer, Jonah. "Steve Jobs: 'Technology Alone Is Not Enough.' " *The New Yorker*, October 7, 2011. https://www.newyorker.com/news/news-desk/steve-jobs-technology-alone-is-not-enough. Accessed September 2017.
7. Christensen, Clayton M., Taddy Hall, Karen Dillon, and David S. Duncan. *Competing Against Luck*. HarperBusiness: 2016.
8. Drucker, Peter F. "The Discipline of Innovation." *Harvard Business Review*. August 2002. https://hbr.org/2002/08/the-discipline-of-innovation. Accessed September 2017.

# Demand-Based Cost Reduction

---

### The Big Ideas

- Cost control is paramount for most companies as many industries continue to experience very low rates of growth.

- Traditional cost reduction initiatives have not improved companies' competitive positions because they all follow the same playbook.

- The demand business system offers a new approach by quantifying which products and product benefits deliver little incremental value to both you and your most valuable customers.

- As a result, companies can restructure their portfolios, redesign their products, and remove fixed costs from their business systems that are the underlying cause of cost inefficiencies.

---

Cost reduction is back on CEO agendas – or maybe it never left. In the slow-growth environment that characterizes many industries today, cost control is one of the most reliable paths for profit improvement. Not surprisingly, according to a survey conducted by Strategy&, 71% of

187

CEOs, responding to a recent survey plan cost-cutting initiatives over the next year.[1] For most leadership teams, this is far from the first time that they have launched broad-based efforts to resize and streamline operations. Despite endless initiatives, companies always seem to find themselves behind the curve because either cost reductions do not stick or customer demand shifts and prior cost savings actions prove to be insufficient. This is not for lack of trying: Most companies have applied every approach promulgated by industry consultants. Starting thirty years ago, the big push was "lean" operations popularized by the Toyota Production System and its originator, Edward Deming. Then process re-engineering came into vogue and companies unleashed armies of Six Sigma Black Belts. In its latest reincarnation, cost reduction is flying under the banner of "Zero-Based Budgeting." Leadership teams looking to improve margins have a menagerie of choices, each branded by its own well-known acronym: Total Quality Management (TQM), Business Process Reengineering (BPR), and Zero-Based Budgeting (ZBB).

These approaches are often effective at eliminating costs in the near term. However, in the medium-to-longer term, costs tend to creep back up. Various studies have shown that cost savings targets are realized only 10% to 25% of the time.[2] The bigger strategic issue is that no approach has been able to establish a compelling track record at sustaining cost savings while also supporting top line growth. The reasons are twofold: First, most cost reduction approaches do not fundamentally change a company's competitive position; and second, most cost initiatives become disconnected from a company's growth strategy. As a result, they do not reduce the downward pressure on sales. Thus begins the following all-too-familiar cycle: Slow growth → excessive costs → broad-based cost reduction → near-term margin enhancement → resources misaligned with demand → slow growth → another cost initiative.

The first reason behind this all too common cycle – that most cost reduction approaches do not fundamentally change a company's competitive position – may be news to many, particularly Wall Street analysts and activist investors who vociferously advocate for aggressive cost programs. The problem with these cost programs is their formulaic nature, for the core toolkit is explicitly or implicitly anchored in benchmarks (see Figure 10.1). Benchmarking and best practices, by definition, cause a company to mimic the practices of competitors or industry leaders. Other tools in the kit, such as "spans and layers" analysis or process redesign,

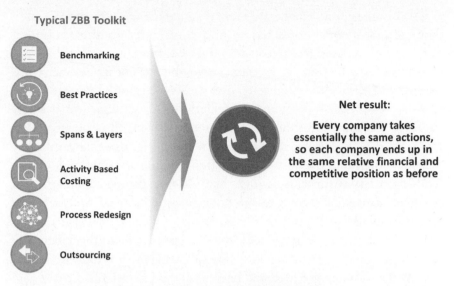

**Figure 10.1   Typical ZBB toolkit.**

rely heavily on observed practices, so it should come as a surprise to no one that, after exhaustive – and frequently, culturally wrenching – efforts, companies find themselves having to launch yet another cost reduction program. If every company takes essentially the same actions, each company ends up in the same relative financial and competitive position as before. Margins may have improved, but performance gaps will inevitably re-emerge. The company that had insufficient funds for new growth initiatives before the restructuring program was launched will still have relatively fewer funds than top-performing competitors after the program is completed. Growth will stall, margins will again erode, and investors will make calls for more restructuring.

In some cases, a cost reduction effort anchored in best practices and benchmarks will make the competitive situation even worse. Just because the most cost-efficient competitor spends 3% of net sales on advertising or 4% on R&D does not make those targets relevant for all companies in the industry. At its core, business strategy is defined by the guidelines that people use to make decisions and allocate resources. Thus, in practice, the use of benchmarks and best practices drives all companies to effectively adopt the same strategy. And you can guess which company will win in that competitive dynamic: The one that sets the benchmark, not the ones that adopt it.

The strategic dissonance inherent to the use of benchmark-based cost reduction underscores the second contributor to the frustrating cycle of cost cutting: Most cost initiatives become disconnected from a company's growth strategy. A recent survey by Accenture among senior executives showed that only 36% of the C-Suite—and only 25% of VPs—believes that their reinvestment priorities are aligned to business strategy.[3] Obviously, this disconnect is not by design, but aggressive KPIs and hard deadlines can overwhelm task forces. In the race to deliver promised near-term results, teams often default to simple decisions like across-the-board cuts, which may cripple prospects for growth, or small actions like new travel policies, which never truly change operating margins.

Numerous times we have seen the inadvertent disconnect between growth and cost initiatives, and the following is a typical example. The director for a major food and beverage brand has planned to capture demand for an emerging flavor palate with innovation. At the same time, the supply chain team is taking aggressive actions to reduce material waste while the sales team is pulling back trade rates to increase margin. Everyone involved recognizes the inherent conflict, but what can be done? Each organization has performance targets to hit, and, within their frame of reference, the actions make sense. Confronted with a mature market, the brand manager feels the need to go after any pocket of demand. Conversely, the supply chain planner sees the need to standardize bills of material as he or she struggles to contain production costs for a fragmenting product line. Meanwhile, the sales team must focus trade spend on the few items that retailers are willing to stock. Eventually, the incongruities are glossed over during the planning reconciliation process, when best-case scenarios in terms of customer orders, plant efficiencies, and product distribution become the base case necessary to square the circle. Not surprisingly, no part of the company actually achieves its plan.

The core issue is the way that cost reduction initiatives traditionally have been managed. Most cost-saving programs are too focused on *how much* to cut – and not focused enough on *what* to cut. Senior executives announce aggressive, high-level targets, such as $1 billion or a five-point increase in operation margins. A large number of task teams are then established, frequently overseen by a project management office (PMO). The PMO chiefly acts as a reporting organization that delegates decisions on what to cut to the individual working teams. The theory is that

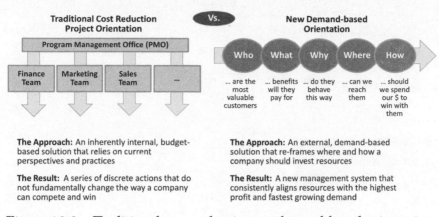

**Figure 10.2   Traditional cost reduction vs. demand-based orientation.**

employees closest to a particular function or activity will have the most detailed and accurate understanding of day-to-day operations and thus are most qualified to decide the best actions to reduce costs. While it may empower employees, this approach requires herculean efforts to coordinate initiatives and align each of them with business strategy. In contrast, a demand-based approach takes a value chain perspective to cost reduction that is inherently anchored in business strategy (Figure 10.2).

The key to strategic alignment is the common "mental model" for managing the company that is the defining feature of the demand business system. Each function or department uses the same frameworks, data, and assumptions for understanding customer demand and defining action plans to capture a greater share of it. The consistent use of this mental model and its underlying data naturally align cost initiatives with growth strategy in the same way that a single, common forecast helps to align supply chain activities.

Tightly aligning cost initiatives with business strategy is a breakthrough feature of the demand business system. Beyond ensuring that cost reductions do not work at cross-purposes with top line growth, a demand-orientation directly addresses structural cost drivers, which are the underlying cause of cost inefficiencies. Operating cost drivers fall into one of two categories: Structural or executional. The concept is explained in more detail in Figure 10.3.

Structural drivers are those factors that define the cost parameters that constrain operating efficiencies. These factors include the offering (e.g., brand portfolio breadth, product line breadth, product attributes),

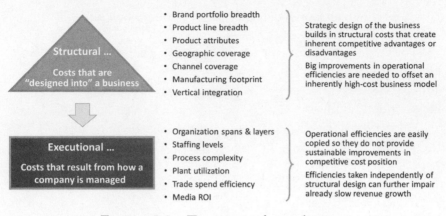

**Figure 10.3　Two types of cost drivers.**

how the offering is produced (e.g., manufacturing footprint, degree of vertical integration), and how it is brought to market (e.g., channel coverage). Taken together, these factors build in the structural costs that create inherent competitive advantages or disadvantages for a business. Big improvements in operational efficiencies are needed to offset a structurally high-cost business model. As every line manager can attest, painful – and potentially crippling – reductions in SG&A are necessary to offset a structurally high-cost product.

In contrast, executional drivers are those factors that reflect how a company is managed. They often define the core operating metrics tracked by companies. These factors include organizational spans and layers, department staffing levels, plant utilization rates, and trade spend efficiencies. Given the ready availability of data and their frequent use as performance benchmarks, most cost reduction efforts focus on executional cost drivers. The immediate impact can be dramatic: Many companies report cost reductions of 300 to 500 basis points of margin. It is pretty obvious why most companies start with an execution-based program.

However, in our experience, a purely execution-based program inevitably leads to the type of never-ending cost cutting that we described earlier. In most industries, structural factors drive the majority of costs, and examples are plentiful: Overdesigned products with attributes that customers won't pay for, legacy products with incomplete benefit bundles that customers will not buy, and new products that divert resources and cannibalize the core, complex product portfolios that are costly to manage at the shelf. Companies that leave these unaddressed will always find themselves unsuccessfully chasing more efficient competitors.

At this point, you may be asking yourself, "If addressing structural cost drivers is so important, why don't most companies focus on them?" Simply put, it is not easy. Structural cost reduction requires a deep, quantified understanding of demand that most companies do not possess. And acquiring new insights is rarely part of the typical cost reduction program. It is this reliance on incomplete or outdated legacy understandings of demand that cripples the ability of most companies to effectively address structural cost drivers – and ultimately contributes to the lack of alignment between cost reduction efforts and growth strategy.

Specifically, structural cost reduction requires knowing which products deliver little incremental value to you and your customers. For your brand and product portfolio, this means identifying three key aspects of your product line: First, which products' incremental sales (net of cannibalization) exceed their margin contribution; next, which products have the greatest return on marketing and promotion spend; and, finally, which pipeline innovations have the potential to tap into the most profitable customer demand. For the design and attributes of individual products, this means quantifying the following: First, which products over-deliver benefits that exceed benefit thresholds that customers are willing to pay; next, which products fall short of minimum benefit thresholds; and, finally, which products could profitably increase benefits delivered.

Most companies have big opportunities to more profitably align their brand and product portfolios with demand. Performance differences are less relevant than in the past, as innovation in both product and business model have narrowed the gap between "good-better-best" in many categories. In fact, mainstream products in many categories have become too good at their core missions – but also not good enough. While this assertion may seem counterintuitive, given that mainstream products are under pressure, it is the case that mainstream products in many categories are competing in a very difficult part of the market today, which we call the "benefit plateau." This concept is one that former colleague Steve Carlotti expanded on in a piece called "The Disappearing Middle Is a Real Market Threat – Here's What Firms Can Do" (Knowledge@Wharton, June 12, 2014). While they continue to perform better than lower-priced products, the difference in performance is not creating much incremental value as perceived by their customers. It is, however, adding meaningful amounts of cost. As a result, many customers develop a preference for the lower-priced offering – not because it is better or cheaper, but because its price is more in line with its benefits than is the case for the mainstream product. This dynamic can be true even if the mainstream product improves its absolute performance advantage. Customers' evolving definition and perception of value can erode brand equities if the benefit and price equation becomes misaligned. This effect is shown in Figure 10.4.

The Great Recession put a fine point on this issue. The rapid change in many consumers' financial circumstances forced these individuals to reconsider a large number of product and service choices that they had not considered before. We know based on purchase behavior that, in many categories, customers choose from a very small number of products, whether we are discussing the chips they eat, the bank they use, or the television channels they watch. For one of our clients in the food and beverage industry, we discovered that although more than 300 different products were available in the market, 50% of people purchased three or fewer of these offerings in a given year. As a consequence, customers' understanding of the breadth of offerings available in the market is not very broad – despite huge investments in advertising and the vast amount of information available on the Internet. The dramatic change in circumstances caused by the recession forced people to reconsider their choices in category after category. Customers learned that lower-priced products were not as bad as they had thought. After experiencing the new choices, customers discovered that their value – as defined by the benefits received relative to the price paid – was actually better. For many, the new choices stuck.

Figure 10.4   Assessing where and how to take action.

The good news is that the demand business system fully captures and quantifies these insights' core to better understanding your product portfolio's and business system's benefit and cost curves, as you may recall from Chapter 2.

The experience of one of our clients highlights the benefits of a demand-based approach to cost reduction. Our client participates in the food and beverage industry, and, like many large companies with mainstream brands, came to us for help when it was struggling. Its categories had lagged population growth for years, and the company's share was under attack from the many small entrants that were attracted by the categories' large size, despite their slow growth. Over the prior two years, the company – like every major competitor – had launched a cost reduction program with the stated purpose of reinvesting the freed-up funds to reignite growth. And like its competitors, these efforts had gone for naught as sales flat-lined and margins continued to erode.

Our client had fallen into the typical growth trap. In search of increasingly smaller pockets of opportunity, the company had proliferated its product portfolio. What had started as a well-planned program to expand distribution into growing retail channels through package and product form innovations had devolved into a "check every box" approach to cover the category landscape. As store shelves became crowded with hard-to-distinguish offerings, sales incrementality plummeted. For nearly one-third of products, 80% of their sales came from cannibalizing other items in the company's portfolio. While these innovations inched revenue forward, they decimated margins. In an attempt to appeal to as many customers as possible, the new products offered a laundry list of benefits that merely served to confuse shoppers while increasing material costs by two times that of the legacy brands. A supply chain designed for long runs of similar products suffered big drops in utilization and yield, as the attribute-heavy innovations quadrupled changeovers. The company soon recognized that value was being destroyed by this strategy, but it felt trapped: Rationalizing the product line would drive down costs but also revenue. Without a growth story for investors, the leadership team feared a loss of market value. Confronted with a seemingly intractable problem, company executives decided to launch a demand-driven transformation.

The executive team established three core objectives: First, a 500 basis point increase in operating margins; second, flat sales during the first year of restructuring and 0.5 point gain in share annually in subsequent years; and, finally, a brand portfolio and product pipeline that would "future-proof" the company with anticipated shifts in customer demand. Three years after the company launched its demand crusade, it achieved these objectives. The turning point was the adoption of the demand-based business system.

The first year focused on first stabilizing, and then reversing, revenue declines. Using the toolkit discussed in Chapter 2 and more fully articulated in subsequent chapters, the company charted a precise roadmap for growth by identifying current, latent, and emerging demand in their categories, quantifying the growth and financial opportunity for each customer segment, defining the total proposition, which maximizes demand capture with the highest potential customers, and specifying the actions needed to deliver the new propositions. As the end of the first year came into sight, the team shifted priorities to margin enhancement.

The central issue was the brand and product portfolio. After much rigorous analysis, the company finally quantified the extremely low productivity of its "long tail". However, chopping off the entire tail was not an option, as some of the products were targeted at emerging demand while others were the only foothold in new distribution channels. A reasonable degree of rationalization was, of course, necessary, but it was more important to change the margin structure so that strategically important but currently low incrementality products could remain in the portfolio. This required a quantified understanding of the drivers of sales incrementality for over 1,000 different products.

There was no shortage of opinions. Marketers believed that brand awareness and brand perceptions drove sales incrementality. The sales force pushed price, promotion, and distribution. The insights and strategy function placed its chips on demographic shifts and competitive intensity. And the innovation team, not surprisingly, felt that product attributes, benefits, and "newness" were the reasons why customers purchased a product. Unlocking the algorithm would equip the leadership to make the difficult portfolio rationalization and resource allocation decisions. So sales and marketing analysts collaborated to build a dynamic econometric model that pinpointed the factors that determined sales incrementality for every item the company produced.

The results clearly reinforced the central role of product design. The appropriate combination of product attributes and customers' perceptions of how well specific attributes deliver desired benefits had the most decisive impact on sales incrementality. And the ideal product attributes and associated benefits varied significantly by customer segment. Unfortunately for the company, sweeter tasting food – which dominated its portfolio – was preferred by the least profitable customer segments, and the segment among which sweeter food had the greatest sales incrementality also had profit margins 800 basis points lower than average. The lower margins were due to these customers' tendency to load up on products when they were on promotion and the higher material costs associated with "amping-up" sweetness to the desired levels. The leadership confronted the unpleasant truth that the most effective way to increase sales was also the most value destructive. And given the very heavy weight of their portfolio toward sweet food, the only way to meaningfully increase margins would be to gut near-term revenue – which would make margin improvement ultimately unattainable due to the high fixed costs in the business system.

But the demand business system offered a solution to this apparent conundrum. The precise insights incorporated into the demand framework quantified the impact of each product attribute and benefit on sales. Using these insights, the company determined the most profit accretive way to reformulate current offerings. Applying the same insights, the company optimized its innovation pipeline. The result was a phased transformation of the portfolio that let the company preserve its core customer base while gradually gaining a foothold with new customers. And the program achieved strategic alignment – margin enhancement actions were directly linked to growth with the core customer segments. Figure 10.5 captures the company's application of demand insights to margin enhancement actions.

As was the case for our client, cost control is paramount for most companies. However, traditional cost reduction initiatives do not improve most companies' competitive positions because they all follow the same playbook. The demand business system offers a new approach because it starts by identifying where profit is located and the customers with which you need to win. It then quantifies which products deliver little incremental value to both you and your most valuable customers by answering the questions foundational to robust portfolio management: What products generate truly incremental sales? Why are these products incremental (or not)? How profitable could they be? What actions should we take to restructure our portfolios, redesign our products, and remove fixed costs from our business system? The result is a cost reduction program that directly matches margin enhancement actions with your company's growth strategy (Figure 10.6).

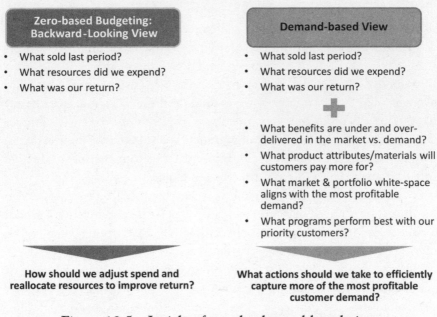

| Zero-based Budgeting: Backward-Looking View | Demand-based View |
|---|---|
| • What sold last period? | • What sold last period? |
| • What resources did we expend? | • What resources did we expend? |
| • What was our return? | • What was our return? |

**Demand-based View (continued)**

• What benefits are under and over-delivered in the market vs. demand?
• What product attributes/materials will customers pay more for?
• What market & portfolio white-space aligns with the most profitable demand?
• What programs perform best with our priority customers?

**How should we adjust spend and reallocate resources to improve return?**

**What actions should we take to efficiently capture more of the most profitable customer demand?**

Figure 10.5   Insights from the demand-based view.

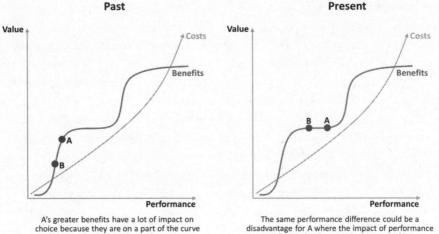

**Past**

A's greater benefits have a lot of impact on choice because they are on a part of the curve where value is rising faster than price

**Present**

The same performance difference could be a disadvantage for A where the impact of performance is low and costs are rising more quickly

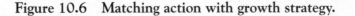

Figure 10.6   Matching action with growth strategy.

## Questions for Monday Morning

1. Do you know where profit is located across both your current and prospective customer base?
2. Do you know how profitable your business with them could be?
3. Do you know how your current product portfolio and routes-to-market influence the structural factors that are the underlying cause of cost inefficiencies?
4. Do you have a roadmap that fully integrates and aligns margin enhancement actions with your company's growth strategy?

# Endnotes

1. Howell, Rodger. "How to Turn Your Cost-Cutting Strategy Into a Growth Strategy." *Forbes*. 11 August 2016. https://www.forbes.com/sites/strategyand/2016/08/11/how-to-turn-your-cost-cutting-strategy-into-a-growth-strategy/#5cd58de37fc6. Accessed October 2017.
2. Agrawal, Ankur, Olivia Nottebohm, and Andy West. "Five Ways CFOs Can Make Cost Cuts Stick." *McKinsey & Company: Strategy and Corporate Finance*. May 2010. https://www.mckinsey.com/business-functions/strategy-and-corporate-finance/our-insights/five-ways-cfos-can-make-cost-cuts-stick. Accessed October 2017.
3. Pearson, Mark, Bill Theofilou, and Kris Timmermans. "The Broken Link: Why Cost Reduction Efforts Fail to Fuel Growth." *Accenture Strategy*. 31 March 2017. https://www.accenture.com/t20170331T025702Z__w__/us-en/_acnmedia/PDF-4/Accenture-Strategy-The-Broken-Link-Point-of-View.pdf. Accessed October 2017.

# Winning in a Digital World

---

### The Big Ideas

- Digital is disrupting and reshaping most industries and has the potential to drive even more dramatic changes to the competitive landscape going forward.
- Digital strategy should not be a siloed effort for the digital team, but a comprehensive strategy for winning in an increasingly digital world.
- Digital approaches can play vital roles, ranging from identifying trends to building brands to acting as a sales channel to enabling entirely new business models.
- Identifying and understanding the leading edge digital consumers among your most attractive target segments is the starting point for maximizing digital opportunities.
- Mapping the digital path to action in detail highlights options to influence purchase decisions and remove barriers at key inflection points.
- Given all of the potential opportunities presented by digital, a robust portfolio of digital initiatives is most likely to maximize results.

---

*"We must move from numbers keeping score to numbers that drive better actions."*
                    —David Walmsley, chief customer officer, House of Fraser[1]

Consumers increasingly live their lives online. As they post photos, review restaurants and vacation spots, rate products and services, support their favorite causes, and go shopping, they create a digital mosaic of what they like, what they dislike, where they have been, and where they may be heading next. This transition is playing a significant role in disrupting traditional approaches and is fundamentally reshaping almost every industry vertical, including media, financial services, healthcare, and retail. The disruption being caused by digital technologies and approaches is not limited to consumer-oriented businesses, as B2B industries quickly adopt digital approaches as well. Stepping back and reviewing all of these changes makes a compelling case for every business to thoroughly assess its current digital capabilities and to carefully plan for a digital future.

Think of all of the ways digital approaches have impacted the retail landscape to date and of all that is yet to come. The first wave of digital retail moved many purchases and even entire categories, such as music, from brick and mortar stores to online sites. Many retailers, including music retailers, bookstores, travel agencies, and video rental chains did not survive this first round of digital disruption.

Now, newer technologies are being used to improve the shopping experience on mobile devices, to enhance the in-store experience, and to solve for the "last mile" by delivering products right to the consumer's door. In-store technologies include robots like Pepper from SoftBank Robotics, which are in the store aisle to assist shoppers,[2] virtual reality devices that allow the consumer to walk through their new kitchen or try on a new outfit virtually, and "scan and go" checkout to make the purchase almost seamless. Consumers can make their purchases in-store, by going online on a computer or a mobile device, or by simply asking a smart speaker or virtual assistant powered by artificial intelligence (AI) to make the purchase. Once an item has been bought, retailers are exploring driverless vehicles, drones, and other innovative approaches to deliver items to the consumer's home. Behind the scenes, digital and other technologies are also driving improvements to retailers' supply chain capabilities, including sales forecasting, optimized product assortments, and labor productivity.

As the world goes digital, many businesses are undergoing significant digital transformations in an effort to catch up with the digital consumers leading the way. We have pointed out how analysis of Big Data, including digital data, can be used to enrich and optimize growth opportunities throughout this book. Now in this chapter we want to pull all of that together and focus on "digital strategy" in greater detail. Importantly, we believe that the days of thinking of digital strategy in isolation or as a separate functional area in the way that pricing strategy or channel strategy might be approached are over. Instead, we think of digital strategy as developing a comprehensive set of successful approaches to win in an increasingly digital world.

## Driving Digital Innovation

At this point, digital is virtually synonymous with innovation. One client friend jokes that there is now a sure-fire way to get funding from senior management for any initiative: Just put the word "digital" in front of the name of the effort you need funded.[3] His joke, while an overstatement, does reflect a new reality, for digital approaches are driving substantial amounts of innovation across industries and creating everything from innovative new offers to entirely new business models.

The financial services industry is one of the many industries undergoing significant changes driven by digital approaches. One example of digital innovation within the financial services industry is PayPal, which offers a great case study of a company addressing latent and emerging demand to become a significant competitor in a mature industry that is dominated by traditional incumbents. Today, PayPal has emerged as a global leader in online payment processing, providing an alternative to traditional methods like checks and money orders. Although they were almost perfectly positioned to address this demand, traditional competitors, including retail banks like JPMorgan Chase and payment processors like Visa, failed to realize the growing need for online money transfers. Despite already having a relationship with almost all of the consumers who would become PayPal's customer base, these firms ceded a significant portion of the market to an upstart who understood the emerging, unarticulated needs of customers. Although it was founded less than two decades ago, the failure of major players to address latent and emerging demand allowed PayPal to grow into a major competitor in payment processing.[4]

At the same time, PayPal's story reinforces the belief that many people have that digital business model innovation is only possible among small technology start-ups. Clearly, this perspective is not shared by Goldman Sachs. In October of 2016, Goldman Sachs, which is far from a scrappy little start-up, launched a digital lending platform called, Marcus by Goldman Sachs. The new digital lending business is named for Marcus Goldman, who founded what would become one of the world's largest, most famous financial services firm in 1869. As an online platform for making personal loans, Marcus by Goldman Sachs competes in a total U.S. loan market, excluding mortgages, which is estimated to be worth about $1 trillion.[5] Personal loans specifically are estimated to constitute a market that is just over $100 billion dollars per year.[6] Goldman Sachs' new lending business now competes in this market with the many existing online lenders including SoFi, Lending Tree, and Lending Club, among others. Many of these competitors operate as "alternative" or "peer-to-peer" lending models that source the funding for their loans from non-bank alternatives or individual investors. Unlike these existing online lenders, Marcus by Goldman Sachs has the advantage of built-in funding from Goldman Sachs and its relatively new online retail bank, GS Bank USA.[7]

After conducting research with over 10,000 consumers, the team at Goldman Sachs felt it had a compelling opportunity to launch Marcus by Goldman Sachs in the consumer lending market.[8] One thing their research found was that many creditworthy consumers with relatively high FICO scores, which is one widely used measure of a consumer's ability to pay for loans and how much credit can safely be extended to them, were carrying high-interest debt, including credit card debt. On average, credit cards were charging an interest rate of 16.4 percent. The team at Marcus by Goldman Sachs realized that they could build an attractive business while helping qualified consumers save money on the high-interest loans they were repaying. Marcus by Goldman Sachs would do this by offering creditworthy consumers personal loans of up to $30,000 at rates that were 300 to 500 basis points lower than what the credit cards were charging.[9] According to Harit Talwar, the financial services veteran and former CMO of Discover Card who now leads Marcus by Goldman Sachs, the average interest rate for their personal loans is about 12 percent, and ranges from 6.99% to 23.99%.[10] For the consumer paying off high-interest debt over a period of several years, refinancing that debt at an interest rate that is even a few points lower can add up to thousands of dollars in savings.

In addition to offering compelling interest rates with the potential to save consumers significant amounts of money, the Marcus by Goldman Sachs team has worked to eliminate consumer pain points while creating an excellent customer experience. Consumers told the team loud and clear that they hate being nickel-and-dimed with fees, and find inexplicable jumps in their loan rates to be unfair. As a result, Marcus by Goldman Sachs has none of the fees other lenders impose for late payments, early repayment, or opening an account. Additionally, because they offer only fixed-rate loans, the monthly payments consumers make never increase unexpectedly. With a simple-to-use online loan payment calculator, a straightforward online application process, and real people who answer calls to the customer support line, Marcus by Goldman Sachs strives to deliver an outstanding customer experience. All of this effort behind digital innovation seems to be paying off as the team at Marcus by Goldman Sachs had already reported generating $2 billion in personal loans about thirteen months after its launch.[11]

# A Digital Early Warning System

One of the most valuable uses for the oceans of digital data available to be assessed is to enhance the type of "early warning system" we discussed in Chapter 4. Digital listening, web scraping, and other approaches can be used to gather digital data for analysis. By knowing what to look for in terms of the forces and factors shaping demand and the Demand Triggers that lead to purchases or other actions on the path to purchase, the digital data collected can be put into context in ways that generate powerful insights. Do the digital data confirm an important trend or indicate that a new trend is emerging? What insights can be gained from positive or negative reviews of your products and competitors' offers? Can the data be organized into segments of consumers to help understand the differences in opinion and in behavior by key segments? Ideally, any digital data collected can be organized into the segments identified from your Enhanced Demand Landscape. Short of that, it may be possible to create demographic or behavioral segments of customers or to use that information to infer to which segment from your own Demand Landscape each customer belongs.

One reason digital data can be so critical to an effective early warning system is that the information often reflects what is happening in real time: Few other resources can provide as much detail that is as close to real time as the digital information consumers generate. As a result, digital insights can provide a preview of critically important shifts in demand. It can also provide metrics related to product consumption in ways that identify replenishment cycles, such as a wireless printer that either informs the user of the need for more ink or actually automatically reorders ink. The real-time nature of digital data can also flag potential problems to be resolved quickly before they have time to become much bigger issues. For example, analysis of digital data might catch a spike in complaints posted online for a specific product, allowing the manufacturer to take action before more customers are disappointed by the same issue.

In addition, digital data sets can provide extremely insightful longitudinal data as key metrics about consumers are tracked over time. Tracking and analyzing consumer ratings and reviews over time could provide new insights and reveal interesting trends. Consider a scenario in which sales are trending down in certain markets or with certain segments of consumers relative to historical sales gains. Drilling down deeper into ratings and reviews from markets with declining sales might identify a quality issue in one of your products, or reveal that a new regional competitor has entered the market. On the other hand, the longitudinal data might show that those markets always show a dip in sales during this time of the year. The whys behind these trends are critical to understand so that managers take appropriate actions to address any issues at hand.

As digital data expand to include metrics from the increasingly wide range of smart devices, from printers to refrigerators to street lights, that make up the Internet of things (IOT), the potential for developing greater insights increases even further. At the same time, as the availability of diverse data sets increases exponentially, there is a very real danger that more becomes less and that potentially valuable insights are lost in an overwhelming sea of data. Clearly, the need for analytic frameworks and for the capabilities to make sense of rapidly expanding data sets will become increasingly critical to businesses of all types.

# Identifying and Understanding Target Consumers

The mistake we see most frequently when it comes to developing a robust digital strategy is the assumption that digital is so ubiquitous that the target should include "everyone" or should be "all Millennials." By definition, having everyone as the target of digital efforts means there is really no targeting strategy at all. And yet, across industries, businesses that are seeking to win with younger consumers will frequently claim that the target of their digital strategy is all Millennials. The flaw in this thinking is the assumption that all Millennials, or any other broadly defined demographic group, will have the same level of interest in a given category or offer. Identifying and understanding the target consumer with pinpoint accuracy is a critical driver of the success of any strategy, including any digital strategy.

Digital data can help identify potential target consumers or enrich your understanding of your current target consumers. Once again, ratings, reviews, posts, and behaviors can all be assessed to determine what is most and least important to consumers and to potentially identify to which segments they belong. For example, TripAdvisor rewards reviewers with points and ranks them on criteria including number of reviews written, number of readers, and how many reviews were rated as helpful. Details about each reviewer are also shared in a searchable database, in part to ensure that these are real people, not the owners of the hotels, restaurants, and attractions being rated and reviewed. Reviewers share where they are from, why they made each trip, where else they have traveled, as well as other reviews that they have written. Some reviewers include other details about themselves such as their age group and a profile of their travel interests such as "foodie," "art and architecture lover," or "family vacationer." All of the reviewers provide an e-mail address for contacting them with questions about the hotels they have reviewed.[12]

Analyzing the reviews and ratings on TripAdvisor could help identify the major segments of travelers that exist in the market, which might include occasional business travelers, road warriors, luxury travelers, foodies, and experience seekers. Importantly, the reviews and ratings can help bring these potential segments to life with insights about their specific decision-making criteria such as price, "must-have" amenities, and proximity to major attractions. These insights can be enriched further by their specific likes and dislikes regarding hotels.

Forms of Machine Learning, such as Text Analytics, can be used to analyze all of the reviews and posts from a given reviewer or from a group of reviewers who are in the same segment to identify key themes and the most commonly used phrases and words. This type of analysis could reveal important drivers of choice or add nuance and new dimensions to known drivers of choice. For example, the analysis might pinpoint exactly what a given segment of traveler means by a high-quality hotel gym or precisely what aspects of hotel dining options are most critical to them.

Now the hypothesized segments developed or the segments identified from the Enhanced Demand Landscape can be found online. One approach for doing so is to build what are called "look-alike" models, which start from the known characteristics of defined segments and then use other information to identify additional consumers who "look like" those segments. These models are typically developed by analyzing online data along with data from third parties with extensive consumer information such as Nielsen, Acxiom, or Experian. When completed, the model assigns consumers to the segments they fit best based on the available data.

Going forward, the look-alike model can be tested and improved based on actual responses from consumers by segment. Essentially, ongoing data collection is used to determine what percentage of those consumers assigned to the "foodie" segment really seem to behave as expected. One potential approach to this type of testing is to advertise your brand or to provide offers aimed at foodies. Does the ad motivate the foodies to click through to your site or to get more information about your brand? Do they open e-mails designed to interest them? What kind of response rates do the specific offers designed for foodies generate among the consumers thought to be in the foodie segment? Is the response significantly different from response rates across consumers in other segments or across consumers as a whole? All of these metrics can be used to refine the segmentation itself, to improve the accuracy with which consumers are assigned to segments, or to enhance the messaging and offers sent to each segment.

Several other approaches can be used to identify and understand the most attractive consumer segments on which to focus. Some websites ask a few questions to help make it easier for consumers to find what they are looking for or to flag something new that might interest that particular consumer. These questions might ask about favorite home décor looks, clothing styles, or wine preferences. Another approach is to ask consumers to join a loyalty program or to sign up to receive additional information or special offers by e-mail or direct mail. What these approaches have in common is that they all gather more information about consumers that helps to build a richer understanding of who they are, which segment they are most likely to belong to and how to win with them.

Simply determining a consumer's zip code can unlock a wealth of information about that person, including average household incomes in that area, demographics, home values, education levels, and more. If someone shares their full name and address, even more details become available. One example of how powerful this information can be is easily found on many car insurance sites. On many of these sites, consumers looking for a better policy only need to provide their full name and address to have the make, model, and year of every car they own automatically filled into the application. This process makes it as seamless as possible to get an insurance quote on any or all of those cars. Connecting name, address, and potentially e-mail address with information about prior purchases, likes, dislikes, and ratings provides an even richer profile of consumers that could be used for developing segments and understanding those segments in greater detail.

## Mapping Digital Purchase Decisions

Mining digital data can also provide a picture of the consumer's path to purchase and the decision points along that path. Today's digital path to purchase looks significantly different from the traditional purchase decision path or customer decision journey looked in the past. The traditional path to purchase was characterized by relatively few data sources and a fairly straightforward, but sometimes lengthy, process of elimination that brought consumers to a final choice to be purchased. Moreover, consumers might have turned to newspapers or magazines focused on product ratings to help with purchase decisions. If the purchase being planned was significant enough, consumers might also seek advice from trusted friends or family members about it. The path to purchase was fairly linear in that the process tended to narrow choices from the many options of which consumers were aware, to fewer choices that they would seriously consider, to the finalists that met their key criteria, to the offer they would ultimately buy. The process could also be time consuming, as data sources were not always readily available, and understanding all of the details, options, and price points for a given purchase could entail multiple trips to different retailers. Prior to having online retail options, the purchase made almost always took place in a store or perhaps through a catalogue.

In contrast, the digital path to purchase has many more data sources, enables easy access to consumer reviews and ratings, is generally a much less linear process, is often completed quickly, and certainly does not have to end with a purchase in a physical store. Figure 11.1 describes the new digital path to purchase.

Figure 11.1 shows that the new path to purchase is more complicated than the traditional path to purchase. It is also more important to understand today's digital path to purchase in detail because there are so many more inflection points for winning or losing with the consumer, many of which can happen very rapidly. It is possible that your brand and offers might lose out right from the start if competitors have superior search engine optimization (SEO) and dominate the terms consumers use most in their initial online searches. Poor reviews, not having enough reviews, or a sub-par mobile experience that makes information difficult to view on a smartphone could all bump your brand out of the consideration set among

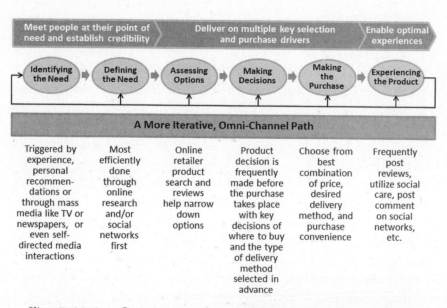

Figure 11.1    Consumer path to purchase – the new paradigm.

your most attractive consumers. All of these factors make it increasingly critical to understand the most attractive segments of consumers for your offers and exactly how their unique path to purchase unfolds.

## Using Digital Tools to Build Affordable Housing

The CMO of a major nonprofit organization we worked with asked, "How do we engage people under the age of fifty-five to support our mission?" Prior to our involvement, the organization had tried almost everything, including SEO, aggregators, partnerships, and other traffic-building approaches to get younger donors to give more volunteering time and more money to help develop affordable housing around the globe. The CMO ticked off a long list of initiatives they had implemented with the objective of engaging younger donors, but none had moved the needle.

One of the organization's biggest disappointments had been a splashy digital campaign, targeting Millennials, that showcased the many ways that access to affordable housing had created meaningful, positive impacts for people across the U.S. and around the world. The primary objective of the campaign was to get Millennials involved, as the nonprofit's current donor base was aging. As current donors aged, they spent much less time volunteering, and they often donated less. As a result, Millennials were literally the future of this nonprofit. However, like their other efforts, the digital campaign had not increased engagement among younger donors.

Why didn't these efforts work? Not surprisingly, one of the major reasons they did not work as planned is that not all Millennials are interested in supporting charities, just like all Boomers are not interested in supporting charities. Even among those Millennials who do want to support charitable organizations, there are many potential causes to support beyond affordable housing.

Now that we had this context, our next step was to identify the segments of younger donors who were most interested in supporting affordable housing. By understanding their motivations and characteristics in greater detail, we were able to create "look-alike" models to find more like-minded young donors, as well as their older counterparts. Importantly, we also understood which segments of donors were least interested in supporting our client's cause so that resources would not be wasted trying to reach them.

As we talked to target donors, it became increasingly clear that our client was not reaching them in the right places or with the right message. The client team had been targeting all Millennials because they had not yet identified those donor segments who were most interested in supporting their cause. Now that we understood who to target, we were able to reach them much more effectively and efficiently.

However, it was also clear that potential donors were not being reached at the right time. The unfortunate reality is that natural disasters, including hurricanes, earthquakes, and wildfires, generate significant news coverage while also motivating charitable giving. Rebuilding, including affordable housing, is one of the most critical recovery needs in the wake of a natural disaster. And yet, our client had almost no outreach or awareness during these tragic events and therefore did not realize any substantial increases in donations despite the overwhelming need for shelter that natural disasters caused. Using digital platforms, our client could now reach the right segments of consumers during the events that both create the greatest need and motivate the most generous giving.

The last barriers to donation success stemmed from misperceptions about the organization itself. Younger donors were highly motivated by the idea of helping people in need around the world with the support required for long-term success. They were much less motivated by the idea of focusing only on the U.S. or by providing only emergency cash for short-term needs. Younger donors did not realize that our client was doing exactly the things they were most interested in supporting. In fact, most younger donors thought our client operated only in the U.S. and that it only provided what amounted to handouts. Since the client did not know who the right target donors were, they also did not realize that the most compelling messages for them were communications that dispelled these misperceptions and spoke directly to their key motivations for giving.

Now that they could get the right message to the right audience at the right time, our client was able to engage younger donors much more effectively. Ultimately, that engagement translated into much higher levels of financial support and of volunteering among younger people. Winning with younger donors was not only important for the near-term health of the nonprofit, it was critical for the future of the mission as the majority of the existing donor base skewed to consumers aged fifty-five or older.

# Digital Collaboration

Digital approaches are not limited to identifying customers, building brands, driving traffic, and creating innovative new offers; rather, digital collaboration can also be used to significantly improve the physical supply chains that turn raw materials into finished goods and move finished products through distribution channels to store shelves. Specifically, digital approaches and digital collaboration across the supply chain can be used to increase data accuracy, enhance forecasts, integrate shopper insights, optimize the digital store shelf, and improve marketing and promotional efforts. Going forward, retailers across channels and the manufacturers that sell their products through those retailers have significant opportunities to optimize their shared supply chains by making greater use of digital approaches.

One of the major areas for improvement is forecasting, for an inaccurate forecast can drive substantial amounts of otherwise avoidable costs. On the one hand, forecasting issues cause lost sales for both the retailer and the manufacturer because the item the consumer wanted to purchase is out of stock (none in the store) or on back order (none available online). Beyond losing that one sale, an out-of-stock situation can mean losing a formerly loyal customer. If the product is unavailable, the consumer might try a different product and decide to switch to that brand going forward. Alternatively, the consumer might try a different retailer and decide to switch to that retailer going forward. Conversely, an inaccurate forecast can result in carrying too much inventory that does not sell but does tie up funds that could have been invested in other opportunities.

Collecting and sharing digital data create one option for improving forecasting accuracy. Increases in search activity for a certain category or a specific product might signal an important uptick in demand. Conversely, a meaningful drop in search activity could foreshadow an impending decline in demand. The volume of purchases conducted online and how these volumes have trended over time can also provide an important input into forecasting models. Sharing this information across all supply chain participants can have two important benefits. First, this data sharing can help improve data accuracy. Multiple players at different steps in the supply chain may have data that help corroborate, refute, or revise the data provided by one of the participants. In addition, the shared data can better prepare all of the participants across the supply chain for what is ahead.

Another opportunity that is often overlooked is to improve digital promotions and campaigns for the benefit of both manufacturers and retailers. The starting point for improving these efforts is to identify and understand the most attractive target consumers in the market. As we have noted previously, when it comes to digital efforts, there is often a temptation to simply target "all Millennials." Sharing robust consumer segmentation data and consumer insights between retailers and manufacturers is critical for successful digital campaigns. With a focus on the right target, the messaging and creative used in digital communications now have to be designed for the specific dynamics and use of digital in order to break through. Finally, impact has to be measured over time in order to drive continuous improvement. Are the digital campaigns reaching the right audience? Is the message compelling to the target? Are sales improving? Digital approaches create opportunities to track these metrics and take action nearly in real time.

## A Mission to Win Consumers Back to the Store

Here is a digital case study that flips the script. Our client, a large retailer of consumer electronics and appliances, had been losing share to online players for years. In contrast to the online giants, our client sold products through a national network of brick and mortar stores as well as online. Despite the potential advantages of providing consumers the option of ordering online and picking up in the store soon after, our client had been losing share of market to the online giants just like most other traditional retailers.

The driver of the successful strategy for winning consumers and market share back from online competitors was going deep to understand segments of shoppers and the most important "shopping missions" they experience in our client's retail categories. Not all consumers – and not all Millennials – find online shopping to be the best solution for everything they buy or for every shopping occasion. Some segments of consumers prefer to see, touch, and feel certain products in person in order to get a better sense of their potential choices. This fact is particularly true for the many categories of consumer electronics that our client sold. These technologies were changing rapidly, and it was hard to get a real feel for how much better the picture quality of the latest generation of a particular product is by looking at one on a tablet or smartphone.

In addition, many of these new technologies, from wearable devices to drones to smart home systems, were both unfamiliar to most consumers and relatively expensive. As a result, lots of consumers wanted to see these new technologies and learn about them in person at a store, given how expensive they are. Going to our client's stores allowed consumers to watch product demonstrations, hear someone explain what the device does, use the product, ask questions about it, and get advice. In too many cases, it also allowed the consumer to get to a decision and then purchase that new item from one of our client's online competitors. The task now was to figure out how to win the actual purchase among consumers who came into the store to fulfill specific shopping missions, especially among those consumers in the most attractive consumer segments.

What we found was that there were several levers available for our client to win with the most attractive consumers, if they could be motivated to come to the store. One of the drivers to bring them into the store was the dynamic we just mentioned: Many people want to experience exciting, relatively expensive new technologies firsthand before they buy. With that insight, our client successfully positioned their stores as *the* authority for certain new technology categories that consumers generally wanted to experience in person. Interest in these categories, along with advertising and promotions related to them across media types, helped drive target consumer segments to the store.

Once in the store, our client could win with these consumers by providing a great experience and a compelling value proposition. We learned that one of the ways to make the in-store experience better was to ask a few questions to understand the customer's specific type of shopping mission. A consumer on an "explore and learn" mission, for example, typically wanted lots of details about the new technologies, wanted to compare a lot of potential options, and wanted to play with the new technology. Meanwhile, someone on a "replacement" mission or a "gifting" mission generally wanted to be guided to a decision quickly. They wanted advice and a recommendation from someone they could trust, and they often wanted to know what option was most popular and why. Importantly, the team on the store floor learned to ask the right questions to understand which segment the consumer was in and what mission they were on. With that context, they could provide the help those customers sought in ways that made for an outstanding shopping experience.

However, a very helpful shopping experience that delivered on the consumer's shopping mission might not actually result in a sale; rather, it might simply put a smile on the consumer's face as he or she rushed home to purchase that new technology product at a competitor's online site. As such, beyond a great experience, our client also had to provide compelling reasons to make the purchase with them. Fortunately, our client had several ways of winning with their most attractive consumers, but consumers did not realize these attractive programs existed.

One of the most compelling reasons to buy was our client's long-standing commitment to matching competitors' prices. Suddenly, consumers who were really excited about getting their hands on a new technology wondered why they should wait several days or even a week to have something shipped to them when they could have that exciting new technology right now for the same price. At the same time, the local store provided a place to return, fix, or exchange the new purchase if anything went wrong. This was a comforting thought for those consumers who were about to take the plunge into uncharted tech waters. Additionally, for larger or more complicated purchases such as a big 4K television or a home security system, the local store provided installation services. Now consumers had lots of compelling reasons to purchase the technologies they wanted right in our client's stores.

The strategy worked. Traffic to the stores increased, especially among the most attractive segments of consumers who were the focus of outreach campaigns by our client. The campaign reached target consumers and reinforced a persuasive message that positioned this retailer as the authority for the latest technologies. It also communicated elements of their value proposition, such as matching prices, returns, and installation services, of which consumers were generally unaware.

Traffic to the stores increased, the in-store experience and value proposition delivered, and store sales rose for the first time in several years. According to a third-party research firm that tracks the retail sector, our client was one of a very few retailers to win share back from online competitors. The competition has noticed, and in the battle to create ever greater levels of convenience, some online competitors have opened "ship to storefronts" that allow consumers to place an order before noon and pick their item up at the "ship to storefront" location on the same day.

These new storefronts are also marketed as a convenient way of handling returns when needed.

## Conclusions

Leveraging digital approaches is increasingly important as customers and consumers become increasingly digital. As new digital approaches disrupt and replace traditional approaches to consuming media, purchasing products and services, accessing information, and conducting financial transactions, expectations and the opportunities for winning with customers and consumers are being reshaped. Digital approaches can be used to enhance growth efforts across the existing business model and even by moving your firm to an entirely new business model. Leveraging digital approaches is now a requirement for continued success across industries and across the business life cycle from the smallest start-up to the most established, global firms.

---

### Questions for Monday Morning

1. Is digital part of your overall strategy for winning in the market?
2. Is your digital strategy and the distinct initiatives that support it a set of disjointed, siloed activities?
3. Who is your digital consumer target? Is it more specific than "Millennials"?
4. How could digital approaches be used to create a more effective early-warning system to anticipate changes in demand? What techniques, including social listening and web scraping, are you using as you predict where customers are headed next?
5. Are digital approaches being used to improve forecasting, understand consumers at a deeper level, enhance inventory levels, and enhance your supply chain by collaborating across members of the integrated supply chain to share data?
   a. How can you apply supply chain thinking if you are in a service business?
   b. What critical partners are involved in your "supply chain" and how can digital collaboration improve results for all partners?

---

6. How well do you understand your target consumers' digital path to purchase?

   a. What are the major implications for your business from the new digital decision journey?

   b. Can you identify the major inflection points throughout the journey and how you perform at each one versus competitors?

7. How can digital approaches help improve your innovation efforts?

   a. Can digital be used to improve your offer or aspects of your value proposition?

   b. Could digital enhance marketing or promotional efforts for your offers?

   c. How can digital be used to build your brand?

   d. Can digital move your business to an entirely new business model?

# Endnotes

1. Levenson, Larry. "38 Inspirational Marketing Quotes." *Alaniz Marketing*. 25 July 2013. https://www.alanizmarketing.com/blog/38-inspirational-marketing-quotes/. Accessed October 2017.

2. Outing, Steve. "Your Future Companion in Your Old Age Could Be a Robot." *MarketWatch*. 13 October 2017. http://www.marketwatch.com/story/your-future-companion-cool-socially-adeptand-a-robot-2017-10-13. Accessed October 2017.

3. Interview with client.

4. Rampton, John. "The Evolution of the Mobile Payment." *TechCrunch*. 17 June 2016. https://techcrunch.com/2016/06/17/the-evolution-of-the-mobile-payment/. Accessed October 2017.

5. Harris, Ainsley. "Will You Trust Marcus (and Goldman Sachs) With Your Debt?" *Fast Company*. 13 October 2016. https://www.fastcompany.com/3062537/will-you-trust-marcus-and-goldman-sachs-with-your-debt. Accessed October 2017.

6. Dickler, Jessica. "Goldman Sachs Makes a Bet on Consumer Debt." CNBC. 27 February 2017. https://www.cnbc.com/2017/02/27/goldman-sachs-makes-a-bet-on-consumer-debt.html. Accessed October 2017.

7. Harris, Ainsley. "Will You Trust Marcus (and Goldman Sachs) With Your Debt?" *Fast Company*. 13 October 2016. https://www.fastcompany.com/3062537/will-you-trust-marcus-and-goldman-sachs-with-your-debt. Accessed October 2017.

8. Frankel, Matthew. "How Goldman Sachs Is Disrupting This $1 Trillion Industry." *The Motley Fool*. 24 July 2017. https://www.fool.com/investing/2017/07/24/how-goldman-sachs-is-disrupting-this-1-trillion-in.aspx. Accessed October 2017.

9. Ibid.

10. Dickler, Jessica. "Goldman Sachs Makes a Bet on Consumer Debt." CNBC. 27 February 2017. https://www.cnbc.com/2017/02/27/goldman-sachs-makes-a-bet-on-consumer-debt.html. Accessed October 2017.

11. Turner, Matt. "Goldman Sachs' New Online Lending Business Just Hit a $2 Billion Milestone." *Business Insider*. 14 November 2017. http://www.businessinsider.com/goldman-sachs-marcus-closing-in-on-a-2-billion-milestone-2017-11. Accessed December 2017.

12. Millwood, Aimee. "A Top TripAdvisor Reviewer Talks About How Reviews Work, for Good and Bad." *Entrepreneur*. July 2015. https://www.entrepreneur.com/article/278954#. Accessed October 2017.

# INDEX

3-D Printing, 9
3G Capital, 21

A/B Testing, 118
Acxiom Corporation,
    The, 208
Advertising Metrics, 13
Airbnb, Inc., 15, 74
Allstate Insurance Company,
    The, 7, 8, 17, 29,
    36, 46, 75, 152, 156,
    168, 172
Amazon.com, Inc., 13, 80,
    88, 119, 132, 133, 153
American Broadcasting
    Company (ABC), 14
Anheuser-Busch InBev, 21,
    47–50, 54, 58, 61, 62,
    76, 135
Apple, Inc., 16, 88, 131–133
Artificial Intelligence (AI),
    74, 202
Atlantic, The, 12

Baby Boomers, 11, 49, 76
Bayesian Methods, 97

Bezos, Jeff, 132, 135
Big Data, 15, 17–22, 32, 34, 35,
    45–46, 62, 80, 90, 91, 93,
    117, 118, 127, 146,
    178–179, 203
Bilbrey, J.P., 30
Black Belts, 188
Bloomberg Canada, 17
Blue Apron, Inc., 73–74, 180
Boulder Brands, 14
Bowen, Kevin, 168
Brand Economics,
    131–146
Brand Value Proposition
    (BVP), 136–138,
    145–146
Briggs, Gary, 141
Buck, Jim, 72
Buffett, Warren, 15, 16, 21, 149,
    151, 154
Bureau of Labor Statistics, 71
Burger King, 21
Business Metrics, 16, 33, 144
Business Process Reengineering
    (BPR), 188
BusinessWeek, 70

Business-to-Business (B2B), 15, 134, 139, 177, 202
Business-to-Consumer (B2C), 15, 134, 140

Cambridge Group, The, 168, 171
Campbell's Soup Company, The, 15
Celestial Seasonings, 14
Christensen, Clay, 171
Churchill, Winston, 18
Coca-Cola Company, The, 133
Cold War, 86, 87
Columbia Broadcasting System (CBS), 14
Comer, Gary, 86
Competitive Advantage, 151
ConAgra, 14
Conference Board, The, 10
Consumer-to-Consumer (C2C), 15, 74
Corona, 49, 77
Cox, Chris, 141
Customer Demand Analysis (CDA), 173
Customer Relationship Management (CRM), 90–91, 95–106, 114, 126–129

Data Dashboards, 93
Data Visualization, 18, 92
Demand Landscape, 33, 38, 50–54, 85–108, 120, 123, 171, 175, 180, 205
Deming, Edward, 188

Diapers.com, 73
Digital Strategy, 201, 203, 207
Dollar Shave Club, 74
Drucker, Peter, 168, 173, 182

Econometric Modeling, 113–116, 196
Economic Indicators, United States, 9, 10
Economist, The, 132, 134
Emergent, 14
Enhanced Demand Landscape, 85–108
Experian PLC, 103, 208

Facebook, Inc., 13, 14, 133, 140–145
Federal Reserve Bank of San Francisco, 12
FedEx Corporation, The, 153
FICO Score, 204
Financial Crisis Inquiry Commission (FCIC), 16
Financial Times, The, 21
Folger's Coffee, 79
Forbes Magazine, 133, 139
Forces and Factors, 69, 75–79, 124, 179, 184, 205
Ford, Henry, 120
Fortune Magazine, 14

GEICO, 7
Geo-location Tools, 94
Go Fund Me, 15
Godin, Seth, 132
Golden Globe Awards, 141
Goldman Sachs Group, Inc., The, 204, 205

Google, Inc., 13, 133
Great Depression, The, 11
Great Recession, The, 194

Hadoop, 91
Hall, Taddy, 171
Harvard Business Review,
     The, 17
Harvard Business School, 76, 151
Hitachi, Ltd., 88
Hughes, Steve, 14

International Business Machines
     Corporation (IBM), 134
Internet of Things (IOT), 206
Internet Trends Report, 4
Isaacson, Walter, 16, 176
*Ivey Business Journal*, 30

Jobs Theory, 177
Jobs, Steve, 16, 17, 131
Jobs-To-Be-Done, 177–178

Kash, Rick, 5
Kraft Heinz Company, The, 21
Krating Daeng, 77
Kun-hee, Lee, 138

Lending Club, 204
Lending Tree, 204
Levitt, Theodore, 76
Lyft, 15

Machine Learning, 18, 92, 93,
     103, 106
Marketing Segmentation,
     Traditional, 85, 88–89

Markov Chain Processes, 97
Mateschitz, Dietrich, 77
Maxwell House, 79
*McKinsey Quarterly*, 15, 21
Meeker, Mary, 3–4, 9
Microsoft Corporation,
     The, 133
Millennials, 11, 12, 71, 79, 171,
     178, 207, 211, 214, 217
Miller Chill, 77
Morrison, Denise, 15

Nanotechnology, 9
National Broadcasting Company
     (NBC), 14
National Public Radio, 17
Nestle Company, The, 20
Net Promoter Score, 123
Netflix, Inc., 13, 119
Nielsen Company, The, 9, 56,
     103, 118, 173, 208

Paris, Lufi, 142
PayPal, Inc., 203
Pet Economy, 70, 72
Petco, 72
Porter, Michael, 151
Precision-Demand System
     Benefits of Data-Driven
          Approach, 121–124
     Current, Emerging, and Latent
          Demand, 75, 184
     Demand Landscape, 32–43
     Enhanced Demand Landscape,
          86–108
     Demand Profit Pools, 51, 167,
          175–176
     Demand Segments, 51–63, 65

Precision-Demand System
(*Continued*)
Demand Trends, 69, 73–74,
79, 81
Demand Triggers, 69,
79–81
Forces & Factors, 69, 75–79,
124, 179, 184, 205
Right at Retail, 57–58
Steps for Implementation,
98–99, 124–130
PricewaterhouseCoopers'
(PwC), 10
Pricing Strategies, 161, 163
Project Management Office
(PMO), 102, 190
Python, 103

R, 103
Randomized Control Trial (RCT),
116, 130
Red Bull, 49, 75, 77, 78
Richardson, Lewis Fry, 112
Robotics, 9, 202

Samsung Group, The, 133,
138–139
Schneider, Ulf Mark, 20
Schultz, Howard, 78, 79
Seagate Technology, 88
Search Engine Optimization
(SEO), 210, 211
Seeking Alpha, 20
Sharing Economy, 15
Shinola, 74
Six Sigma, 188

Social Media Management,
13, 18, 55, 117, 119
Social Network, The, 141
SoFi, 204
SoftBank Robotics, 202
Sony Corporation, The, 138, 139
Spark, 103
Spending Trends, United States,
9–12, 70–73
Spinbrush, 176, 177
Starbucks Coffee Company, The,
75, 78, 79
Statistical Modeling. *See*
Econometric Modeling
Student Loan Debt, 12

Talwar, Harit, 204
Tesla, Inc., 17
Text Analytics, 208
Thompson, Derek, 12
Tim Horton's, 21
Total Cost of Ownership, 154, 162
Total Quality Management
(TQM), 188
Toyota Production System, 188
TripAdvisor, 207
Tropicana, 14

Uber Technologies, Inc., 15, 73,
74, 152
United States Census Bureau,
11, 23–24

Value Equation, 143, 144, 149,
154–161
Visa, 203

Wall Street Journal, The,
    23, 46, 65, 84
Walmsley, David, 202
Wanamaker, John, 112, 130
Weather Forecasting,
    113, 117
Wheatley, Bob, 14
White Wave, 14
Whole Foods Market, Inc., 13

World Bank, The, 10
Wozniak, Steve, 17

Yager, Floyd, 17

Zero-Based Budgeting (ZBB),
    20–22, 188
Zuckerberg, Mark, 140, 141,
    143, 145